# Witness to the Truth

# Witness to the Truth

My Struggle for Human Rights in Louisiana

*- To Andrew Blankenship -*
*May you find gems of wisdom*
*in an old man's story.*
*Be blessed!*
*Cleo Scott Brown*

## John H. Scott *with*
## Cleo Scott Brown

University of South Carolina Press

© 2003 Cleo Scott Brown

Published in Columbia, South Carolina, by the
University of South Carolina Press

Manufactured in the United States of America

08  07  06  05  04    7  6  5  4  3

The Library of Congress has cataloged the first printing as follows:

Scott, John Henry, 1901–1980.
   Witness to the truth : My struggle for human rights in Louisiana / John H. Scott
with Cleo Scott Brown.
      p. cm.
   ISBN 1-57003-489-3 (alk. paper)
   1.  Scott, John Henry, 1901–1980. 2.  African American civil rights workers—
Louisiana—Biography. 3.  Civil rights workers—Louisiana—Biography. 4.  Bap-
tists—Louisiana—Clergy—Biography. 5.  African Americans—Civil
rights—Louisiana—History—20th century. 6.  Civil rights movements—
Louisiana—History—20th century. 7.  Louisiana—Race relations. 8.  East Carroll
Parish (La.)—Race relations. 9.  East Carroll Parish (La.)—Biography. I. Brown,
Cleo Scott, 1954–  II. Title.

E185.93.L6 S28 2003
323'.092—dc21                                                          2002015055

*To this end was I born, and for this cause came I into the world, that I should bear witness unto the truth.*

—John 18:37b

*History is of little value unless it inspires one to greater endeavors, or serves to guide against the mistakes of the past.*

—John H. Scott

To my parents, John Henry and Alease Scott

To my sons, Marlon and Devin, and my granddaughter, Tania

In memory of my nephew, Kendall Terrell Pullen
January 26, 1980–January 23, 2002

# Contents

# Illustrations

# Acknowledgments

I am deeply indebted to many for their assistance, contributions, and encouragement that made this book possible. Though it is not possible to mention everyone, there are some I would like to give special recognition.

First I must recognize and honor God for giving me the patience, wisdom, and skills to complete this project and for bringing the right people into my life to make this book happen.

Special thanks go to University of South Carolina Press acquisitions editor Alexander Moore and his wife, Suzanne Krebsbach, and to former managing editor Barbara Brannon.

Special acknowledgment also goes to the late Dr. Joseph Logsdon, who gave me the gift of my father's life through the recorded interviews he conducted with my father, and for permission from the University of New Orleans for their use.

Many thanks go to my critiquers, Thomas Richardson, Sam Booke, Charles James, and Kato Singleton, and members of the South Carolina Writers' Workshop; thank you, for your time and valuable comments.

I am especially indebted to the reference librarians at the Otranto Branch of the Charleston County Library who located almost every document, newspaper, and old book I requested, and who always served with a smile. I am also indebted to the librarians at the Goose Creek Branch of the Berkeley County Library, who also provided me assistance and a quiet place to write, and to the research staffs of the following libraries: the Amistad Research Center, Tulane University; Special Collections, Manuscript Division, Library of Congress; National Archives, Southwest Region, Fort Worth, Texas; Archives and Manuscripts Department, Earl K. Long Library, University of New Orleans; the Carter G. Woodson Regional Library, Chicago; and the public libraries of Baton Rouge, Monroe, and Lake Providence, Louisiana.

I give special thanks to my family: first, to my sons, Marlon and Devin Brown, who never complained about the many hours I wrote and researched and the many times I asked, "How does this sound?" Thank you for letting me know you believed I could do this. Next, I thank my sisters and brothers, who provided important input to complete and improve the story: Leon, Leotis Tyrone (who passed away April 2001), Johnita, Elsie, Amatullah, Louis, and Harriet. Special thanks to Amatullah and Elsie, who went more than the extra mile in critiquing and making suggestions for revisions to the manuscript.

I also acknowledge special people like William "Bill" Brown who taught me professionally in ways that changed all other aspects of my life and prepared me to do greater things; Ellen Hyatt, who gave me valuable writing advice at the beginning of this project and introduced me to world of writers; my brother-in-law Dr. Imari Obadele and author Ralph Keyes, two people who actually gave me the courage to tackle this project; Kathy Alexander, who taught me the importance of a writing schedule and kept me on task; Johnny Barnwell, who chauffeured me from research center to research center, never complaining once; Vera Polite, who helped me better understand my father's spiritual walk; Wanda and Wilken Bradley, who provided me laptop and printer for out-of-town writing trips; the wonderful staff at Hedgebrook on Whidbey Island, Washington, who created and provided to me the perfect writer's retreat; Poyas and Jennifer, who always encouraged me to think big; and the many others who provided encouragement along the way.

# Introduction

For about four years of my childhood, I went to bed each night with the thought that I might be murdered in my bed or trapped and burned in my house by morning. I remember that after being baptized at age ten, I began praying a nightly prayer: "Dear God, if this is the night they come to kill us, please take me into your kingdom to be with you." Then I would climb into my place in the little rollaway bed we let out each night in the living room and go on to sleep.

From my childhood until my mid-thirties, I never spent much time thinking about those bad years. They held too many memories I preferred not to recall. Besides, until I was in my mid-thirties, I might have felt less inclined to think about the events of the 1960s and before. I was living in a special period of time, the '70s and the early '80s, a time that turned out to be the only years of my life when I did not receive regular reminders that my skin color made a difference.

As an adult, when I started to reflect on my childhood, I began to consider my childhood behavior odd. What manner of man was my father, Rev. John Henry Scott, that I should become comfortable with climbing into bed and going to sleep, not fully expecting to die, either because Daddy wasn't scared of anybody or because Daddy and God seemed so close? Why was I as a child comfortable with the fact that "the cause" might require so high a price, that it should be important enough to require my very life? Why didn't I resent in my young years my father's choices that put me in harm's way? Did others in my family feel the same way?

I remember a family gathering of my brothers and sisters, after our parents were no longer living, when the conversation turned to those really bad years right before the 1965 Voting Rights Act passed, a time that we had never discussed before. I was surprised at how others had felt during that time. I remembered being scared of all the guns and hiding under the bed when my older siblings had target practice to protect the family. I recalled moving into my first apartment after college and realizing that I still rushed past windows at night the way I had learned to do when shadows on a curtain could mean I had become a target. My brother Louis, who was next in age to me, had spent endless hours thinking of possible ways we could get attacked and creating almost superhero-type plans for saving the family. One plan included digging a tunnel from under the house to the woodpile so that we would always have a way of escape. My next oldest sibling, Amatullah (Sharolyn), talked of her periodic dreams of being shot, which persisted over fifteen years. She spoke of her fear of policemen that had developed after a childhood police interrogation, and although she had had almost no adult experience with policemen, for many years the sight of flashing lights in the rearview mirror, or just the thought of being pulled over by an officer, filled her with terror.

After my parents died, I became custodian of my father's papers. I, like my father, loved history, and I thought it would be fun to look through all the things my father had collected through the years. I drove to Louisiana and loaded the car with boxes of pictures, clippings, tapes, papers, and letters.

Several years passed, and the boxes remained untouched and unsorted at my house. One day someone called to tell me about a *Time* magazine article on my hometown of Lake Providence, Louisiana. Lake Providence was attempting to become classified as an economic empowerment zone, but certain of its citizens wanted to block such action. When I read the article, one comment by a prominent Lake Providence citizen (to whom I will refer later) stuck in my mind. He remarked how he understood blacks because his ancestors had owned them.

This comment started me to thinking about Lake Providence and its continuing struggle with issues of race. That evening, I decided to pull out the boxes and see exactly what was in them. I sat down in the bed with a large stack of papers, close to two hundred pages of transcribed interviews with my father, conducted by University of New Orleans professor of history Joseph Logsdon. I laughed and I cried as I found myself on a journey from slavery to freedom, to slavery again as created by Jim Crow laws to freedom of a sort in the 1960s. As I traveled down the road of my father's life, a new level of understanding opened to me. For the first time, I understood my father, a man unlike any I have heard or read about. But even more important, I understood the connection between the past and my future. I began to clearly understand how black Americans got in the position they are in today and why we have had so hard a time getting back out of this position. Although my father's narratives focused on his twenty-five-year struggle to obtain the right to vote, they also covered stories and events from right before the end of slavery through the major events of the twentieth century. I could finally make sense of a history that happened all around me and understand how what was *not* taught had substantially affected everyone who had grown up in America.

All my life, I had always heard the general public speak of slavery as something so long ago that it wasn't supposed to still have a major impact, but as I read, I discovered just how closely I was linked to slavery. It was early 1994 and I was still in my thirties, yet here I was reading about the people who raised my father—his grandparents, people born in the 1840s and '50s. How could I not be tied to slavery if the things my father learned and passed to me, right or wrong, about being a parent and taking care of children and being responsible to the community, were learned from people who lived in slavery times?

In the early morning hours I started toying with the idea that my father's interviews should be compiled into a book, because my father still had something significant to say to another generation. I had no memoir writing credentials but, like my father, I figured I could do anything I put my mind to. I located Dr. Logsdon's phone number via directory assistance. I started the conversation with, "This is Cleo Scott Brown. You probably don't remember me because it has been so many years since you have seen me." To my surprise, he responded with, "Is this Rev. John Henry Scott's daughter?" More than thirty years had passed—but Dr. Logsdon identified me immediately. He was ill at the time but nonetheless took a strong interest in the project. He encouraged me to write the story he had intended to but had never had time to undertake. He provided me a listing of research resources, and I was on my way.

So I began a five-year research journey that started with sorting all the papers and individual stories into chronological order. To my surprise, a story about a unique town and a unique man unfolded before me. I had always been in awe of my father, a man of uncommon bravery and tenacity, a man cordial and comfortable with both beggar and high governmental official, a man totally committed to his community. But as I researched, I found I did not know the half of who he was.

My research revealed a story about a man born in 1901 in a small, almost all-black Northeast Louisiana parish where black businesses, schools, and communities thrived without much contact with the white population. But one significant problem remained from the 1870s. Blacks were still not allowed to vote. The papers told the story of how my father's perseverance, even in the face of death, was instrumental in persuading the federal government to bring suit against the town and the state and break an eighty-four-year system of exclusion. In the process, doors were opened not only for blacks in Lake Providence but also for blacks throughout the South.

I have attempted to validate the account in the transcripts by comparing it to information in publications, cassette tapes, court transcripts, pension records, and oral histories. Where these sources offered greater details on a particular story, I have done my best to incorporate that detail without altering the intent of my father's original narrative. Fortunately, there were many people still around Lake Providence in their late eighties and nineties who were directly involved in the struggle to gain the right to vote—people like Rev. Francis Joseph Atlas, Mr. Benjamin Blockwood, Mr. Adam and Mrs. Julia Millikin, Mr. Frank Nervis, and Mrs. Gardenia Johnson, some of the elders mentioned in the book. Their minds and memories were all still sharp. I will never forget how Rev. Atlas, in his early nineties at the time, broke down and cried. He told me, "You just don't know what it was like. You don't know what it is like to try to help the people and when the trouble comes, they leave you all by yourself. I was all by myself."

I then began to feel that lonely place where my father must have been too many times, when he had to fight alone against obstacles that must have seemed insurmountable. Yet his passion for the people never ended. He served as pastor for twenty-five years, president of the East Carroll Baptist Association for thirty-one years, president of the local NAACP for thirty-three years, and chairman of the East Carroll Ministerial Alliance for about five years, and all that time conducted regular visits to hospitals, senior citizens' homes, and prisons.

Though my father often walked in danger, he bore a confidence that came from having a walk so close to God that he was always willing to leave this place, but always mindful that no man could take his life until God gave permission. It made him bold in a way that no one, black nor white, was accustomed to. He aroused intense hatred and fear, but at the same time, respect and awe from white men who did not like him because they could not figure out how to control him. But through it all, he remained steadfast to his beliefs and principles. He tells his story through the wisdom of one who has sat between two centuries and as one who can provide firsthand accounts of actual events, recounting them without bitterness and anger.

As I traveled coast to coast for this project, I was continually amazed at the number of people whose lives were positively touched by my father. I believe that his voice, his simple language, his belief in God, and his vision for humankind will inspire another generation to be better, to do better, to become change agents of tomorrow, just like he inspired thousands of young people who left a small town to rise high in their chosen professions. Welcome to my father's world as he tells you his story in his own words, as only he could tell it.

CLEO SCOTT BROWN

# Witness to the Truth

# ONE

# The Beginning

I reached over to touch the throbbing spot on my left arm as I ran fast as I could along the dark highway. Warm blood was already starting to flow through the strips of fabric that just a few minutes ago had been the sleeve of my favorite dress shirt. My mind told me that I'd better find a hiding place fast, so I ran down the steep embankment toward the cotton field that bordered the highway. As I glanced back in the direction I had come, I caught sight of the headlights of a slow-moving car. It was the same car. It had to be the same car. The headlights were shaped the same as the car that had trailed us out of town.

I ducked into the cotton field, crouching down between the cotton stalks, my heart racing, every beat pounding in my ears. The ditch was deep, and it was pretty dark, but I worried that they might still be able to see my white shirt in the moonlight. I figured they were inching along, peering into the darkness looking for my car, trying to see if I had lost control and turned over in the ditch when they had shot into it as they had passed earlier. Then an even worse thought struck me. Maybe they were looking to see if they needed to finish the job. Maybe they wanted to make sure that we were all dead—my wife, my children, and me.

As I tugged at my bow tie, struggling to get my breath, words I had told myself through the years came rushing back to me, repeating over and over in my mind—A cause worth fighting for is a cause worth dying for. *A cause worth fighting for is a cause worth dying for.*

I was sixty years old and for the first time in my life I felt the full weight and implication of these words. Then just as suddenly, it was as if a window of knowledge opened to me. It became clear on that muggy August night in 1962 that sometimes plain and ordinary people are given extraordinary jobs to do and they are blessed with the skills and courage necessary to do them. I had been in preparation for this time all my life. All my experiences, both the bad and the good, taken altogether, had made me ready for the work I had been assigned to do, for surely without my life's experiences, they would have broken me.

———————— ∎ ————————

I feel compelled to put my life's story on paper, to be shared with generations to come. I am old now, but the Lord has blessed me with a very good memory, and I believe he has reserved my memory for a great purpose. I must start my story at the beginning of my life because so much of what we will become depends on how we start. Our conditions and circumstances are not of our own choosing, so we are either made or broken by what we are given.

I was born not long after the turn of the century on December 30, 1901, in East Carroll Parish, Louisiana. On the map, East Carroll Parish is located in the top right-hand corner of the state, bordered by Arkansas to the north and the Mississippi River and the state of Mississippi to the east. Although there were more than 11,000 people in East Carroll Parish at the time I was born, they were so scattered over the parish that there were not enough people living in any one place to form what could be called a town. I was born near a riverboat stop called Atherton, on the Mississippi River in the southern part of the parish. It was one of the places where mail was brought in by boat.

I was a little skinny, light-skinned, sandy-haired boy loved by all my relatives. My parents, John Henry Scott, Sr., and Lucy Conn Scott, named me John Henry, Jr., after my father. I had a sister named Geneva who was two years older than me, and later another sister named Azzena and a brother named Buddy were born. My sister Geneva did not live with us but lived with my father's parents, Harriet and Charles Scott.

When I was three, my mother and father separated and my father moved to Edwards, Mississippi. Mother took me to live with her father and stepmother. Because times were tough and my mother had to work hard for a living, her stepmother suggested, not long after we had moved in, that I should be sent to live with my father's folks. It grieved my mother very much to let me go, but she had no choice but to send me away. So one Sunday morning she dressed me up as if I was going to church and we all went out to where the horse and buggy were waiting. They set me in the buggy on a little box at their feet and we took off down the long dirt road that led from Stamboul plantation.

After we had ridden about ten miles out in the country, we came to this big house with a long row of cedar trees in front. It was the house where my sister Geneva and my father's parents lived.

My mother said, "Get out, Son, and stay here until we come back for you and be a sweet little boy." She gave me hug and they left.

Evening came and then night, and I kept going out on the porch looking for them to come back, but no one came for me. Soon I began to cry. I cried every day no one came.

I was only about three years or so when I was sent to live with my grandparents, but I remember that my grandmother tried her best to console me and make the best of a hurtful situation. I remember how she always made things extra special for me. I guess it was because of the way I had come to live with her. Sometimes I think maybe she made an idol out of me, always fussing over me and doing things to make me happy, trying to make my life as easy as possible.

In later years when my mother remarried, she wanted me back, but she couldn't get me away from my grandmother. So my mother would come to see my sister and me, and we would go to see her in St. Joseph, Louisiana, where she lived with her new husband. She would always relate the incidents that separated us. I guess that was why I remembered so clearly the story of our separation even though I was so young. Mother still wanted us, but she couldn't afford to take us from my grandmother. The last thing I heard my grandfather say to my mother when she had come to visit us was, "As long as I got a house, you are welcome and you will always feel like my daughter. I don't want you to feel no ways bad about comin' here. You come and stay just as long as you want to."

So I settled into life at my grandparents' with my sister Geneva and my grandparents' youngest son, Charley Jr. My grandparents had moved to north Louisiana from Salem, North Carolina, in 1872 when my grandfather was about thirty years old. My grandfather, Charles Henry Scott, or as we called him, Papa Charley, had ended up in north Louisiana after joining one of the colored regiments organized by the Union army during the Civil War. His regiment, the 20th Regiment, Company C, had been involved in garrison duty up and down the

Mississippi River. After the war ended, he came back down to Louisiana and looked things over and decided this was a good place to live. He went back to North Carolina and married my grandmother, Harriet Sides, who was only about fifteen years old at the time.

My grandmother Harriet was what I call a moralist. She didn't want anything wrong. She had been reared by her white mistress during slavery back in North Carolina and I believe it was her mistress who put a lot of those moralistic ideas in her head. Grandmother spoke good English although she could barely read and write, and she would tell me, "I don't want you talking like these bad-speaking people." She didn't believe in people drinking. In fact, the scent of whiskey would pretty well make her drunk. She wouldn't allow Papa Charley to grow tobacco on our farm. She had been around tobacco farms in North Carolina and she said the very scent of it gave her a headache. She didn't like rough people, those who used bad language, or women who wore their dresses too short or acted vulgar. She didn't want them around. She was a strict moralist.

Grandmother was also flighty and excitable, afraid of most everything. She was afraid of snakes and witches and ghosts, but to have me along seemed to give her quite a bit of comfort. So she took me with her everywhere she went. She called me her "little man." Soon I took on the nickname "Man," which later was changed to Mannie by my friends when I started school. The name carried over into my adult life.

My grandmother was cheerful most of the time. In fact, she seemed to find humor in most things. She had a loud laugh that she exercised to its fullest. Grandmother always got up early in the morning, and year round she had breakfast ready on time. We never had to go to Sunday School or regular school without breakfast. When we got back home, we always found a hot meal ready—baked sweet potatoes and so on.

Although my grandmother was very affectionate, once in a while she would pull a switch off the peach tree and do some whipping. She always gave us what she promised. If Grandmother told me I was going to get a whipping if I didn't do something, I could guarantee she would do it. No need to try to explain my way out of it. I was going to get it. My sister Geneva would always start crying before she got her whipping. I'd tell her, "You ought to wait till you get it. You'll be all cried out before you get the whipping." I would always wait until I got mine before I started crying.

My grandfather, Papa Charley, was very short for a man, only five feet two inches tall, with very light brown skin, dark eyes, and graying hair. He was jolly and playful, but at the same time he could be very serious. At home he was positive but quiet. He never fussed. When my grandmother squabbled, he'd never talk back. Aggravated, she'd say, "Charley, you shouldn't do this" and "Charley, you shouldn't do that," and he'd just sit there and pat his foot. He seemed unconcerned about the fussing. What he said he meant, and he just wasn't going to fuss about it. You knew the first time he spoke he meant what he said.

Papa Charley was an unusual character to me. Considering his age and small size, he was actually much of a man. He could climb a post and then come down like a cat, head first, even though he was in his sixties. He was friendly with all the men—and charming with all the women. In fact, it made my grandmother jealous most of the time because he would get on the horse and ride through the plantation, stopping at practically every house he passed, and would have something to say to everybody. All the ladies would run out smiling to see "Uncle Charley" or "Woodrat" or whatever pet names they made up to call him. He always had a sack of greens on the horse and something to give away and something to sell. It just made him a very notable fellow in the community. He could always supply some laughter or a story to listen to. The neighbors looked up to him and he was well respected.

My grandparents lived close to the Mississippi River, which was both a blessing and a problem. The Mississippi would sometimes overflow its banks, or the poorly constructed levees would break, allowing the muddy Mississippi waters to flood miles and miles of land. Of course, it was also this flooding and dumping of new soil by the Mississippi River that had created the rich, fertile farmland of the Delta.

When I was still young, the levee broke north of where we lived. The floodwaters made their way down to our settlement so we had to move to higher ground. My grandfather found us some rich farmland on high ground in the woods and began clearing us a plot. He built our house out on a ridge overlooking a bayou called Otter Bayou.

Every morning except Sunday, my grandfather would leave out from the house carrying a fishing pole, a gun, an ax, and a shovel so he could fish a little, hunt a little, and clear a little more land.

When you got to our house out on that ridge, you couldn't go any further and you couldn't look but one way and that was straight up. The cypress trees grew as wide and tall in that bayou as the giant sequoias and redwoods grew out west. The trunks were so wide that when a tree was cut and down on the ground, men could stand on each side of it and not see each other.

All around our house between the trees grew thick underbrush filled with all sorts of creatures to fill a little boy with wonderment. This was the environment where I was reared—out in the woods, two and a half miles from our church and the nearest store.

I enjoyed being outside. I learned the language of the birds and watched the squirrels play up and down the trees, and I had a time keeping the bobcats and the minks from killing our chickens. I'd go out at night and scare the raccoons out of the cornfield, where they would be fighting over ears of corn.

My grandmother taught me how to fish when I was only five. We would catch catfish, trout, and perch and bring them home to cook for supper. There were plenty of snakes on the fish banks and almost everywhere in those woods. I felt brave because I wasn't afraid of snakes and I could protect my grandmother who was deathly afraid of them.

When we weren't fishing, Grandmother liked to go visiting. She'd take me with her from house to house. I had an opportunity to listen in on practically all the conversations—even though children weren't supposed to listen in on older people's conversation in that day. In fact, in that time if a youngster listened in while grown-ups talked, he'd get slapped in the face, driven off like a dog. "What y'all doing listening to grown folks talk?" they'd yell, and we'd run away because we knew someone was about to get hit.

So I got to enjoy a status different from most children. Because my grandmother took me everywhere she went, I got to be a part of the group. I was often the only child around, because most of grandmother's friends were too old to have young children. Most of the time they didn't even seem to be aware that a child was around, and they would talk about all kinds of things in my presence. They would give me a box in the corner and an apple or a piece of bread or something to play with, and I would just sit there and listen to their conversations. Of course I hated apples—but I learned that I could fake a serious involvement in apple eating and the old folks would soon forget all about me and get deep into their conversations. So that's how I came to know so much about what was going on back then.

The women never spoke of politics because of the troubles they had suffered after Reconstruction. Mostly they talked about the different struggles they were having. They gossiped about their husbands and who their sweethearts were (at that time it seemed nearly every man had one, or was accused of having one). Then they would tell their dreams and someone would explain the meaning.

I was reared superstitiously, because there were quite a few "isms" and "signs" and other such things. At that time, ghosts were still living and the witches hadn't died, because they were "riding" people. To sit and listen to the strange stories would make the hair rise on your head and keep you from sleeping at night—such stories as the witch getting out of her skin and coming through the keyhole scaring you and going up the chimney saying, "hi-ho and over the latch." All these were terms supposedly used by witches.

It was this same superstitious belief that allowed the Ku Klux Klan to control the people when I was a child. The Klansmen would put a sheet or other white covering over themselves and slip into black people's houses. This was easy because most of the houses had no locks, or if they did the Klansmen had keys because they owned most of the houses where the recently freed blacks lived. Once inside, they would pretend to be the ghosts of old slave masters. Of course the old people had feared their masters when they were alive, but nothing compared to how much they feared them as dead men. The Klansmen also knew all about guns, and most blacks didn't even own guns, and even if they did, they were afraid to shoot, because they couldn't kill a ghost. And so black people were filled with superstitions and afraid of just the idea of a ghost coming to get them in the night. And all the children could be run off just by telling them about it, because the children had learned to see ghosts too.

Sometimes when the older people got together, their stories would turn to recollections of slavery days. Some of them had fairly good masters, but others had it rough. An old black man named Dan Willis, who visited our house from time to time, would make me hot mad just to listen to him. He would tell how he had held people to be whipped. He described how the overseers would tell him to go catch other blacks, people in bondage just like him. He would strip all their clothes off, men or women, and stretch them across a barrel and beat them until the blood ran or until a man cried and humbled himself. He would drive the other slaves to the fields, handling them like cows—he was what they called a driver, the black man chosen by the master or the overseer to control the other blacks. Of course anyone who lived long enough to see how black people were handled on the old-time chain gangs could about see what the old people were talking about in slavery.

Other than old Dan Willis's story, I do remember that their recollection of slavery didn't seem bitter. They had a new freedom and they were enjoying it. Most of them never expected to be free, so they chose not to dwell too much on the past. They said there were too many bad things to see looking back and so many good things to see looking forward. So they mostly just looked forward. Some of them had never been allowed by their masters to participate in church, because some masters found religious people harder to control. But once they had gotten the church, they also got joy and hope. They would get together and sing and tap out a tune called, "Thank God Almighty, I'm Free at Last." It had no religious significance, just that their bodies were free.

# TWO

# Grandfather

Being sent to live with my grandparents started me down a road far from where I would have traveled. It was my grandparents' great love for me and their examples of courage that prepared me to meet the challenges I would face later in life. They were very independent, a trait that set them apart from most people of their time. Since this was the early 1900s, most of the older people in my community had grown up under slavery and had lived completely dependent on other people. For several generations, overseers had whipped away any thoughts about being independent, so hardly anyone had any real-life experience with living without a bossman.

One of the things that made Papa Charley and Grandmother different was that they both had been free blacks before the Emancipation Proclamation. Papa Charley had been born free, so he had had a chance to see a slightly different kind of life than most of our neighbors. He had been born around 1842 in Salem, North Carolina, to a free mother named Isabella Scott and a slave father known as Harkless. The custom at that time was for children to take the status of their mother rather than their father, so that's how Papa Charley got to be free.

I can remember when I was a boy, on cold winter evenings, Papa Charley would oftentimes pull his wooden chair up close to the fire to rest a bit before turning in for the night. I'd pull my stool up close beside him and beg for a story. Of course telling stories was Papa Charley's favorite thing to do, so it didn't take much urging. So there we'd sit and he'd talk until the cinders turned from bright red to gray.

Although Papa Charley's Civil War stories were my favorites, the stories about him growing up in slavery times always aroused my curiosity because his childhood was so different from mine. He had grown up with his two half brothers, Henry and Richard, but without his parents. Of course this wasn't such an unusual thing during slavery, as parents and children were often separated when they were sold off to different masters. Papa Charley's daddy had been sold to slave traders from Richmond in 1846, and soon afterwards, his mother left him and his brothers and went off to Richmond to follow Papa Charley's father. To get the money she needed to get to Richmond, she had "bound out" Papa Charley and his brothers for a hundred dollars to a small farmer named John L. White in Wilkes County, North Carolina. Papa Charley never heard from his mother again.

Being "bound out" was like being a servant except you didn't get any pay. In North Carolina, poor free children, regardless of color, had to learn a trade under a system on the order of indentured servitude. So even though Papa Charley was only about five years old, he had to start working for this Mr. White because his mother had bound him out. The way Papa Charley pictured it, you were supposed to be like part of the family you were bound out to. He went to church with them and he said that Grandmother had even been allowed to sit in the family pew with the family she was bound out to, right along with the bossman's children. Although Papa Charley said the family he lived with treated him very nice, he still had to come and go at their command, even though he was freeborn. Whenever he went out alone, he had to have a special written pass or some kind of papers. The arresting officers would stop him and say, "Let me see ya papers, boy." If any free black children were caught out without their papers, why, they'd be hauled off to jail to stay until someone came down to say they had permission to be out unaccompanied.

Once I asked Papa Charley if he had ever thought about being free, really free, like the free blacks in the north. "Son, ev'ry man wants to be free," he said. "The good Lord created us that way. I was always thinkin' 'bout bein' free, goin' up north if'n I had a chance. We had this underground movement, a way for us to find out when there was a chance for us to 'scape north. It gave us somethin' to hold on to, somethin' to keep us thinkin' freedom was possible. But the bossmen kept most coloreds ig'nant. Slaves didn't even know where they was, what things looked like outside their own plantation, so most of them couldn't even 'magine runnin' away—runnin' to where? Besides, I reckon most of them was jest too scared of what would happen to them if they got caught. I slipped off myself a couple of times befo' the War broke out, sleepin' in old cotton houses and corn cribs, but they always found me and brought me back to the person I was bound out to."

I was curious and wanted to know everything. I would urge Papa Charley to tell more stories. I remember him telling me the story of how he ended up in Louisiana during the Civil War.

"Well, it happen'd like this." I could see Papa Charley settling back in his chair the way he did when he was about to tell a long one. "Up 'til the time the Civil War broke out, I was workin' from one fam'ly and then another, 'bout seven or so families by the time I turned twenty. But then the war broke out and white men started goin' off to fight. I heard that Captain William Wheeler was lookin' for a waiter and a cook, so I decides to hire myself out. He was a confederate captain for Company G, 2nd Battalion, North Car'lina Infa'try. Now you know Captain Wheeler wanted me 'cause ev'rybody knew what a good cook I was.

"I cooked for and waited on Captain Wheeler straight through the summer of 1862, but at the end of the summer, he quit and his brother Mr. Henry took over being captain. So I started cookin' and waitin' on him."

"Was there fighting going on when you were with Mr. Henry?" I asked.

"Boy, there was plenty fightin' when I was with Mr. Henry—real fierce battles. I missed that battle at Fredricksburg when all them boys got killed in late '62. I had gone back home to Salem. Was too sick to wait on Mr. Henry then. But after I was gone a couple of months, Mr. Henry sent for me to come back to work for him. I shoulda stayed where I was 'cause they was jest startin' to get into the real thick of things. Mr. Henry was ordered to Pennsa'vania 'bout the time General Lee was makin' his final raids. I met up with him right 'fore he took his regiment to Gettysburg.

"The first, second, and third of July of '63, I'll never forget. The fightin' was so fierce at Gettysburg, I thought for sure ev'rybody would get killed. Captain Wheeler got wounded on the third and commenced to retreatin' on the fourth. But when we got to Maryland, we all got captured and thrown in prison in Baltimore. And you know what?" Papa Charley said with a laugh. "They threw me right in jail too along with all those Rebel boys.

"They kept us locked up at Fort McHenry the rest of the year. Somebody told the Union officers I was a good cook and a good waiter, so they got me to come work for the quartermaster. Somewhere 'round Christmas, they called all the colored prisoners out and made us stand in a line before this Fed'ral officer. I thought we was in trouble but they jest told us to repeat this oath—'I promise I will never rebel again against the United States.' Then they told us we was free. Jest like that, they let us go."

"What did you do then Papa Charley?" I asked. "Where did you go? You couldn't go back to North Car'lina, could you?" I wondered what would a person do if they couldn't go back home.

"Well on Christmas Day, me and a sharp-headed fellow we called 'Goose' and another fella named George Davis got together after they let us go and we decides we'd go some place up north. We didn't right know where, we jest knew we should go north and try to find us some work. Somewhere we hear that New York is lookin' for coloreds to join a new colored regiment. They had this thing called a draft where they had to find a certain number of men to go fight the rebels. So they decided to let the coloreds join the Union army so they wouldn't have to send so many of their boys to fight and die. But we didn't care 'bout that part. We jest wanted the chance to help fight for freedom. So we caught a train from Balt'more to New York City to go join up.

"We got to New York during the Christmas holidays. There was people and buildings ev'rywhere, nothin' like you ever seen around Louisiana or North Car'lina. We found the enlistment office, but the sign on the door said 'CLOSED UNTIL JANUARY 1, 1864.' So we stayed 'round New York City and had us a good ol' time until the new year. We made us up some new names to use when we went down to the enlistment office, in case someone from Car'lina might be lookin' to send us back. That turned out to be a big mistake, but that's another story for another day."

Papa Charley stopped to put more wood on the fire and stoke the flames.

"Papa? What happened next?" How long was he going to stay over there messing with that fire?

"Hold ya horses, boy. I'm goin' to finish this story in due time. You don't want the fire to go out, do ya?" He settled back down in his chair. "Now back to where I left off."

"When the enlistment office finally opened, we was there to sign up early that mornin'. The doctor checked us out top to bottom. I was so scared I wouldn't git in 'cause of that piece missin' off the end of my finger here." He held his finger out in the fire light.

"But the doc, he says, 'As long as it ain't ya trigger finger, you can still go.' When that doctor told me I'd make a fine soldier, I was grinnin' from ear to ear. Me and my friends was all goin' to be mustered in that day as soldiers in the 20th U.S. Colored Infa'try. I left New York City that same day for trainin' camp at Riker's Island, about ten miles east of New York City, with my new name of George Wilson and my $25 enlistment pay in my pocket.

"I got there none too soon 'cause the regiment was completely filled jest three days later. I trained with the other soldiers 'til March and was issued my weapon, an Enfield .577. Then on March fifth, they brought us into New York City for a big sendoff parade. I remember it like it was yesterday. We made formation at the East River and marched with our muskets and bayonets down to Union Square. The streets and all the windows was filled with people of all races, wavin' flags, yellin' and cheerin' us on. Some people was even in the trees and on top of houses. We marched down the street, left, right, left, right, all one thousand of us marchin' in time."

I looked over at Papa Charley. Even in the dim light, I could see that his eyes were closed but he was smiling to himself.

"We looked so good in our Union army uniforms and we was jest so proud, proud to be soldiers, proud to fight for the freedom of colored people we had left behind in the South. They fed us in the Square and then we was off again marchin' down Broadway on to the North River where they had a steamer waitin' for us. We boarded the *Ericsson* that took us down to Camp Parapet, some eight miles above New Orleans, Louisiana. And that's how I found out all about Louisiana."

Papa Charley used to tell some real hair-raising stories about his time in the war but he mostly saved these stories for when he had an audience. Grown folks and children alike would gather around to witness his performances. Over time, the stories got more and more grand until you would have thought Papa Charley had won the war all by himself.

He told stories about the cavalry and the infantry, how they would get on hills and battle one another. The band would be playing and they would be yelling before the campaign started. He told about the old-fashioned cannons, how they would pull the trigger after they had charged it with powder and then they would leap away to keep the cannons from jarring them too badly. And he told about the cannon-balls he'd see coming red hot, knocking off the limbs of trees. He said that once on a bridge they were attempting to cross, somebody let loose a cannon and swept the bridge practically clean.

He told stories about General Grant and his attempt to seize Vicks-burg, Mississippi, how they tried to come north, up from the mouth of the Mississippi River but were stopped before they could get to Vicksburg. He told about how General Grant had come to make camp in the town of Lake Providence, in the parish where Papa Charley had made his home after the war, and how the slaves had come off the plantations to join the Union Army. He told about the fifteen-foot-wide canal that General Grant had had the men try to build from the lake in Lake Providence to the Mississippi River so that he could send troops and gunboats through to invade Vicksburg, and how this strat-egy had been unsuccessful.

Of course Papa Charley wasn't the only one telling stories. There were plenty enough Civil War stories to go around because quite a few black Union soldiers had settled in East Carroll Parish after the war. A place called Milliken's Bend, past the southern end of the parish, had been the scene of the first Civil War battle where black soldiers had outnumbered whites and where most of the soldiers were ex-slaves. After the war ended, with the small pensions they received for their military service, many black soldiers were able to buy land and homes and start businesses, and quite a few of them settled in an area of the parish we called Soldiers' Rest.

On the thirtieth of May each year, the old black Union soldiers would all get together in Vicksburg, Mississippi, for a celebration of the Grand Army of the Republic, as they called themselves. The whites would also take part in these Memorial Day ceremonies at the Vicksburg Civil War Cemetery. There would even be a few Confeder-ate soldiers around, but there just weren't many Rebels left. A few cap-tains of the Confederacy were still around, such as Captain Keene and Colonel Buckner, but they didn't appear to resent the celebrations. Everyone seemed to treat one another with respect. The old soldiers seemed to take great pleasure in having good times together and talking about the war.

As a child, I loved listening to the war stories. These war tales impressed me and the men of the community because Papa Charley would make us feel like we were there. As a boy, I imagined Papa Charley fighting all those battles as a Union soldier—when actually he never got to participate in real combat. I learned later that he was just describing the bloody battles he had witnessed while working for the Confederacy. The story about General Grant in Lake Providence and the capture of Vicksburg had actually occurred the year before my grandfather joined the army. He was probably recounting stories that had been shared with him by other soldiers while he performed garrison duty in north Louisiana.

But at that time, none of us knew that these stories were not all his own. The recently freed men who had been on the plantations of north Louisiana all their lives were in awe of someone who had been so many places and had done and seen so many exciting things. Through my grandfather, they could see outside their limited experiences in the cotton fields of Louisiana. He sparked in them dreams of possibilities, and in me, a desire to travel all over and to be very brave like my grandfather. I noticed how the people respected and looked up to him. It gave me a picture of the kind of man I wanted to become.

# THREE

# A Different Kind of Place

When the Civil War ended in 1865, Papa Charley mustered out of the army in New Orleans and worked his way back across the country to his home in Salem, North Carolina. He worked there a while, making sure that he didn't let anyone know about his service in the Yankee army. He said that the white people put such great confidence in him as being a good trusty waiter for the Rebel army that he thought it best not to let on that he had actually been on the other side too.

After a couple of years at home, Papa Charley happened to meet Andrew Calhoun, who was a labor agent from South Carolina. Labor agents were traveling throughout the states that had been under slavery looking for newly freed blacks to come work the many abandoned farms throughout the South. Mr. Calhoun was trying to fill the labor needs of Captain William Bodien Keene, a confederate captain who, along with his father and siblings, owned Transylvania, Sauve Terre, Stamboul, Atherton, and Mound plantations in Louisiana in East Carroll Parish. He told Papa Charley there was a great demand for labor so he wouldn't have to worry about running out of work to do. Papa Charley had also heard that Louisiana was moving right along politically and that Louisiana's 50% black population had already elected America's first black Congressman, even though Congress never did let him take his seat.

Papa Charley figured that Louisiana would be a good place for a black person to live. Besides, they wanted him to work in an area he had already seen and liked when he was in Louisiana during the war. So in 1872, Papa Charley decided to move to East Carroll Parish along with my grandmother, Harriet Sides Scott, whom he had married the year after he got out of the army.

It has always been interesting to me how one event, one decision sets the stage for the right people to be at the right place at the right time, years into the future. Take the Bible story of Joseph, for example. If Joseph's brothers hadn't decided one day to sell Joseph into slavery, Joseph wouldn't have been in the position later to save them and many others from starvation during the famine. So that is how I have come to look at Papa Charley's ending up in northeast Louisiana. It was meant to be because years later I would need to be there to perform the job that had been assigned to my hands to do.

No one can really understand life in East Carroll without understanding its beginnings. The parish Papa Charley moved to was different from most parishes in Louisiana because it had a whole lot more black people living there than whites. The other parishes in that northeast corner of the state were mostly black too. This had all come about starting in the 1820s and '30s when big plots of land in the parish were distributed to white planters under a land grant program. Because the area was so sparsely populated at the time and because farms in excess of a thousand acres required a lot of manual labor, the planters had brought in thousands of blacks whom they enslaved to do their farm work. They hired overseers to take care of the day-to-day operations. Many of the families receiving this free land and practically free slave labor eventually became the ruling class of East Carroll. These were also the families that seemed to brag the most about how much they had accomplished on their own and complained the most about any amount going to the Negro, after they themselves had been given so much.

This combination of fertile land and free labor created quite a bit of wealth. In fact, before the Civil War, the parishes in the northeast corner of the state were the wealthiest in Louisiana, producing a quarter of the state's cotton crop off the labor of their majority black populations.

The new landowners put so many black people in slavery until by the time the Civil War started, the black population of 11,000 was more than three times that of the white population. This fact never ceased to trouble the whites of the parish. During the war, the younger white men had been required to join the Confederacy. The white women had been sent away to live with relatives in other places, while the older men and boys had to do patrol duty. So hardly any white people were left in the parish during the war.

With no masters around, many black men either ran off from the plantations or joined the Union Army through the many army camps set up in Louisiana. In fact, so many blacks joined across the state that

Louisiana ended up with more blacks enlisted in the Union army than the states of Alabama, Arkansas, Florida, Georgia, North Carolina, and South Carolina combined.

In 1872, when Papa Charley got to Carroll Parish (as it was known before it split into East and West Carroll in 1877), it wasn't like he expected. Northeast Louisiana had practically been in a race war after an election when blacks had voted solidly for and elected the governor who had a black lieutenant governor on his ticket. Right after the election, the Ku Klux Klan organized and immediately started a campaign to break the political power of the Negro by killing black people and northerners all over the state.

What the Klan had not expected, though, was an organized resistance from blacks living in northeast Louisiana. Many of the northeast blacks were ex-Union soldiers who had moved in from other states because they had been given an opportunity to buy and rent land in Carroll Parish. These ex-soldiers also knew a little about fighting and about hiding out and ambushing the enemy. There were frequent confrontations, which created a lot of fear among the whites, especially in the majority black parishes along the Mississippi River such as in Carroll, which by now had a seven-to-one black population. Papa Charley said that the white folks had somehow gotten the notion that the coloreds were going to try to make white people into slaves, so all of the white people carried loaded pistols that they were quick to use.

The Klan was outlawed right before Papa Charley moved to Carroll, Louisiana. After things settled down a bit, Papa Charley was able to settle in for a few, almost peaceful years of farming. He told me how schools sprang up everywhere and how former slaves, both children and grown-ups, flocked into the one-room schools to learn to read and write. All the black people were trying to go to school while the white children stayed at home because the black superintendent of schools, Judge Jackwith Clay, refused to operate separate schools for the races. In fact, at that time, when blacks had some political power at the state level, they had created a new Louisiana state constitution that prohibited separate schools based on race. They had also written other requirements into the new constitution that guaranteed the freedom of the people and allowed the ex-slaves the opportunity to become self-sufficient over time. It was the constitution from their time in office that had established the requirement for state-supported education, a requirement that was kept even after the blacks lost their power.

Papa Charley told me about how black people could actually vote back then and how most everybody, both free-born and ex-slave, participated in politics. They had big open-air political rallies and organized political groups, and black people just naturally seemed to take to politics. The year Papa Charley moved to Louisiana, blacks were elected to the offices of lieutenant governor, secretary of state, superintendent of education, and U.S. Congressman. The state already had a black treasurer. In Carroll Parish, they elected a black sheriff and a black representative to the state legislature. There was a black clerk of court, and all the justices of the peace except one were black, and all the constables were black. They almost elected a black state senator from the area, but the white votes from another parish in the district prevented this.

Blacks across the state got so active in the Republican Party, the party of Abraham Lincoln, until they got to be the majority at almost all the parish conventions. The white Republican politicians, who were just using black people to get themselves elected, starting worrying that blacks were getting too politically powerful and independent, so they decided they'd better join up with the Democrats, the former slave masters, to keep blacks from taking over all the elected offices.

Papa Charley said that black people had believed in the Republican Party until President Lincoln was assassinated and his vice president, Andrew Johnson, took over. The new president, a southerner, made a deal with the southern whites, and after that, black people lost their protection *and* the forty acres and a mule Congress had promised all the ex-slaves.

"Those was some terrible times after the last Federal troops pulled out," Papa Charley recalled. "I believe it was 1877. The old Klan members got together and started them a new organization called the Bulldozers. Those Bulldozers burned the places where we was havin' school. They wouldn't let anybody give lodgin' to those white teachers who came down from the north to help us get some learnin'. Colored folks was so scared of those crazy white men that they was lined up at the river, trying to ketch a boat goin' north."

"'Round about '79, they ran all the colored people out of office in East Carroll. A group of white men busted into the police jury meetin' room and held all the colored officers at gunpoint. Made them sign a letter to the gov'nor sayin' they resigned their posts 'cause they couldn't do their job properly."

"Back then, if anybody spoke 'gainst them Bulldozers, they might find themselves at the wrong end of a gun barrel or in the woods in the middle of the night gettin' a beatin' they wouldn't soon forget. Sometimes they'd string 'em to the trees with their manhood cut off, hang 'em up in places where colored people was sure to pass by. It was terrible times. Colored people stopped even tryin' to vote 'cause of the threats and the hangin's."

"There was some evil white men 'round here after the war. Po' white boys mad 'cause they done gone and got shot up for nothin'. The ones that used to have money meaner than snakes 'cause they done lost the war and their slaves done run off and they don't know how they goin' to make it without somebody else doin' their work. Some of them used to havin' us wait on them hand and foot didn't even have a pot to pee in. And the way they acted, you woulda thought ev'ry problem they had, a colored person was the cause."

After the black people were scared away from the polls, it wasn't long before the Republican Party was broken and the former slave masters got back all their political power using tricks, deceit, and violence. At times, gangs of white men rode through the woods killing ex-slaves trying to leave the South, all for the sport of it. In fifteen short years, black people went from slavery to high level political offices to no right to vote to hanging from the trees, and it was more defeat than the human mind could bear. There was no more fight, and there would be little fight in East Carroll blacks for decades to come.

Blacks understood from slavery days that most southern whites considered them less than human. It was something white children had to be taught from birth in order for their minds to easily accept without guilt doing such evil things to other human beings. Since many former slave owners believed blacks had no souls, they could commit guiltless murders, especially when after slavery, they weren't murdering something that meant money to them. A black man who "got out of his place" could be killed to make him an example, and another cheap laborer could easily be found to take the dead man's place.

Most blacks found themselves with no real choices. They could go back under the master's rule and control, or die of starvation because these were the terms for getting hired. So they resigned themselves to working on the plantations. Actually the black man became a slave again. He belonged to the man in the manor. He gave the bossman his labor, and in return, the bossman advanced him food and shelter for which he would have to pay later. But most of all, the bossman provided him protection from random acts of violence, if he submitted to the bossman's rules. If anyone on a place got put in jail, the bossman would go and get him out. A sheriff couldn't even come on a plantation and arrest anyone until he consulted the bossman, and if the bossman told the sheriff not to come, he couldn't come.

The ex-slave masters seemed to like the new system. They didn't have to buy people, clothe them, or pay for their medical treatment, and if their work didn't suit, they could just turn them off the place. And all the bossman had to do was pay a wage so low that all the worker would ever be able to buy were his bare necessities. The worker would never be allowed to make enough to buy anything he needed to make his own living. The workforce was guaranteed.

So after Reconstruction ended, the blacks worked the crops through the spring, summer, and fall. At Christmas, after all the crops were in, the bossman would furnish them a Christmas celebration. He would give them a nice time, such as it was. He'd provide some whiskey, and they'd have a big bonfire and a dance and otherwise enjoy themselves together. But they were still just like his slaves.

The black man was freed with nothing but his labor, and the white man's need for it probably saved black people from annihilation. Cotton was still profitable, but it took a lot of hand labor to operate a plantation. The farms, the levee camps to keep the Mississippi flood waters back, and the log camps to clear the virgin forest lands—these labor-intensive systems are probably the only things that kept black people from being killed off after the Civil War.

Actually we have to give credit to some white people, because they all weren't bad. If they had been, why, all black people would have been killed. All blacks would have been killed, and there wouldn't have been anything done about it.

# FOUR

# Rabbit, Possum, and Coon Brains

By the time I was born at the turn of the century, blacks and whites in East Carroll Parish had settled into a peaceful coexistence. The burnings, shootings, and hangings had slacked off. The white man seemed satisfied that he had gotten back most of what he had lost during the war and Reconstruction, and the black man had resigned himself to providing the much-needed labor that whites could not provide for themselves. But of course I was just a little boy and not so aware of grown folks' problems. I was too busy learning all about life at Papa Charley's.

My grandparents lived in the southern part of East Carroll Parish in a community called Transylvania, a word that meant "across the woods." Although our house was down on a bayou, set way off by itself at the end of the woods, it was still the center of social life for the area. People came by all the time to buy vegetables from Papa Charley, but it was the combination of my grandmother's good cooking and my grandfather's great stories that made it hard for people to leave once they stopped by. The grown-ups would end up sitting around under the shade tree telling tales, swatting flies and mosquitoes.

Grandmother and Papa Charley belonged to their lodges and Negro secret societies—the Knights of Pythias, the Courts of Colanthis, and the Odd Fellows. These were fraternal organizations patterned after similar ones in the white community. The black community operated these organizations somewhat like an insurance company where you paid your dues and in return received financial assistance when you were sick or in financial trouble. There were no insurance or medical benefits available to blacks in the area in the early 1900s, so these organizations filled that need.

The members met at our house. They would put the other children and me out of the house during these secret meetings, but I would try to listen in on what they were saying. The members went through secret rituals that no non-member was to ever know. They also had special rituals for new members. I would overhear them laughing, talking about someone "riding the goat."

Children always seemed to be around our house. They loved to visit because Grandmother enjoyed children and she gave them plenty to eat. When we would be outside playing, she would call us in and give us these flat square cookies called tea cakes, hot right out of the oven. She even had candy pullings and other fun activities to keep youngsters entertained.

Papa Charley had two sons other than my father. His youngest son, Charley Jr., still lived at home. He was in his early twenties, and he would take me around with him like I was his little brother. He showed me how to hunt and taught me all about trapping animals. We spent a lot of time together out in the woods.

At our house, we had a big hole up in the loft where my Uncle Charley told me Santa Claus lived. When we would be sitting by the old fireplace at night, my uncle would throw an apple or a bag of peanuts up into the hole and let it fall as if it had been thrown out of the hole. He would say, "Red" (that's what he called me because of my reddish complexion and sandy red hair), "You have been a good boy today, so Santa is giving you something." Because I really believed Santa was up there watching me, I was a lot better than I would have been.

My other grandfather, the one on my mother's side, spent a lot of time with me too, up until he died during the scarlet fever epidemic about the time I started school. Granderson Conn, or as everyone called him, Elder Conn, lived on Stamboul plantation, the next plantation over from where Papa Charley lived. He pastored the local Baptist church, Seven Stars, and he would often come by in his buggy and take me with him to visit his church members.

Elder Conn was half black and half white. He had been born in Kentucky in the late 1830s, his white father a member of a land- and slave-rich family. During slavery, a plantation owner could just walk around his yard and pick out any female, didn't matter whether she was grown yet, and use her for his pleasure or to produce more children to sell or to work his fields. The person he picked out could be a man's mother, sister, or daughter, and sometimes even an enslaved man's wife. And this is what happened to my great-grandmother. The owner picked her although she already had a husband.

So that's how my grandfather got to be half white. When his white father left Kentucky to settle in the Delta area of northeast Louisiana, he brought my grandfather with him. He took him away from his mother and raised him in the big house with his white brothers and sisters, who were all younger than he was. But it wasn't like he was one of the family. He just lived up at the big house like a house servant. He played with his white brothers and sisters, and they taught him how to read and write by drawing out the letters in the dirt. Although teaching slaves to read and write was generally not allowed, for some reason around East Carroll, quite a few bossmen allowed their slave offspring to learn to read and write, which all helped to spread literacy faster after slavery ended. So my grandfather was quite educated for his time, and as an adult he was well respected by both blacks and whites.

Although Elder Conn came by for me often, I do remember one time in particular. He came by in the buggy and took me to a lady's house. While we were there, the woman served us some lunch. Then she put a kettle on the wood stove and brought out a bottle, some glasses, and some sugar. She poured something out of the bottle into the glass, and when the water was hot, put in the hot water and sugar, and gave me a little taste. After a while my head began to swim. But I didn't say anything.

On the way home, I was so dizzy, I fell out of the buggy and my grandfather didn't even miss me. A lady who lived nearby saw me sitting there in the road in the dust and started running after the buggy, yelling "Elder, you lost your little boy!"

He came back and picked me up and dusted me off. He said, "Boy, now don't you say anything about this." I promised him I wouldn't.

Later in the evening, after Elder Conn dropped me off at home, my head started aching, so I went to my grandmother and said, "Grandmother, my head is hurting real bad."

"What do you think is the matter?" she asked.

I said, "I think grandfather lost me out of the buggy."

When Elder Conn came to pick me up again, my grandmother asked him if he had indeed lost me out of the buggy. He said, "You little rascal, didn't you promise me you wouldn't tell anybody?" I promised him I wouldn't tell anything anymore.

In the early 1900s, each area of the parish had its own school that was held at the nearest church. I started school at age five, bundled up to make the daily two-and-a-half-mile walk in the winter cold to the church in Transylvania, which served as the schoolhouse during the week. Black children were allowed to attend school only during the winter months because we had to be available to work in the fields the rest of the year.

Even before I started school, I knew lots of children, because of the many people who visited my grandparents and because my grandmother always carried me with her when she visited other farms. So I looked forward to going to school, and I was eager to learn. I had already learned my alphabet before I started school, but in the first grade, we learned to recite the letters all kinds of ways, backwards, forwards, and divided in half like this—AN, BO, CP, DQ, ER, FS, and so on. Then we moved to the second grade, where we got three textbooks that our parents had to buy.

We had to memorize practically all our studies, and we had to stay in a book until we could recite it. There were no blackboards, and we wrote our lessons on old-fashioned slates because we didn't have much paper. Of course we had to memorize our lessons because we would soon have to erase the slate in order to copy down the next lesson.

All our classes were held in the same room. The children in the higher grades assisted those in the lower grades. There were no desks, so we sat on the hard wooden benches used for church services on Sunday. The church was cold and drafty, and many days it would be so cold that the teacher would have to let us take turns warming our feet and hands by the potbellied wood stove. The boys had to take turns going outside to gather more wood for the fire. At lunchtime, we ate the lunches packed by our parents, which for most children were molasses and biscuits carried in a pail.

At the end of each school day I would have to hurry home to help with the cows and do my other chores. I'd finish the day off with a hot meal—steaming pots of vegetables, baked sweet potatoes, and meats with cornbread or biscuits on the side.

Our teachers would sometimes bring the newspaper and read us stories about Uncle Wiggly Long Ear and Nurse Jane, Fuzzy Wuzzy, and the Muskrat Lady, all of which I found quite interesting. On Friday evenings, we would have some kind of program or a spelling match. In spelling, they would call us to the front of the room and give us words to spell. If the person beside me missed their word and I spelled it right, I could move up to their space. I could keep doing this until I finally worked my way to the head of the class or time ran out. We would always end the school term with a big concert, with all the community in attendance.

All the time I was in school, I tried to stay on the good side of my teachers. I tried to obey. I always stayed on the good side of my classmates too. In the early 1900s, we had plantation gangs. The boys from one plantation would fight the boys from another plantation. A good many of my classmates' parents were sharecroppers, living about as poor as it was possible to live. Because of their poverty, my classmates seemed to have a great need to defend what little they had and take power the few places it could be found.

Sometimes the boys from different plantations would meet up and start yelling insults at each other, the worst of which was to call a fellow schoolmate black. The other person would yell back, "Who you calling black?" and the fight would begin. Being as light-skinned as I was, I knew better than to call anyone black because they were sure to beat the living daylights out of a light-skinned boy.

At the time, I couldn't see a reason for them to be fighting each other, considering that none of us owned much of anything. I could sense that white people treated lighter-skinned blacks better, acting like we were automatically smarter and cleaner than blacks who were very dark-skinned, but I figured white people probably did that just to cause confusion. I figured God was smart enough to know what he was doing. He created black folks in a bouquet of skin colors, so any shade should be good. It just didn't make sense to me, this fighting over skin color. Of course when I became a man, I was able to figure out what all the plantation gang fighting was about. I came to understand that when people can't get basic needs met and when they aren't given fundamental power, they will create their own power, if only by bullying the people in their own family or in their own neighborhood.

Because of the plantation gangs, boys couldn't go from one place to another to see a girl without permission from the gang of that place. I found myself in a peculiar position because of my grandparents. Because of them, most of the boys from the different plantations already knew me, either through Papa Charley and my grandmother or through my grandfather, Granderson Conn, who had baptized most of the people in the community. I could go pretty much wherever I wanted to.

So I ended up with a special standing among my peers. I had friendships in all the gangs and used my friendships to help keep peace among my classmates. This special standing even carried over into the organizations and clubs I joined. I was always voted the head of something—the 4-H Club, the Boy's Corn Club, and many other organizations, when I was in school.

My grammar school education was probably the best they could offer under the circumstances, since we didn't attend a full-length school term like the white children. Our parents didn't have to send us to school at all if they didn't want to, since it was only against the law for white children not to attend school. The white school board paid black teachers $20 per month for the three months, but from time to time, our parents were able to raise another $40 through some kind of educational association to keep the teacher there an extra two months. The community would also help support the teachers by sharing what we had at home. I would bring them vegetables and eggs from my grandparents.

Our parents required teachers to be a part of the community, because teachers were considered an extension of the home. Teachers were looked up to and held in the highest regard. Unlike today, the teachers' job was to develop the total child. Our teachers understood that there were lessons children needed to learn before they could properly learn reading, writing, and arithmetic. They helped mold our lives by teaching us to expect a little more from life than the plantation system. They taught us manners, respect for older people, and how to be neat. Because they understood the importance of these lessons, they found many ways to mix instructions about reading and writing with lessons about good behavior.

Our school was on the order of a Christian school where they read the Bible and said prayers each morning. When we arrived at school on Mondays, the first thing our teacher, who was a minister, would ask was, "Who went to Sunday School yesterday?" Children who didn't go to church were considered bad.

Our teachers gave wholesome instructions. It was inspiring to me when they read from the psalms of David: "The Lord is my shepherd, I shall not want"; "Blessed is the man that walketh not in the counsel of the ungodly"; and "The earth is the Lord's and the fullness thereof." It gave me a pickup or something to hold on to, made me feel unafraid of the bad things that could happen, to know someone absolutely good was in charge.

We would sing "Be a sunbeam, Jesus wants me for a sunbeam," and "Be a hero on the battlefield of life," and "Count your blessings." The schoolbook we used contained many quotations such as "As you would have men do unto you, do unto them" and "Work while you work, boys, play while you play; this is the way to be happy and gay."

When I was in school, there wasn't an abundance of well-educated people around East Carroll, black or white, due to the impact of Reconstruction on schooling. During Reconstruction, many white parents had kept their children home rather than send them to school with the newly freed blacks, so as it turned out, most whites who grew up from the beginning of the Civil War to about 1890 had little or no schooling.

We were lucky, however, because the teacher at our school was very well educated. When I finished grammar school, our teacher, who was a Methodist pastor, decided on his own to add another grade to take us further. Higher education wasn't considered all that important at the time. In fact, even in the late 1920s, there were only four black state-supported high schools in the entire state of Louisiana—three run by the state and one by the black state college, Southern University. So our teacher helped East Carroll Parish move educationally ahead of many parishes in the state.

Any student who finished this new grade—the eighth grade—could go before the school board and take a teacher's examination. Anyone who passed could become a teacher. Most of my classmates took the examination, passed, and started teaching. I took the exam, too, but decided I wouldn't teach because I liked freedom too much. Besides, the salary was only about $40 a month at the time I took the test.

I could make that much in a week hunting and trapping. So I figured I would do that for a while.

About the time I finished grammar school, our local Baptist Association decided to open a high school for blacks. The association was an organization of all the black Baptist churches throughout East Carroll Parish. The East Carroll Baptist Association, back in 1896, had been a part of the Ninth District Association of the state assembly, which back then also included all the black Baptist churches from Madison, Tensas, and Concordia Parishes. Although there weren't any real roads between the parishes in the late 1800s, in order to meet, the Association members would have to ride their horses long distances down the narrow paths that snaked through the dense woods.

The four parishes had organized for the purpose of operating a Christian school, which they named the Broomsy School. The District had raised $4,000 for the project, but unfortunately, the parishes couldn't agree on how the money was to be spent. In 1906, the District had a big split that ended in a lawsuit. East Carroll received $800 from the money on hand, which they used to purchase sixty acres of land about two hundred yards from the Lake Providence city limits, the county seat of East Carroll Parish. They formed their own association called the East Carroll Baptist Association in 1907 and not long afterwards opened a high school on their newly acquired property. All the Baptist churches in the parish helped to support the school.

Our new school was called the East Carroll Baptist Normal and Industrial Institute. East Carroll became known in all the surrounding parishes as the progressive parish because it was the only one with a black high school. Children flocked into Lake Providence from all the surrounding parishes.

The more progressive-minded members of the community believed that education was going to be the key to getting respect, so they willingly opened up their homes to these children from other parishes. Some families lived in one- or two-room houses, and money was always scarce, but there was a generous spirit that led people to share whatever they had. They let children live with them during the school term and in return, the boarders helped the families with the chores such as tending the pigs and the cows. Their parents provided vegetables and whatever small amounts of money they could afford.

Some parents even sent their younger children to live in East Carroll because some of the black schools in the surrounding parishes were pretty bad. Some grammar schools didn't even have a system of promotion where children could move from one grade to another. So there was a constant influx of new children into town.

I actually liked going to school and learning new things, so when I heard about the high school, I decided to reconsider my plans for a life of hunting and trapping. After giving it a little thought, I decided to try out the new high school.

The new high school was in Lake Providence, which was about eight miles north of where I lived in Transylvania. I attended the new high school for a short while but soon started having second thoughts. For one thing, I kept having trouble getting a ride from Transylvania to Lake Providence. Not many people owned a car in 1916. Besides, it was hard for us to see a practical reason for pursuing higher education at that time. There just wasn't much mental-type work to do around a farm, and we didn't know anything about what was going on in other places. This was before we had tractors—and no one needed to have an education to drive a mule. You could easily learn "gee" to make a mule turn right and "haw" to make him turn left, and "whoa" to make him stop. You didn't need an education to drive some cows to a pasture or to chop weeds out of the corn. You always had a bossman to tell you, so you didn't have to think for yourself. Not that you couldn't think for yourself—it was just that the bossman wasn't interested in what you had to contribute. That's why so many black children didn't try to go any further.

So after putting in a little more time in the ninth grade, I quit. I had reached the top. I left the classroom and went into the woods. But I still wasn't satisfied within myself, because I really wanted to learn all the things being taught at the high school. Even if I didn't know how I would use the information, I just liked knowing new things. So whenever I could catch a ride, I would go up to the high school and just sit in and listen to the classes.

Sometimes I would do substitute teaching at a new school near my home, the Transylvania Rosenwald School. Our community had been lucky enough to get one of the schools built with funds from the Julius Rosenwald Fund, founded on profits from the Sears,

Roebuck Company. Unlike the church school I had attended, this new school had blackboards, desks, and separate classrooms, and teachers who were sometimes trained and paid by the fund. Eventually I was made an honorary member of the faculties of Transylvania and a new school the parish opened in 1937, the East Carroll Parish Training School, which was run under the direction of Professor G. W. Griffin.

Although I loved school, working there failed to give me what my heart so desired—which was freedom and independence. I knew I didn't want to be like the boys I met on the plantations who were always at the beck and call of the plantation bossmen. Hunting and fishing were the keys to my independence.

I loved being in the woods. Growing up, I spent so much time there that I felt I was almost one with the animals. I could look at an animal track and tell the male from the female. I could look at a rabbit running down the road and tell you whether it was a he or a she. While hunting at night, if there were coon eyes, I'd say, "That's a coon in that tree," and if it was a possum, "possum eyes," or if it was somebody's cow across the field, I'd say, "That's cow eyes."

I was also a great fisherman. I got fish all kinds of ways, at night and in the day. I learned to know just where the fish would be biting and what type of fish would be on my line before I pulled it up from the water. Now you might think that this is a fable but all that I'm saying is true.

My Uncle Charley Jr. bought me a couple of animal traps, and I became a great mink trapper. Since we lived on the bayou, right near the woods, I could catch maybe four or five a week. I'd bring the mink skins into town to Lake Providence to sell to a storekeeper named Mr. Leach. He'd tell me, "Ol' boy, ol' boy, they ain't worth but six bits (seventy-five cents), but I'll give you a dollar because you bring them all to me."

One day, a new fur buyer came through the country and I had six mink furs at home at the time. He stopped by our house and when I came out, he said, "I heard you trap. Do you have any mink?" I mumbled yes but I didn't really want to tell him, because I planned to take them to Mr. Leach. Mr. Leach had told me he'd give me a dollar for them and "don't let nobody else have them."

My grandmother told me, "You can let him look at them. It can't hurt for him to look." So I went and got my furs. The fur man turned my furs over, inspecting them closely. Finally he said, "Son, what you want for them?"

I said, "You're in the business. Will you make me a deal?"

He looked them over again. "Well, I tell you, some of them are sorta small," he said.

I thought to myself, he'll probably offer me fifty cents.

Finally after what seemed like a long time, he said, "About the best I can do for you is six dollars apiece."

Six dollars apiece! Thirty-six dollars total! That was quite exciting. I'd only been getting a dollar for the lot. Mr. Leach had been beating me out of my furs.

So hunting and fishing became the way I made my livelihood. Some nights I'd go out coon hunting and I would kill five or six coons, which would be about $30 a night. That was big money then, and the next day I would be all dressed up walking around. Nobody saw me doing any kind of work. They were wondering how I was living.

My life in the woods not only affected my pockets, but it also influenced my behavior. I spent a lot of time observing animal behavior, and I tried to imitate the characteristics I admired. Since I was raised superstitiously, I thought eating animal brain would help me be like them in some way. So I ate the rabbit head because I wanted to be able to run fast and be cunning. I ate the squirrel head—I wanted to be frisky. I ate the opossum head because I wanted to be sly. And finally I ate raccoon brain because when you get a coon cornered, he will always fight his way out. I wanted to be able to fight my way out if I was ever pushed into a corner.

# FIVE

# A Matter of Respect

We lived in Transylvania on a section of the 10,000 acres of land owned by a company called Abston, Crump, and Wynne. The owners, who lived in Memphis, had turned over management of the land to a local bossman. The bossman had hired some independent farmers like my grandfather, but mostly he just let the same families stay who had worked the land during slavery when the Keene and Constant families had owned it.

When the old folks had been freed from slavery, they were just told they were free. Someone came up one day and announced, "Oh by the way, you are free as of today. You don't have to work for the master anymore." Nobody offered them anything to start off with—no house, no money, no land, no cooking equipment, no education, nothing to make a living with. All they owned were the clothes on their backs.

Congress had voted for each of them to get forty acres of land, but apparently the new president didn't see much economic value in over two hundred years of free labor. So he gave the land back to the very same group who had enslaved the people, and the old folks were left with nothing. To keep from starving, most of them had had to go back to work on the same plantations where they lived before the Civil War. They became what were called sharecroppers, some of them staying in the same old, one-room dirt-floor cabins they had lived in as slaves. Some moved into other shanties provided by the landowners. This was the economic system under which I grew up in the early 1900s—black people provided the much-needed labor necessary to make the crops while the white bossmen provided the land and the tools.

Because we lived in such a remote area, I didn't get exposed to racial prejudice as much as some children. The Transylvania community was made up of about 250 black families, and as a teenager and young adult, I didn't have many occasions to come in contact with white people. In fact, Transylvania was surrounded by other plantations that were also settled by mostly black families. Before Emancipation, the area had many slaves because the land up and down the river was so rich. After the slaves were freed, most had stayed in the area, so most people I saw were black.

Actually there was only one white family living in our community. The father, Mr. Abe Bass, seemed to be a very nice man, and he taught his children to be the same. The only other white people I was exposed to were the bossman and the whites who came by our house to buy vegetables from Papa Charley. So that made it better for us. Since there were so few whites around to treat us as inferiors, we never got to feel the full impact of Jim Crow laws that required that black people be treated less than any other race.

Papa Charley was a great truck gardener, selling fresh vegetables to anybody who came by—corn, cabbage, mustard and turnip greens, melons, potatoes, and tomatoes. As a child, I found the white people who came by the house to buy vegetables to be very friendly. They would always bring an apple or something for me and would sit around laughing and talking with Papa Charley. So I had no reason to think that they would wish to treat me badly.

In East Carroll Parish in the early 1900s, most blacks lived a distance from any whites. Generally, there would be only two white families on a large farm—maybe the general boss, as we called the landowner who lived in the front house, or the big house, as we called it, and the sub or riding boss who rode the fields making sure that black folks did the work. The riding boss would ride his horse around to the different day laborers' houses, stopping at each of the identical cabins on the row. He'd come up to a man's door and a man could be in his bed and he'd walk right in and say, "Get out this bed and get to work! We need you in the fields." And he'd finish with a "See that your children get to work, too!"

The riding boss didn't have too much contact with independent farmers like Papa Charley. The independent farmers paid rent for the land and owned their own equipment. The boss would just occasionally ride out to their farms to commend them for their work because they knew they were going to get their money. These were mostly blacks who had managed to come out of slavery times with some money or equipment, some of them free-born or ex-soldiers like Papa

Charley. Most sharecroppers were working with the hope that they could make enough off their crops to become independent farmers someday.

The riding bosses generally found themselves isolated from most other whites. The plantation owners pretty much excluded poor whites from farming their land because they considered them troublemakers. And since there weren't enough poor whites to maintain a farm or as they called it, a plantation, they preferred not to have just one or two poor white families around. They also didn't want their black workers exposed to any white people who might be as far down the pecking order as we were. They feared that if we saw white folks without money, power, and authority, we might begin to question what they were always trying to teach us about the "natural order" of things— that white men were born to control and black men were ordained by God to serve.

Most times, nobody was around for a white boy to like but his sister, so he would pick out a black girl and make her his friend. Finally, maybe he would get a child and go ahead and just stick with her on through life. Of course, by law he couldn't marry her, but many whites lived common-law with Negro women as though they were their wives. They bought their homes and reared their children, and no one seemed to bother them about it. Some of the biggest white men in town never had a wife—never had a white wife: Mr. Jim Pitman, Mr. Will Wiley, and some of the Millikins. Then there were others who had their white wives and at the same time reared another family by their Negro sweethearts, and dared anyone to say anything about it.

Most of the big white men had somebody black kin to them, oftentimes children they got by the cook or somebody else who worked for them. Anywhere you went around town, you could see their children, some of them so light-skinned and straight-haired they could pass for white. Some of them did, when they moved away to other areas.

So it made the relationship between blacks and whites somewhat different because so many of us were kin. Since blacks had given up trying to vote, there wasn't much of the violent kind of hostility between the races anymore, unless you did one of two forbidden things—you made an advance toward a white woman, or you tried to take the black woman the white man called his.

When I was growing up, my job was to help my grandfather work the large piece of farmland Papa Charley rented from Abston, Crump, & Wynne. Although Papa Charley had always operated somewhat independently, when I was a teenager, something happened that changed our lifestyle. In 1915, when he was over seventy years old, Papa Charley finally received what was called a bounty from the government for his services as a soldier in the Union army. The fictitious name of George Wilson, which he had used to join the infantry, had cost him years in trying to convince the government to give him the pension he was due. His discharge papers had burned up in a house fire, so he had no easy way to prove he was the same person as George Wilson. Throughout my childhood, he had given deposition after deposition describing times, places, and events, trying to prove he had been where George Wilson had been in the service. The government denied his claim for fifteen years, but they finally gave in and granted him his pension when he was almost too old to use it. He received a big check for his back pay, and a monthly check until his death.

When Papa Charley received his back pay check, he bought his own plow, other farm equipment, and a team of mules. Then he got other blacks to work with him and he furnished them supplies, just like the white and black landowners did for their workers. He brought them up to town in Lake Providence every Saturday evening to get their groceries at the big grocery store owned by a black man named W. E. Boyce. This made Papa Charley even more independent, and none of the owners bothered him.

I was still a teenager at the time, almost fourteen years old. Although most of my time went to helping Papa Charley on the farm, when I could get some spare time, I would go fishing and hunting. One day when we weren't all that busy, my grandfather gave me permission to go fishing. As I walked down the narrow dirt path to the fish bar, dragging my cane poles as I walked, I saw the riding boss coming on his horse in the opposite direction. When he got up beside me, he stopped his horse and asked me in a condescending voice, "Where you going with those poles?"

I wondered to myself why he thought it was his business where I was going. We were independent farmers and no one had bothered me before about my comings and goings. So I said, "Look like when you see a person with poles, you should know they're going fishing."

His face went red with anger. "We don't fish on Saturdays," he said.

I gave him a kind of sideways look, not looking him straight in the face, and said, "Well, *we're* not going fishing, *I'm* going fishing. And my grandfather told me I could go today."

He got to ranting and raving about what I could and could not do on Saturdays, how he wouldn't put up with no trifling boys around his place. Then he said, "Who's your daddy anyway? I'll talk to him about your disrespect."

"You should have talked to my grandfather first anyway," I returned.

He knew I was a minor and my grandfather had told me I could go fishing. I didn't owe him anything and my grandfather didn't owe him anything, yet he thought he should be able to tell me when I could fish and when I couldn't, when I should work and when I shouldn't. So that was the thing that began to open my eyes. I began to feel a little bitterness toward the plantation bosses because they thought they should be able to boss all black people around.

Another incident a few years later reinforced my belief that you should stand up against something you believe is wrong. In this incident, the riding boss shot one of the men who worked on the plantation.

It all started when the black fellow accused the bossman of liking his girlfriend. The bossman fired him on the spot, told him to get off the place, and refused to pay him for the time he had already worked.

The man left but after a while came back looking for the bossman. Across the field, we could see his head over the tops of the cotton stalks as he loped back up the road looking for the bossman. When he caught up with him, he demanded his money. "You done fired me, you gonna pay me now!"

"Now, listen here!" the bossman told him. "You won't get any money till Saturday when everybody else gets paid."

Both of them were good and angry now. "Yeah, but I'm fired and I'm goin' to have my money today!"

One word led to another. The black fellow pulled out a pistol, but the pistol failed to fire. When the bossman realized the pistol wasn't firing, he pulled his own pistol and fired several shots, hitting the black fellow once as he tried to run and hide behind some trees. With a flesh wound in the thigh, he limped over to another worker's house to get help, while the bossman jumped on his horse and made for home to get his shotgun to kill him. When the bossman returned with his shotgun, lots of people had gathered around, and the people in the house wouldn't let the bossman come in.

The bossman left, swearing that he would kill them all, and word spread around the plantation that the bossman was gone to get help. We assumed he would get a mob together and come back to lynch the fellow that night. So Papa Charley and my father, who had recently remarried, along with a bunch of other men, gathered up at the man's house to wait. They took me along with them.

Way late into the night, two deputies, Christ McGinnis and Will Conn, one of my relatives, showed up at the house. Now it was unusual for a black man to be a deputy back then (of course, he didn't look very black), but because Will Conn was a sharpshooter and could outshoot almost anyone around the state, they had given him the job. He made arrests, acted as jailer, and even picked up prisoners from other towns, especially the ones that were supposed to be notorious. He was one of the men who acted as a guide for President Theodore Roosevelt during his trips to East Carroll Parish to bear hunt.

As the deputies came up into the yard, all of us who had been waiting inside came out and joined another group of men now coming around from the back of the house. We stood forming a wall between the officers and the house.

"We come to make an arrest, so you fellows need to step aside and let us go in the house."

We didn't make a move. Somebody said, "Now, you know what's going to happen if we let you have him."

The deputies talked and talked, trying to convince us to let them arrest the fellow. Finally Will Conn said, "We come to arrest this fellow, we have papers. We guarantee his protection. So many of you are around here, what you think?"

I believe my daddy told him what we thought about his guarantee. They talked a while longer, and as day was about to break, the men finally backed down and let them take the fellow off to jail.

The workers on the plantation decided they wouldn't work any more under such a man, a man who didn't show any of the workers their proper respect. The black fellow was the one who had been shot—and who would be dead by now if someone hadn't intervened—but he was the one who would be in jail for a very long time. So when the time came to go to work, everybody—the day hands, the share-croppers, and the independent farmers—all refused.

The riding boss must have gotten in touch with the owner in Memphis, because one day he and the riding boss just showed up where the workers generally congregated. "Why you all not working?" the owner demanded to know.

Somebody answered, "We all decided not to work as long as this man is your agent."

"Well, this man hasn't done nothing and I can't turn him off."

Days passed with nobody working. On Saturday, Papa Charley called a meeting for the workers to talk to the owner. We all met up at the lot where the mules and other animals were kept.

After a while, the owner and the agent arrived. The owner got off his horse and said, "Let us pray."

*He needs to pray,* I thought.

After he finished praying, he made this speech, trying to show us how the black fellow had been at fault and he wasn't going to turn his agent off. He concluded with, "So what y'all going to do about it?"

My grandfather, who was our spokesman, said, "Well, we decided not to pick any more cotton as long as he's here." He motioned toward the agent.

The owner tried to convince us to go back to work but he couldn't, so he set another meeting for Monday. We hadn't worked for over a week, and the owner couldn't make any money with the cotton still in the fields.

On Monday, we all met back up at the mule lot and the owner made another speech, trying to convince us to go back to work.

Papa Charley told the owner, "We have told you we're not going to work as long as he's your agent."

The owner called the riding boss up front. "Come on up here," he said, slapping him on the shoulder. "I want you all to know that I'm not going to fire him."

The riding boss, who hadn't spoken a word throughout the different meetings said, "Well I tell you, if y'all don't want to work under me, I don't want to be your agent, so I'm resigning."

So that's the way we got rid of him. I learned an important lesson from this as a youngster that proved true through the years—if people stick together, they can pretty well get what they need.

A new boss (just about as bad as the last one) came on the place, and soon afterwards, a lot of new workers. The new bossman let the new workers borrow just as much money and run up just as much credit as they wanted, and of course the workers were obligated to work in the fields to pay it back. He actually encouraged them to run up their credit accounts, the same way that he encouraged them to drink. Often he would give out free liquor at the end of the work week after knock-off time, supposedly as a reward for good work.

Many sharecroppers didn't understand that these things were done to control them, and they would be around bragging about how good the new bossman was. They didn't realize that sharecroppers in debt meant guaranteed workers for the next year, because sharecroppers weren't supposed to leave a place if they owed the owners any money. Sometimes sharecroppers would try to leave anyway, but the riding bosses and owners would put the sheriff and the deputies on their trail until they tracked them down and made them sorry they had tried to leave. A runaway sharecropper could end up hung, or even worse, get sent to the feared state penitentiary to work on a chain gang, where he'd be chained and whipped and made to sleep in filth by night and work in filth by day. In some ways, the early 1900s seemed to me to be a lot like how the old folks described living under slavery.

I had heard about the new boss and had seen him around, but he had never said anything to me. One day I was coming from the store when I saw the new boss headed my direction.

"Hey boy," he called. "Why aren't you out there in the fields with the other boys? I been noticing you walking around here, not working."

I replied, "I don't work by the day. I am a farmer with my grandfather. When he doesn't have anything for me to do, why, that's nobody else's business."

I thought the bossman would about come out of his skin, he was so mad. "Oh, so you are one of those smart-a—— uppity niggers," he said. "I don't care what you do with your old grandpappy. If you aren't in the field by the time I finish getting my supplies, I'll be by your place and I'll make it so hot for you, you'll be sorry you didn't come."

I went on home and told my grandmother what the bossman said. When I repeated what I had told the bossman, she looked like she might faint dead away. "That white man will come down here and kill you for your biggity talk," she said. She insisted that I go on down to the field.

My father, who happened to be visiting us at the time, told my grandmother, "Don't tell the boy that. What business the white man got doing anything to him?"

So I made up my mind not to go. My daddy said I shouldn't go, and since I didn't owe the bossman anything, I shouldn't have to go. So I got ready to defend myself. I had been studying the coon to learn just how to do it. You get a coon cornered and he will almost always fight his way out. I had eaten the coon brain for just such a situation as this.

It was now past the time I was supposed to be in the field. I kept looking out the window waiting for the bossman to come after me. After a while, I looked and saw him coming, just a stepping. I felt uneasy, not all together because of what he would do to me, but what he might make me do to him. My heart pounded as he came near the house. There was a ditch bank that ran not too far from the house, and when he got close, he just followed the ditch on around and never came by the house to say anything.

It was a scary feeling standing up to the bossman because grandmother was right. The bossman would just as soon have killed me as looked at me. But something moved in me that day. I knew I had to stand up and keep on standing up, because if they caught me bent over, they just might climb on my back and keep me bending and scraping all my life. I didn't want to become just another day hand, living a life of submission under the control of someone else—someone who would never allow me to become a real man.

On April 14, 1921, Papa Charley died, somewhere around the age of eighty. Nobody knew his exact age for sure. My father and his two brothers from Mississippi came for the funeral. My father tried to talk my grandmother into moving to Mississippi to live with one of her children, but she refused saying, "No, me and my boy are going to stay together. We can make it all right."

So the two of us lived there together until November, when my sister Geneva and her husband separated and she and her two children came to live with us. The following April, just one year and two weeks after Papa Charley passed, my grandmother passed on too, and left just my sister and me there to try to carry on the farm. The bossman at that time asked me what I intended to do, would I attempt to carry on. I decided that I would. The people told me, "You can stay there, and if you'll be the man that Charley was, why you'll always get along with people."

Although I was only twenty, I tried to step into my grandparents' shoes and run the farm the best I could. I even tried to keep up my social standing, though the life of the house, my grandmother, was gone. My house became the place where young Christians would meet. We would play and sometimes do a little dancing, away from the deacons of the church. Every once and a while, we would allow a deacon to come who wouldn't talk and who liked those kinds of things. During the late summer, between cotton chopping and cotton picking time, we would have a good time with our fish fries and other socials.

On the plantation, there was a system called "furnishing." This meant the owner would furnish each family who farmed for him so much meal, so much flour, some clothes, and things like that. He would provide seed money in the spring and groceries starting in March on through a little after cotton picking time. Most people kept a small garden to avoid having to get too many groceries from the bossman.

Each plantation had a store called a commissary where everybody picked up their food and supplies. The commissary owner had certain things for the poor. For instance, he had high-class flour for cash-paying white customers. Sharecroppers had to get the old flour that was often filled with bugs.

Since I was a trapper, during the winter months I made extra money. For fear I would spend it before summer, I decided to buy some things at this store up town in Lake Providence. I bought enough flour to carry my sister and her children and me through the year.

I'd still go to the commissary from time to time to get other things. Whenever I would go up to the counter to ask for what I wanted, they'd say, "Meat? How much? Sugar? How much? Flour?"

"No, I don't need any flour," I'd say.

Each time I went there and said no, they'd ask me, "Why don't you get any flour?" I'd just say I wasn't out yet. Finally I got tired of them asking so I said, "Well, I don't want that old, bad flour and that's the reason I don't get it."

The next time I went to the commissary, the owner called me off to the side and said, "Man (short for Mannie), tell 'em to let you have this good flour but don't tell the others about it."

Whenever anybody got groceries or supplies from the commissary, the person behind the counter wrote it down in an account book under each person's name. They didn't tell us how much our things cost, nor were we told how much interest we were being charged. And we didn't get to see our account sheets until after the crops came in, when the bossman would settle up the accounts with all the workers. He would total up how much money was made off the bales of cotton sold from each family's acreage and subtract out the gin charges. Then he would subtract the amounts we owed through the commissary. If a farmer worked on the half, he would get half of what remained; on the fourth, one-fourth of what remained.

Many people couldn't read or write, not to mention add and subtract, so they didn't know whether their accounts were right or wrong. Most of the time, the bossman would tell the people they owed more than what the crop brought in, so after working a whole year, many families had to stay on another year to pay off their debts. Sometimes the bossman would take the people's livestock, saying they had to take it because they just owed too much money.

Of course there were some fair bossmen, and in a really good year, why, a farmer might get maybe five hundred dollars, especially if he had a gang of children or other kinfolk to help him bring in the crop. Then there were other bossmen who in a good year might find a way to get rid of the sharecroppers and hire more day laborers so they could keep the profit.

For some years after my grandparents passed, I worked toward maintaining an independent farmer status, but I was unsuccessful. Over time I found myself in a sharecropper status and eventually in a day-hand status.

A new man I had once had a big run-in with took over as agent of our place. I was worried because I knew he would remember the run-in and would most likely throw me off the place. He came by the house and he said, "Now, Man, you can just stay right on where you are. You don't have to worry. I know you and you know me, and we'll get along all right together." I was surprised—I had done all that worrying for nothing.

In the summer, we worked about nine hours, with everybody generally starting about daybreak when the cotton plants were still wet with dew. We worked into the full heat of the afternoon, chopping weeds and grass out of the cotton fields. Other times, we'd have to thin out the cotton stalks when they would come up too thick. The only break we had during the day was at noontime for lunch. Several times a day, we'd get to stop briefly when the water boy walked through the field with his bucket of lukewarm water and offered us a drink from the tin cup reserved for "colored." The other cup was for the white bossman only, and no one dared cross the line to use it.

Some time after the new man took over, his brother got killed, and he turned all the bossing over to me while he took care of his brother's affairs. He said, "You take over there for me. Get them hands out and see that they work."

The sweltering, energy-sapping Louisiana heat, sometimes one hundred degrees in the shade, even with a breeze stirring, could make for some fairly hard workdays. The planters had left very few trees in any field, and the knee-high green cotton stalks ran in straight even rows as far as the eye could see. The only protection between the sun and our brains was the wide-brimmed straw sun hats everybody wore. I decided that since I was in charge, I would make work conditions a little better. I would establish some break-time rules.

"If you all work harder, if it gets too hot, we'll stop and cool off," I told them.

That afternoon, we had stopped for a break when I looked up and here comes the bossman on his horse, dust a-flying. Everybody went to grab their hoes and go running back out to their rows. I said, "No, no, we can't do that. We are under the shade and we have to stay here."

He pulled his horse up. "What's the matter, Man?"

"Nothing's the matter. I promised them if they would work hard, if they got hot, I'd let them cool. Don't you see that we got a whole lot more done than they been doing by me promising them that?"

He said, "All right now. I'm holding you responsible for everything." He pointed at the group of people standing in the shade. They all looked a little panicked. "Look over there." He counted the number of people and said, "Five minutes from each one of them, that will cost me . . ." He went to figuring how much I was costing him, although we had gotten much more work done than when he was there.

A few weeks after that, he decided to stop paying us when we knocked off work on Fridays. He said we would have to start getting paid at the big country store where they paid at eight o'clock Saturday night when it was too late for anybody to take care of their business. And the bossman knew that Saturday was the only time we had. I decided that I just wouldn't go get my money. So on Monday morning, I dressed up and went over to the house.

"Where are you going?" the bossman asked.

"I couldn't get any money Saturday and I got to tend to my business today."

Later that week, he called me off to the side. He said, "Now you come over here Saturday morning and get your money, but don't tell them others about it."

Finally we had another run-in about some rule that didn't make sense to anybody, probably not even to him. He had backed down in previous encounters, but this time he said angrily, "You think you a d—— white man, don't you? You ain't no d—— white man."

Something inside pushed me to feel independent, in spite of my environment. I would always stand my ground when I was not being treated respectfully. I remember one situation when I was in my thirties. I had a white neighbor who used to have company outside making noise all hours of the night, and I'd dare not say anything about it.

One night, two of my friends, Harrison Mingo and Cliff Maxwell, came by to visit. Around nine o'clock, they decided to leave. We walked out to the car and we were laughing a little bit when my neighbor came to his door and yelled, "Cut out that racket out there."

He went back into the house and after a while, he was back to the door again. "Cut that racket out I said! If you don't, I'll shoot."

One of us said, "You're not the only one that's got a gun."

After that, my neighbor didn't say anything else and my friends went on home.

I don't know, but there's something inside me that can feel when something is wrong. I felt like my neighbor was going to try to retaliate in some way, so I went on in the house and got ready for whatever might happen.

The next morning I saw him coming stepping and he said, "John, I don't like the way you spoke to me last night."

I said, "No, I don't like the way you spoke to me either. You've had your company over there making racket until eleven or twelve o'clock at night and if I dare say anything to you, it would be one of the greatest insults. My company was just visiting till nine o'clock and you come out there talking like that."

"You must remember I'm a white man," he returned.

"But you must remember I'm a man too, and I want you to respect me and I'm going to respect you."

He looked shocked. He must have been speechless, because he turned and left without saying another word.

No matter where we went, we couldn't get away from the old slavery system mind-set, especially after Jim Crow laws had made discrimination against us the law of the land. We always needed to be reminding white men that we didn't deserve to be treated low-class. We were human beings and men too, just like them. Being disrespectful to black people wasn't something they seemed to really be aware of doing. Disrespect was something most of them did as naturally as waking up in the morning or breathing. They didn't have to deliberate on what degrading thing to say or do or spend any time feeling guilty about humiliating anyone. It was just normal to them because it was what they had been taught from birth to do.

I was visiting my mother not long after the incident with my neighbor and happened to mention it to her. I shouldn't have said anything, because she got herself all worked up and told me I should move before that man and his friends killed me.

I guess she had a reason to get worked up. Something bad *could* happen to me. I had seen it happen several times before. Black men had been killed for a whole lot less. Just looking a white person directly in the eye when you talked to him was considered improper respect, so I had been stepping way over the line all my life. I knew the kinds of things white people expected of me—to duck my head and look at the ground when they looked at or spoke to me, or grin and say "Yessah, Mr. Charlie" no matter how wrong Mr. Charlie might be. I couldn't see myself being like that or living like that, and everything inside of me rebelled against it. I had to be treated with respect. I would not be running from one place to another. They'd just have to kill me. So I made up my mind to stay. Not long after that, the man moved out and another white family moved in.

I had some chickens, and from the time the new family moved in, the lady there commenced to complaining about the chickens. "Got to get rid of them, they messin' on my porch." So I moved the chickens away so they couldn't get over to her house.

Out in my chicken coop, I had one hen setting, waiting for the little chicks to hatch. I went out there one day, and my new neighbor had sprinkled the eggs full of salt. Then next thing, she decided she wanted me to come work for her. She said so nicely, "Henry." She always called me by my middle name, which she knew I didn't like. "I want you to work some for me but I don't have no money to pay you but I'll give you some peaches I got put up and things like that."

I told her, "I'm sorry, but I'm farming and I don't have time to do any outside work."

Then she decided she wanted my house. "I want that house you're staying in. I want to put a cook in it."

"Well, I'm in possession of it for the balance of this year," I said. "And I don't intend to move."

Her son, who was a nice fellow who I went hunting with, told me, "Now, don't worry about mother. She's just like that. She says when we get a cook, we's wasting the money, and when we don't have one, we working her to death."

Finally she decided she would just get rid of me. We had some words and she said some pretty terrible things, so I asked her, "Do you have religion?"

She snapped, "Yes, I got religion."

"Well, you're about the worst Christian I ever saw."

"Well, now I tell you," her anger rising, "I need me a cook and you keeping that house!"

She went on explaining how she really needed my house, and then all of a sudden she quieted down and asked sweetly, "Henry, you got any potatoes?" I told her yes and she said, "Well, bring me some and then I'll fix you some nice pies." So I brought her some sweet potatoes and she fixed me two nice-looking pies. Course I was afraid to eat those pies 'cause something in me said, "If you eat those pies, why, the house is hers." So I didn't eat them, but on several occasions, she asked me about the pies.

"How was the pies?"

"They were really good," I would tell her.

Actually, I took those pies and buried them to make sure that no dog or nothing wouldn't get them and die.

There was another incident in the forties at a little country store owned by a black fellow named W. L. Kennedy. Whites liked to hang around the store talking and drinking cold drinks. I was outside the store one day when Mr. J. D. Winters and Dr. Davis, who had an office in Transylvania, came over. There was a fellow who played the piano named J. C., who regularly hung around there. Somebody asked the doctor, "What's wrong with J. C.?"

"Nothing's wrong with him," Dr. Davis said. "He just done broke himself down at those nigger parties."

I thought to myself that it was a pitiful person who could have so much book learning yet didn't seem to have enough sense to learn how to treat his fellow man. So I decided to take a really bold step and remind the doctor, in an offhanded way, that he should be more intelligent than that.

I said to Mr. Winters, "Why, I thought doctors were too intelligent to use slang."

He looked at me funny. "What you talking about?"

"The word Dr. Davis just used."

"Nigger? Course he said nigger. Nigger is a pet name. Listen now, where you think you are? You not in Chicago."

I said, "No, I've never been to Chicago. I've never been North, but I know slang when I hear it, and doctors are always refined people." I walked away.

After the exchange, I thought to myself, now I've lost two friends. They'll be around telling everyone how I had the nerve to be telling them what they shouldn't be saying.

The next day I went back to the store, and Dr. Davis and Mr. Winters were there again. They said, "Oh, here comes the preacher. Come over here and have a cold drink with us." So I took a soda and joined them.

I never sensed any ill will. I mean speaking out to people who were being disrespectful, I've never seemed to suffer from it like most people. Other people I know could have said some of the same things and they would have been put off the place or run out of town. Actually, I believe speaking out put me at an advantage over blacks who would take any thing white folks put on them.

I always had this independent spirit—this need to be free and respected like a man. The other workers always seemed to appreciate my taking a stand, although they were afraid to do it themselves. It just seemed to make them feel better that somebody could take a stand and still not get fired or run out of town. This encouraged me to keep pushing the boundaries of acceptable behavior as defined by the white agents, bosses, and businessmen.

For some reason, I never had a chance to be brainwashed like many blacks who grew up in the early 1900s under a system of severe racism. I know that some of it was due to my ability to earn money outside the plantation system. But mostly, I believe it was because my grandfather's pension allowed him more control over my life and kept me from spending my impressionable childhood years under the control of bosses and agents who still saw black people as slaves. My grandfather taught me how to be strong and how not to be afraid to stand up for what was due me—and most of the time that was simply a matter of respect, what white folks called "acting like a white man."

# SIX

# Running When You Can't Hide

Go to church for this, go to church for that—when I was a child, I thought I spent just too much time at the church house. Five days a week I went there for school, every Sunday I was there for Sunday School, and once a month I'd have to stay all day for communion service. The church even sponsored most of our social gatherings, like our picnics and ballgames. It was the center of the community.

Most people in my community attended church. As a child, I attended Seven Stars, located at the north end of Transylvania Lake, the first Baptist church in both East and West Carroll Parishes. Seven Stars was a big white wood-frame church with a steepled bell tower jutting out to the front left side. Every Sunday, the best-sounding bell I've heard anywhere would be rung to call the members to church service. It could be heard for miles around. It would also be tolled to announce whenever anyone died in the community.

Seven Stars was organized in 1867 by my great-grandfather on my mother's side. His name was Louis Taylor, but everyone called him Daddy Lou. Daddy Lou had started organizing Baptist churches right after the Civil War, and pretty soon he had established a church on every plantation from Transylvania northwards to the town of Lake Providence (after slavery ended, each section of the parish retained its original pre-slavery plantation name).

Although the people attended different churches, they were all connected through Seven Stars. It was considered the mother church, and the other plantation churches were considered branches. The branches had Sunday School and weekly prayer meetings and sometimes preaching services, but every first Sunday of the month, everybody from the branches came down to the mother church to partake of the Lord's Supper. This was when we would get together and share bread and juice in memory of the broken body of Jesus Christ.

On each first Sunday, the big open meadow around Seven Stars would be filled with horses, buggies, and wagons from the surrounding plantations. In the summer, it would be very hot, with all of us so crowded up in one church. People would come early, hoping to get a seat and catch an occasional breeze through one of the six stained glass windows propped open on wooden sticks. Of course it seemed to me that the open unscreened windows let in more flies and gnats than breezes. But the grown folks never seemed to notice that it was too hot, or the wood pews were too hard, or the preacher preached too long. Only us youngsters seemed to notice such things. The grown folks seemed perfectly satisfied to stay there all day, which they did most first Sundays.

Many people arrived early just so that they would have a chance to pass a little idle gossip about people in the community before preaching service started. After all, many of them hadn't seen each other since the last first Sunday service. Groups of whispering ladies gathered in various sections of the church while the deacons, all gussied up in their suits and ties and well-worn but shiny shoes, made their rounds greeting and shaking hands with everybody.

After a while, the head deacon would pull out his pocket watch and, as if on cue, the deacons would make their way to the wooden bench closest to the pastor. This was the signal for church to start. The rest of us would rush to our seats, and the congregation would go silent as a couple of deacons would take their places at the front of the church and start off on a song, stretching each word out into so many syllables that the words became indistinguishable to me.

After the song, the deacons would launch off into one of their long prayers, each line followed by an "Amen" and "Thank ya Lord" or "Ha' mercy" from the congregation. They thanked the Lord for helping them just make it another week and prayed for strength to make it through the next one. They'd say, "I want to thank you Lord that my covers wasn't my winding sheets and my bed wasn't my cooling board." This meant they were glad that in the night they hadn't died, their body laid out for viewing (this was back before embalming).

As far back as I can remember, our church had an organ and a singing choir. In fact, our church promoted music by paying for lessons for any young person who wanted to take them. We had so many girls who could play the organ, sometimes there would be controversy over who would play on Sunday.

Our church sang a lot of songs with a similar theme—life was hard but everything was going to be wonderful on the other side. These songs seemed to say to me that they didn't expect things to get better on this side and that our only hope for an improved situation was to die and go home to heaven. They sang a lot about being tired and weak and about God standing by them as they "traveled on this dangerous journey."

The women would pat their feet in time with the music, clomp-clomp, clomp-clomp, their shoes drumming all cross the church against the wood plank floor. Then someone would just wail out in the middle of a song, and the wailing would take life and move through the church until pretty soon so many people would be crying that no one could hear the singing anymore. Women would run up and down the aisle or fall across the benches, if no one was there to catch them. Sometimes it seemed that most every woman in the church would be crying, and some of the men too. As a child, I wondered why the grown folks were so sad. It was confusing to me that the same people I saw laughing and joking in the fields during the week could cry so hard on Sundays. But I was still young and didn't yet fully comprehend the double life the grown-ups had to live in order to survive mentally.

As in any Baptist church, they had to take up some money. They had a "poor" offering for the sick and invalids and a second offering for the expenses of the church. The deacons would beg for just a little more money, because the first amount they collected never seemed satisfactory to them. That dragged the service out even longer.

Finally, our pastor, Rev. Sam Gaither, would take the stand and read his text from the big Bible on the pulpit. I would watch the hats of all different shapes and sizes moving back and forth with the rhythm of Rev. Gaither's words going out over the audience. He'd preach sermons taken from different parts of the Bible, but they often had the same themes—be encouraged because good and righteousness would be victorious over wrong and evil, and people needed to look up. He'd open the doors of the church, asking for people who wanted to accept Jesus Christ as their Savior to come up front. And

Sunday after Sunday, I would just sit there and never go up and give my life to Christ. I halfway believed, but much of Christianity was a mystery to me.

Service would end with the roll call of all the members of the branch churches. Each member was expected to come up and pay their ten cents church dues to the mother church. Then after a whole day of service, we'd all go outside and have a good time eating from big baskets of food the women had prepared and brought with them.

Sometimes we had what they called testimony services. People would come up in front of the congregation to give their testimony about what God had done for them. Many would start off, "Sistahs and brothers, I come before you today to let you know my mind is made up, my heart is fixed, and I plan on making heaven my home." Then they would proceed with their unusual stories about the presence of God in their lives. I heard them tell about how the Lord had heard them praying and answered their prayers. They talked about how something would wake them up in the middle of the night with answers to their problems. Some said they told the Lord that if he had heard them pray, to make a star shoot, and they said it shot—or let the moon bow to them, or let it rain, or let the sun shout. To them, this was the evidence of God's presence with them. All these testimonies made me look at life and God in a different way.

Our pastor, Rev. Gaither, made a great impression on me. Although I was still a teenager, his words from the pulpit made me think about my life, about the future, and about love for a community. He was the first person I knew who spoke in words the things I felt in my heart. He was unusually well educated for the early 1900s and spoke very proper English. What made him even more unusual was that he was jet-black and spoke of his color with great pride in a day when dark skin was more likely considered a badge of shame. He used to say, "I'm 'real' black, black that won't wash out or fade."

Rev. Gaither was outspoken in the field of human relations and showed a great deal of concern not only for the people in our church, but for all the churches in the parish. He served as the president of the East Carroll Baptist Association throughout my childhood, until he passed away when I was about twenty-five, and through the

Association, he had been instrumental in organizing the Baptist-run high school.

Some people in our church were very progressive-minded, but others seemed to have no direction. Many of Rev. Gaither's members had once been slaves or were the children of people who had been slaves. I could tell they genuinely believed what the bossmen and the other whites around told them. And they acted like people act when they believe they aren't worthy or that they'll never have any say-so in their own lives. They'd tell their children, "Now don't you go getting no big ideas. You know white folks ain't gon' let you do nothing but work in these here fields."

Every once in a while, Rev. Gaither would say some things to the congregation that created controversy between him and the members. I recall him saying, "Some of you are just like crawfish. You'd rather go backwards than forward," or "You're just like a tumblebug." (A tumblebug is a type of beetle that gets in cow dung and rolls it up and rolls it backwards too.)

Rev. Gaither used to take up a great deal of time with the people and have a great deal of patience, but they didn't comprehend what Rev. Gaither meant when he tried to explain how their lot in life could be better than what the white man said. They couldn't see it in their minds. They could only see what was before their eyes. I remember Rev. Gaither disappointedly shaking his head and quoting from Proverbs 29:18, "Where there is no vision, the people perish."

This same group of people used to talk bad about Rev. Gaither, never seeing how they were losing all the time. They convinced me I would never want to become a minister because I couldn't have stood being treated like they treated Rev. Gaither. But my pastor had so much patience, he kept right on trying to help the people, fussing with them about their backwardness and trying to get them to look up and live a decent life.

I used to wonder why people still came to church when they were always talking about Rev. Gaither behind his back. I suppose it was because they needed the church and God more than they were annoyed with Rev. Gaither's chastisements. Life was hard for them, although I didn't fully realize this until I became an adult. Back then grown-up problems and concerns were kept from children so children didn't have to worry about so many things, when they were too young to handle them. It was only after I was in my twenties that I truly began to understand how heavy a load second-class citizenship was.

I listened carefully to what my pastor and the people from the various plantations said, but most of what I learned came from what they *did*, how broken-down some people looked, how they responded to different situations. Slowly I began to understand why grown-ups not only needed but absolutely had to spend time in church. It was a place of restoration, a place where dignity was restored, where life had value and purpose. A man's spirit could sink pretty low knowing he would chop and pick cotton from dawn till sundown all year and still not make enough to pay his debts from last year. Women who tended little white children suffered under the daily humiliation of having children call them by their first names, while as domestics, they had to call the little children "Miss" or "Master." Then they had to smile and say, "Much obliged to you, Mr. Charlie" at the end of the workweek when the bossman paid them in old hand-me-downs or leftover food from dinner instead of the wages he had promised.

And then there was always the required smiling. Not only did we have to pretend we didn't mind how we were treated, but we were also required to smile as if we actually enjoyed it. Old men concealed a lot of depression, anger, and hatred under their smiles after years of being told where to eat, what to eat, where to work, whether to go to school, and when, if ever, they could lift their heads.

Operating down to white people's expectations was mentally exhausting and mind-numbing, especially when black workers often knew more than the owners about farming and tooling. It took a lot of energy to pretend you enjoyed something you actually hated. But pretending was what was required. It wasn't a written rule, but we knew from experience that repercussions generally followed any time a black person expressed dissatisfaction or unhappiness about mistreatment.

But on Sundays, everything was different. When people came to church, I could see that church had power and purpose. It was like church had the power to straighten your back, clean you up, and restore your dignity. Preoccupation with earthly things was left at the door, and the people moved into a heavenly realm. Everybody became a brother or sister in Christ, sharecroppers, maids, and business owners alike. In the black church, black people were in charge. They could head their organizations, keep their records, and say what was on their minds. They could use the talents they weren't allowed to exercise all week. For a few hours each Sunday, people could be what God intended for them to be.

It was our relationship with God that served as a filter through which we passed all that was bad and wrong so we wouldn't be affected so much. We knew someone whose power was big enough that he could even control mean-spirited white people. I compared the people who didn't have a relationship with God to those who did. They seemed to have it so hard, always leaning on something that couldn't hold up under the kinds of burdens we carried. They spent Saturday nights shooting dice and losing their pay, getting drunk and trying to sleep it off all day Sunday, and they never felt any better for it. I could see them getting more and more defeated as they lost their little money, then their wives and children, and finally all their self-respect.

I was greatly influenced by the church, not only because of Rev. Gaither but because I had so many ministers on my mother's side of the family—my great-grandfather Louis Taylor (Daddy Lou), his son-in-law and my grandfather, Granderson Conn, and even my mother's brother. My Daddy wasn't a preacher, but people called him preacher too.

Although my great-grandfather Daddy Lou died in October 1873, almost thirty years before I was born, it seemed that most people knew who he was or knew something about him. He had organized not only the plantation churches in rural East Carroll Parish but also Bethany Baptist in West Carroll Parish and North Star Baptist up in Lake Providence.

He had been so well loved and respected by the people that they still talked about him when I was a child, although many of them probably were not old enough to have actually known him. When old people would see me, they'd start talking about how my great-grandfather had done so much and how I would certainly be somebody when I grew up because I had Daddy Lou's blood in me. So he had become a kind of hero of mine.

I don't know whether Daddy Lou had any kind of formal training as a minister, but the old people would tell great stories about his phenomenal ability to organize and encourage the people. They said his funeral had been the biggest funeral ever in Carroll Parish. The local newspaper at that time, the *Lake Republican,* had said that there had been more than three thousand people present, 1,500 on horseback, 1,800 on foot, and 75 wagons with women and children.

Because there were so many preachers in my family, the people started trying to make a preacher out of me. Everybody called me "Preacher" or "Elder," but I had made up my mind when I was just a boy that I didn't want to be a preacher. I was now almost nineteen and I still hadn't even been baptized, although I knew I believed in Jesus dying on the cross for my sins. So if I wouldn't even walk up the aisle to the front of the church and say I believed, then why did they think I should be in front of a congregation trying to be a preacher?

Of course when God decides on something, you don't have any control over who and when. I certainly didn't have any control over God's call, because on the same night I prayed and accepted Jesus as my savior, I also heard God's call into the ministry.

So on the fourth Sunday in September, 1920, three months before my nineteenth birthday, I went before the New Jerusalem Baptist Church congregation and told them of my conversion, how I believed in Jesus and wanted to be baptized—but I refused to tell them about my call to the ministry. I figured you couldn't control being called, but you could control whether or not you answered the call.

I was wrong there too. I went on with my normal routine, pretending like I hadn't heard God. Not long afterwards, I got low sick. I went from doctor to doctor, but nothing they gave me made me feel better. I just couldn't get well. I felt so bad all the time that I decided that life wasn't worth living and I might as well give up and die. I sent a friend to the store to buy me a suit to be buried in. My sister, who was living with me at the time, asked me what I was doing. I said weakly, "I'm getting ready to leave you."

That night, I got a young fellow to come and spend the night with me, as I was sure death would take me before morning. In the middle of the night, this vision came to me. I was standing before God. It was so vivid that when I woke up the next morning, I was surprised I wasn't in heaven.

Weeks passed, and then I had another vision. In my vision, two men came in to arrest me. One looked angry and the other one looked pleased. They asked, "Why aren't you working?"

I said, "Well my crop is clean as anybody else's."

"We're not talking about anybody else!" they said angrily. "We're talking about you!"

The angry one gave me this fierce look. "We've come to arrest you!" But the kind-faced one began to plead for me to be given another chance.

Finally the angry one gave in and said, "If we don't arrest you this time, will you go to work and do what I told you to do?"

I told the man, "Yes sir."

So then I was convinced that my sickness was because of my refusal of the call to the ministry. So I went and acknowledged my calling to the church.

My pastor arranged for my trial sermon. Anxiety, fear, and self-doubt filled my every waking thought. But every time I'd think about running away from the job, I'd see that angry face from the vision saying, "If I don't arrest you this time, will you do what I told you to do?" I kept thinking, why would God pick me, knowing I don't want to do this?

The appointed day arrived and I went up in front of the people and started preaching. I was looking at the people's faces, searching for a clue as to how I was doing. It seemed like they thought I was doing okay, but I just wasn't preaching to suit myself. So I decided I still wasn't going to preach if I couldn't do any better than that. I refused my calling again.

Several years passed and I still wasn't doing what God had told me to do. I had been seeing a girl by the name of Jessie Mae Attaway and putting most of my attentions there. I thought I was *soooo* in love with her, even though we used to argue much of the time and she smoked, which I hated. I decided that twenty-three years old was time for a man to be getting himself settled down, so right after my twenty-fourth birthday, in January 1926, we got married.

The day after the wedding, we had a fight so fierce I told her, "We might as well call this off right now!" She told me that would suit her just fine. We decided that we just wouldn't turn in the license and that would be that. She packed her things and left but soon afterwards came back. We lived as husband and wife for a while, although the license was never turned in or recorded. After several months, she got mad at me again and left, and then came back again and left again and came back again until we were both convinced that we would never get along. During these comings and goings, we had two children, Cornelius and John, but after she moved away to another state, it was difficult to get to see them with transportation being what it was in the early 1920s.

So time moved on, and I continued doing what I wanted to do, making many bad decisions while I ran from God. I pretended like there wasn't a calling on my life, like I could just ignore the calling and it would go away. One night, a severe thunderstorm rolled in. I was sitting in the dark, listening to the rain pounding on the tin roof. The thunder was rumbling so loud that the windows rattled. The wind continued to pick up until it became a roar, blowing things up against the house. The tin roof began making this awful banging noise as if the nails were pulling out, and the pieces of tin were flapping up and down in the wind. I felt sure the roof would rip loose and fly off any minute, or even worse, the whole house might fly away with me in it. I decided I'd better start praying for God to help me because I didn't want to die that night.

I got down on my knees and attempted to pray. "Oh God, please have mercy and spare my life tonight." But every time I asked the Lord for mercy, something would come before me and say, "You haven't done what I told you to do, you haven't preached."

I begged, "Lord if you just please spare me tonight, I will preach."

He spared me, so I went back and told my pastor I wanted to try to preach again.

Later, when I decided I wanted to leave Lake Providence to go live in California, I had another vision. In the vision, the bossman appeared to me and said, "I heard you were fixing to go."

I told him, "Yes, I plan to leave."

"Well, I don't want you to go," he said. "I want you to stay here and help me gather my crop."

He beckoned to me. "Come out here. I want to show you something."

I went out and looked and the cotton fields were white, all ready for harvest.

He said, "Now, I want you to take your work gang that you have been losing time with and put them to work in my field."

I really didn't want to hear this, because most of the young people were leaving East Carroll at the time for places like California, Chicago, and Detroit. But for me it seemed hard to get away. Every time I would attempt to go, I would have a vision or something would happen in the family. The first time I made up my mind to leave Louisiana, my grandfather died, so I had to stay with my grandmother because she loved me so much. By the time my grandmother died the next year, my sister Geneva and her husband had separated and she had come to live with us with her two children, so I decided I would stay on and help her to see after the children. But it was really within me—my own inner self—why I didn't leave. Every time I attempted to leave, it looked like I got a rejection, like I wasn't supposed to leave—so I stayed.

I stopped fighting my call and began to accept the fact that I would be a preacher after all. I got my preacher's license in January 1927 at age twenty-five, but it took me another ten years before I became an ordained minister. Well, maybe I wasn't as committed yet as I should have been.

Several years after I got my license, the Baptists opened what they called the National Minister's Institute at Leland College in Baker, Louisiana. The purpose was to educate Negro ministers who in the past had not had access to theological training. Ministers would gather each year from across the state for training and study. After the classes ended, Leland would assign a man over each area of the state to continue the training work of the institute.

So I began in 1930, and I continued until about 1940, attending the institutes, taking various courses. I took Church History, The Letters of Paul, Church Pedagogy, Christian Ethics, The Holy Spirit, Worship in the Church, and many other courses. But of all the courses I took at Leland College, the one that interested me most was The Holy Spirit.

Based on what I had seen in my own church, I thought the Holy Spirit meant an emotion when you got happy or what we called shouting, like when the women were running up and down the aisles doing their holy dances. But I learned that the Holy Spirit was God himself living inside of the people who would accept him. The more I learned, the more my relationship with God grew. I could feel his presence with me all the time. I believe that God allowed me a very special relationship, because he knew that only his strength would hold me up under the extreme circumstances I would later have to face in life. He took away from me the spirit of fear and gave me a boldness that could only come from him.

At Leland College, we were advised that when we went back home, we should get acquainted with other preachers in the community, especially the white preachers. So this is how I became acquainted with the first white minister in my life. When I got back home, I went by to visit a white preacher's house. Rev. G. A. Nelson, the pastor of the white First Baptist Church, was the first white Baptist preacher to settle in Lake Providence. I found him to be one of the finest men I had ever met. He would participate in our Baptist association meetings and help us with our training.

From then on, Rev. Nelson, Rev. S. A. Russell, and Rev. Paul Elledge, and then the white ministers out at Transylvania and other places, started to participate with us and we developed a fine relationship. At one time we had an interracial and interdenominational ministerial alliance. I promoted a combined brotherhood, and we started having brotherhood meetings together. Not only did the Baptist ministers come, but the Methodist, the Assembly of God, and the Catholic. One time one of the white Baptist ministers from the nearby community of Melborne even came and brought his whole congregation, and they took an active part on the program. But as time moved on and these ministers died or moved away, the Christian blacks and whites lost their closeness, especially after we blacks started pressing for our civil rights.

During World War II, when men were scarce at southern colleges, the National Home Missions Council set up schools for ministers at various universities. I received one of their grants and got to attend Southern University in Baton Rouge for three years. Then the Southern Baptist Convention, which was the white Baptist organization, operated the School of Prophets, which I attended for several years in the 1950s. Afterward I went to the United Theological Seminary in Monroe, Louisiana, where I received my bachelor's degree in theology in 1953.

Through the years, I have never stopped attending classes, because the Christian educational system is so vast. When I began to study about God and his wonders, it was like sailing a great ocean. I could just sail on and on and on and never stop beholding new wonders.

The whole of life is one big school term with something new to learn every day. That's why I filled my life and my children's lives with books, magazines, and newspapers. When you stop learning, it's like being a dead fish. Dead fish go down the stream, wherever the water takes them. Live fish can go up against the current.

Life is like a story that I remember from my second-grade reader titled, "The Bird Thought." The mother bird had built her nest and laid eggs in it. One day a little baby bird hatched out of the shell. Since all the baby bird could see was an egg, he thought the world was made out of pale blue shell. He was brooded by his mother, and finally she threw the shells out with her bill. He looked at the straw and thought the world was made of straw. He didn't wish for any other place to live. But finally, one day his feathers grew out and his wings got strong, and he decided to fly away from the nest. He began to look around in the world. Finally he reached this thought: "Well, I don't know what the world is made of and neither does my brother."

So that's what has kept me going—my endless journey to find out what the world is made of. When I had only seen plantations, I could only understand life through the eyes of a laborer. But when I read, even before I got to travel, my mind began to open up to new possibilities. I found that many of the bad decisions affecting large numbers of people were made by politicians, leaders, teachers, and preachers who had never been out their nest, who didn't have a clue how much damage they caused daily. They kept the people thinking small, with no vision, because they thought that all of life was like their pale blue shell.

# SEVEN

# An Awakening

As far back as childhood, I was interested in civil rights. I wondered why the Negro was treated differently and why his school term was shorter. I wondered why the way we were raised was criticized, when Negro women were hired to raise most of the white children. I couldn't understand why the Negro had to work so hard and get so little, how he could be considered lazy, when for practically free he built the roads, the levee, and the railroads and worked the crops that produced the money that made the landowners wealthy. But still the Negro couldn't get paid enough wages to feed his family.

As a teenager and young adult, I could never understand why the Negro didn't participate in politics. Blacks outnumbered whites and their relations with them seemed good. In town, they had picnics and rooster fights together, and they played side by side on the same ball teams. People of both races came from far and near to see the birds trained by the famous chicken fighter-trainer who lived in the Transylvania community. Our Coal Tar Baseball Team and the Brass Marching Band that went and played for the different socials and picnics up and down the river also had the backing of the white community. When boxing matches were held in Lake Providence, black and white prizefighters fought each other in the same ring, in spite of Jim Crow laws requiring the separation of the races. Even the housing was fairly mixed in town. But it was just a few Negroes who would even say anything about voting. It was all a mystery to me.

One Sunday when I was teenager, my pastor, Rev. Gaither, brought some Negro newspapers to the church. He told the adults to take them home and read them or if they couldn't read, have their children read the papers to them. This was my first time seeing a Negro newspaper. So I began early in life reading the *Chicago Defender*, which became the most influential black paper during the early decades of the 1900s.

It was the *Chicago Defender* that started the fire for civil rights really burning in me. At that time, the *Defender* featured writers such as Dean Kelly Miller, W. E. B. Du Bois, Roscoe Simmons, Perry Howard, and Charles Houston. In another section, there was Salem Tut Whitney, and a young folks' section by Bud Billiken.

I noticed a big difference between the news in the black-owned papers and news in main town and city papers. Reading the local newspapers, you would have thought black people didn't do anything but commit crimes, and many of those allegations were fabricated. Rarely was anything printed about our accomplishments or about regular black life except maybe when somebody died. So in a subtle way, white people were taught to believe an untruth about who we really were.

Occasionally the white-owned city papers would include something about a lynching, especially if they were particularly proud of what had been done, like the article calling a lynching a "black barbecue" or the time a news article referred to the charred remains of a young boy as a "black steak." They didn't speak or write of murdering black people in terms of criminal or immoral behavior. They spoke of it with the same satisfaction as they would have described bagging a deer. It was like evildoing was taken for entertainment.

In the 1910s and the 1920s, the black-owned publishers printed information the white press wouldn't even acknowledge was happening, such as stories about mysterious, unsolved racially motivated shootings, but more importantly, they carried articles that showed me how the race was advancing. The *Defender* ran advertisements for good-paying northern jobs and featured stories highlighting the achievements of blacks who had moved north. They explained what Congress was doing or was about to do and how it affected the Negro race. They reported on the activities of the National Association for the Advancement of Colored People (the NAACP), an organization my pastor had introduced me to because he said they were about helping the colored man. Early on, I had noticed him asking people to join the organization.

I learned there were progressive black people all over the United States fighting against second-class citizenship. The writers taught me to look forward when most things around the South said to look down.

I slowly began to realize the power of the press. It had the power to make a whole people look up—or the same words and images could be changed around and the same people could be made to look down.

I stayed with the *Chicago Defender* for years until I was introduced to the *Pittsburgh Courier*, a more recent publication that carried a Louisiana supplement providing four pages of state news. It was considered the most militant black paper at that time. I also started getting some of the southern black papers like the Oklahoma City *Black Dispatch*, one of the Scott syndicated papers from Atlanta, Georgia, the *Louisiana Weekly* out of New Orleans, and the *Monroe Broadcast* out of Monroe, Louisiana. I pretty well kept up with Negro life across the country through the Negro newspaper. So it was my pastor, the writers for the *Chicago Defender*, and one of my schoolteachers who kindled the fire of freedom in my soul.

There were certain very progressive-minded people who had made their home around Transylvania and Lake Providence. Blacks who owned the bigger farms were sending their children off to high schools affiliated with colleges such as Southern University, Tuskegee Institute, and Hampton University. After high school, some young people even went back for college, where they learned the business side of running a farm and scientific methods of raising better crops. Some came back to East Carroll after college to take over family farms, while others became teachers and principals. Others started their own businesses.

I reasoned that the thing that could help a progressive-minded person most was what I was reading in the *Chicago Defender*, so I wrote them a letter and soon became a newsboy selling subscriptions and delivering papers for ten cents apiece. The *Defender*, which had a national circulation of 250,000 by 1920, was easy to sell, no trouble at all. I knew who my customers were because at that time only special, forward-thinking people read the Negro newspapers. Later on, I also sold the *Louisiana Weekly*, published in New Orleans, to these same people.

The black press also introduced me to war through its stories of Negroes in the military. During World War I, which was fought during my teenage years, President Wilson announced that blacks would be allowed to join the military. He made promises that made us think that this would be the great turning point for blacks in America. We should have known better, though, when just the year before, Wilson and his administration had decided to segregate black and white government workers, giving them separate restrooms and lunchrooms. But black people were always looking for any kind of sign that things might get better, so in our community, everybody was excited and all the men talked about signing up. They figured that if they showed they were willing to die for America, then maybe America would stop treating black people like second-class citizens.

I was only fourteen or so when the war started, too young to register because they only took men ages eighteen to forty-five. But I was still in tune with what was going on because at school, we were always talking about the war and patriotism. Our teachers taught us patriotic songs such as "Over There" and "If you don't like your Uncle Sammy, then go back to your home over the sea and don't be ungrateful to me." We gave speeches about chasing those Germans to hell, and we felt proud when we heard President Wilson's slogans "Fight for Democracy" and "Make the World Safe for Democracy." My fighting spirit was really kindled when my father took me to see a movie about a cruise ship called the *Lusitania* that had been torpedoed by a German U-boat. To see the torpedo hit the ship and see the people struggling in the water made me mad.

The people who went off to World War I thought they were really fighting for something important. They didn't join up to earn a paycheck or go because a draft said they had to go. They felt like they were going to help make the world safe for democracy, and for a very short while, race relations seemed to improve a bit.

But when the soldiers came back from overseas, they were different from how they left. They told us stories about how color wasn't as important over there as it was in America, how the foreigners treated them with respect, until some white American officer would tell the foreigners to stop treating the black soldiers like they were equal to whites. They said foreigners cared more that they were Americans than that they were black. They had had a taste of being treated like men, and it was good—and they couldn't ever go back to bowing and scraping like they had done before the war.

But in the South, they were still expected to act that way, and that made the soldiers mad. I read in the papers that in the bigger cities in

Louisiana, the soldiers were parading down the streets in protest with signs saying they refused to be treated like second-class citizens anymore.

When the Negro soldiers would parade, it would seem to make some whites lose their minds. They would line both sides of the street and start heckling the soldiers before they even got up to them. When the soldiers would get up close, the white bystanders would spit and curse and throw whatever happened to be around at the time. Most of their insults ran along the same theme, such as "Get back in your place" and "Nigga, you're never going to equal up to white people." And the sad thing was, they made it a family outing. To see the little white boys and girls, with their child-size hate signs and their little faces contorted with hatred for somebody they knew nothing about, made me know we'd still be dealing with this in the 1940s and '50s when they came of age. Prejudice was being handed down to the next generation as if it were a grand inheritance.

After the marches started, there were race riots and increased lynchings in north Louisiana. Rallying white people would get themselves so worked up about some perceived wrongdoing by a black person that they would attack any Negro who had the misfortune of being around at the time. I read stories of all these people getting killed just for being in the wrong place and black soldiers being beaten up when they tried to stand up for their rights. I read about race riots in Illinois, Philadelphia, Houston, Charleston, Washington, D.C., and a lot of other places. Hundreds of blacks were lynched during the postwar years. These things really discouraged me, especially after our hopes had been so high during the war. If we were good enough to die for America, I couldn't understand why we weren't good enough to live in America.

In later years, after I was old enough to join the service, I was walking through town one day when I saw a sign tacked on a pole: YOUNG MEN, JOIN THE ARMY, NAVY. TRAVEL, LEARN, AND EARN. It showed where to write for an application. I wrote for one, and when I started to fill it out, I noticed it had a place for you to write in your race. I wrote in the blank "Colored" and sent it in. They sent it back with a note written across the top, "Sorry, we don't have any place for Negroes at this time." So I never got into the army.

Many farm hands had moved north during World War I, but I had stayed to help my sister out. Since both my grandparents had died not long after the war ended, my sister and I were left alone in their house to try to maintain the same farm they had maintained. At that time, most young people didn't have much responsibility, and here my sister and I were living in a large double house made for two families. I was young for what I was expected to do, and on top of that, I looked even younger than my twenty-one years. The agent who had recently taken over the place liked the strong, strapping types, but I was five feet eight inches tall and weighed only 140 pounds. My twenty-three-year-old sister and I couldn't get a lot of work done each day like the big families could. Families with ten or more children had plenty help with the plowing, planting, chopping, and cotton picking.

I guess it wasn't in me to make a good first impression on the new agent. Spring had come and was almost gone, and everybody was about finished breaking up their land and cutting up the stalks, and I was still rabbit hunting. The agent came along and saw me. He said, "Man, I want to tell you this. You're going to be the a—— of this plantation."

I said, "Yes sir, but I notice all the animals I catch, that's the fattest part of them."

I could see that comment didn't go over too well, and he would probably make me pay for being a smart-aleck.

Later that month, the agent stopped by our house. "Man," he said, "you just not working enough land to be living in a big double house like this. When you make this crop, you're going to have to give this house up. You'll have to take a smaller house."

"If I have to move, I'll leave the place," I said.

He didn't look too moved by the thought that I might leave the place. "Well, you'll have to go," he said, "because I'm going to have to have the house." He walked away, looking very unconcerned.

The rest of spring and on into the summer, I lived a bit uneasily. I'd lived there so long, I hated to go, but I was a man of my word. I said I'd leave if I had to move out my house, and I would just have to find some place else to go.

That summer, some strangers started showing up in town. As it turned out, they were labor agents from the north seeking Negro laborers to work in northern factories. They were shorthanded, and they said southern blacks made better workers and seemed to appreciate a job more. Of course, they didn't have to do much to convince a lot of people to move, because there were many reasons to want to leave. Farm work wasn't the easiest way to make a living, because too many things were outside your control—would you get enough rain to get the cotton plants up out of the ground, would you get enough sun later on to make the cotton bolls open, and if all this worked out, would boll weevils decide your crop was the best place for breakfast, dinner, and supper and eat up five months of work.

Then there was the issue of how we were treated, especially right after the war, all for the magnificent sum of fifty cents a day. These labor agents were offering real wages. They gave people their fares north with a guaranteed job at the other end. People were hopping every train or bus they could catch. One family member would leave, make some money, and send fare back for other family members.

Pretty soon places like Chicago, Detroit, and St. Louis were overflowing with Louisiana black folks, until some cities seemed to start developing Negrophobia over the large influx of Negroes in their midst. My pastor, Rev. Gaither, made up a song about the whole situation, which he sang for the congregation, after chastising them for wanting to leave town. The song went something like, "Too many Negroes in town and I'm tired of these white folks shoving me around. Back to the country I'm bound, because there's too many Negroes in town." But of course nothing he or any of the other ministers could say could convince the people to stay in the South, because we figured northern whites couldn't possibly be as bad as the southern ones.

Black folks had left in droves during the war but never like during the years following the war. Hundreds of thousands left the south during the 1920s, looking for a better education for their children and for laws to protect them from the crimes committed against them in the South. All of this turned out to be lucky for me but not so lucky for our agent.

Many black skilled laborers left East Carroll during this time, and even some of the big black landowners who had worked so long to make enough money to buy their own places. Everybody dreamed of a place where the burden of being judged by the color of your skin didn't have to be carried every day. We figured it must be something close to being in heaven.

Although many people on the place I worked caught the moving spirit, I still couldn't bring myself to move. This was during the years I was fighting my calling to the ministry, but fight as I might, I couldn't bring myself to leave East Carroll Parish. It was getting over in the year, close to cotton-picking season, and two or three houses stood empty on our place. Many sharecroppers and day hands had gone north over the summer, so we weren't the only place with empty houses. Local agents were getting desperate to find enough people to bring in the fall crops.

I knew our agent would be in trouble with the boss if he couldn't get the crops in on time. One day the big bossman came by and told our agent that unless he filled every house by cotton-picking time, he wouldn't have a job.

The agent came and told me, "You don't have to go, just keep your house, and I want you to go ride around with me and help me get some labor." Then he gave me a pocket of cigars, even though I despised smoking.

It was dangerous to fool with anybody's labor at that time, because another agent just might shoot you over his workers. I was nobody's fool, but I did ride around with him a bit and that fall, *he* had to go but *I* got to stay. The scarcity of labor improved the Negro's plight, but after a while, the southern landowners banded together and ran the labor agents back up north.

After several years of living with me, in 1927 my sister Geneva remarried. She and her husband stayed in West Carroll Parish for a while and then decided to move back to East Carroll. They signed a contract to go live and work on this place for a year. When they got to the plantation, they found out the bossman wanted them to move into an old dilapidated house with a dirt floor. When it rained, the water poured in through holes in the rusted tin roof, so much so they might as well have been outside. It was getting near Christmas and my mother was coming to visit them, and the bossman still wouldn't fix the house. They had asked him several times, with no results, so they decided to move to another farm. There were plenty of people around looking for good laborers.

There was a black man who had a plantation nearby, so they decided to move over on his place and work for him. My brother-in-law borrowed the man's mule team and wagon and brought it up to the old house so we could load up their things. I don't know how the bossman found out, but before we could even start loading the wagon, here he comes riding up on his horse. My brother-in-law was in the house at the time and he had told me to stay outside and mind the mules.

I was sitting in the wagon as the bossman rode up on his horse.

"Good morning," he said.

"Good morning, Mr. Wilson."

"What you fixing to do?"

I thought for a minute, realizing that what we were doing could get my brother-in-law in serious trouble. "Fixing to load some corn," I said. I didn't know what else to tell him.

"For what?" he asked unpleasantly.

I couldn't think of what to say next. Besides, I was pretty sure he already knew what was going on, so I decided to just tell the truth. "My brother-in-law said you won't fix the house, and he's not going to stay here any longer."

He was not pleased at all. He shook his finger at me. "You take that team of mules down there and put them in my lot, and turn them loose." He pointed toward a fenced-in area. "I'll show that son-of-a-b—— about letting his team come on my place."

"Who, me?" I said. "Carry another man's team and put it in your lot?"

"Yes, you son-of-a-b——!" Who you think I'm talking to?"

I gave him my "I-can-be-just-as-crazy-as-you-are" look and said, "Are you talking to me?"

His face turned a bright red and his veins bulged in his neck as he yelled, "Yes, who you think I'm talking to? If you don't carry that wagon down there and put it in my lot, I'll fill you so full of these shots you won't wiggle." He had pulled his pistol and was waving it around dangerously.

I stepped out on the wheel and said slowly in a very firm voice (they say I always talk slowly anyway), "Now listen, I wouldn't carry this man's wagon down there and put it in your lot for *hell*. I wouldn't carry it down there if I knew I'd drop in *hell* the next minute. If you're so brave, you pull your trigger."

"Oh, you are crazy!" he said.

About this time, my brother-in-law came out and the bossman started on him.

"You been used to living on peckerwood places, but you don't treat a white man like this. You just moved here and now you talking about you going to move away. No, you're not going! Besides, you've got a contract to work the year. You can't just leave. I can have you arrested!"

My brother-in-law motioned for me. "Go in the house and tell Geneva what's going on out here," he whispered.

I went in and when I came back out, the bossman must have thought I had gone to get a gun or something because he said, "Now listen, God Almighty, let's reason together. I know I made you all mad and you made me mad, but we can settle things better than this. Now, if you just come here to give me a bad name and move off the place, nobody else will want to stay here."

I said, "Well, I wouldn't want to stay with nobody that called me an sob."

He drawled, "Oh hell, I'm a son-of-a-b—— myself. I'm a son-of-a-b—— on wheels."

He kept talking around, trying to persuade my brother-in-law to stay. Finally he said to me, "Now listen, your daddy knows me and if he says I'm a son-of-a-b——, I'm that."

"I don't have to ask my daddy," I said. "That's what you said a while ago, you were one."

We carried the man's mule team back to him and decided to try to get away some other way. We went up to Attorney Wiley's office for some advice as to how my sister and her husband could legally get out the contract.

"Well, I tell you," he said. "I could tell you what to do to get away, but I got a place and the coloreds might use that same trick on me."

He wouldn't tell us, so we went to the high sheriff and talked with him about the situation. He said, "Well now listen, you'll have to be careful because that white man will kill you."

So I asked him, "Mr. Bass, have you ever known a Negro to kill a white man?" He looked at me strangely and I don't remember him returning me any answer but I know he remembered me from then on.

My brother-in-law did eventually move off the place but he had to pay twenty-five dollars to get out of his contract, and the man never did let him get all his things.

The social structure of Lake Providence and the surrounding rural areas remained pretty much the same until Huey Long's 1928 election as governor. Before his election, the upper-crust blacks—and there was an ample number of them mostly in town—and the upper-crust whites always stuck together. We had business people like Henry Jones, president of Standard Life Insurance Company of Louisiana and owner of a general merchandise and grocery store on Levee Street, and W. A. Brannum, insurance agent and owner of a local funeral home and ambulance service, and I. C. Curry, proprietor of the First and Last Chance Store. And there was Andrew Black, a brick mason and carpenter, and big farmers like Bill Hubbard and Andrew Chambers. Money and business gave them a connection that overlooked race, as long as the upper-crust blacks didn't try to vote. Blacks and whites seemed to treat each other with mutual respect and even came to visit each other back in those days.

Of course blacks had made some attempt to register to vote. In 1921, when poll taxes were adopted in the Louisiana constitution, my father and his friends W. A. Brannum and Henry Jones had contacted the NAACP about it. They were told that if people paid their poll taxes, they were supposed to be allowed to vote in the elections. That entitled you. So they started pressing the local registrar to let them vote, and after they started pressing, the local officials just stopped receiving the poll tax from anyone who wasn't white. So now they had still another reason to keep us from voting.

The poor white man had no social standing either, and if he did anything wrong, upper-crust whites came rough on him just like they did blacks. Black people had very little contact with poor whites, who were mostly isolated off by themselves. In fact, when I was coming up, I did not have any social relations with poor whites. My grandmother must have been taught to avoid contact with them, because whenever she looked up and saw a poor white man coming walking, it seemed to create some type of fear. The old people would always say, "A po' white man just won't do right."

I think the upper-crust whites intentionally kept us separated so that we wouldn't have enough contact to find out how much we had in common. We might have joined together to rebel against the big landowners. The bossmen went out of their way to tell both sides stories that would cause us to fear and distrust each another. We learned to look down on poor whites and poke fun at them, calling them names like "po' white trash." Everyone—the wealthy farmers, the upper-crust blacks, the black independent farmers, sharecroppers, and even the day laborers—looked down on the poor white dirt farmer. So even after I went into the ministry and had a chance to associate with quite a few poor whites, I found only a few who wanted to talk and be friendly. There just seemed to be a distance between poor whites and poor blacks that was hard to cross, the distrust and brainwashing were so deeply rooted.

Huey Long ran his campaign for governor on the platform that most people in Louisiana were poor and oppressed and kept that way by a few rich men who owned and controlled everything. He opened the eyes of the poor whites politically, and they played a big part in getting him elected.

At the time of Long's election, East Carroll was still only one-third white, so we didn't have many whites of any description, and we had even fewer poor whites. Prior to Long's election, Negroes had gotten all the jobs from the few highway building projects in the parish. Most jobs were classified as "white" jobs or "colored" jobs, and clearing land and laying roadbeds was considered "colored" laborer work. It was physically exhausting construction work in the hot summer sun.

Louisiana's roads were in terrible condition. Hardly any of them were paved, and when it rained the roads were almost impassable. When Governor Long began his massive highway and bridge building projects across the state, the jobs were taken away from local Negroes and given to the poor whites who elected him. But in spite of this, Long still gave hope to the Negro community. It kindled something in the Negro when they saw seemingly powerless poor whites who had not been voting begin to vote and get recognition and better jobs. It showed me that there was a connection between voting and being respected.

The Great Depression came while Huey Long was in office. In 1930 we could scarcely find any kind of work to do. Cotton prices dropped so low that hardly any landowners could afford to pay wages. Other jobs formerly classified as "colored" work were now reclassified, and these jobs were given to white people. So everyone who found work counted himself or herself lucky.

I had become active during this time in the East Carroll Baptist Association, serving as their missionary. My job as missionary was to visit churches to distribute information and sell religious materials. I still was not pastoring a church, because although I had received my preacher's license in 1927, I still was not ordained. During the Depression, everyone mostly had enough to eat, but nobody had money to be buying clothes. My one suit already had the elbows out of it, and I still hadn't found a job. I went for weeks without work until I finally found an agent who was hiring. He told me I could start work on Thursday.

On Saturday, just two days after I started the job, the bossman announced to the workers, "If everybody's not here in the morning, you don't have a job."

I was working farther down the right-of-way at the time, so one of the other workers came down to tell me what the bossman said. Knowing I always went to church on Sundays, he said, "What you going to do?"

"Oh, I'll be at Sunday School in the morning," I said.

I knew I needed this job, but no one had the right to ask me to choose between church and working on Sunday. I'm sure the bossman knew that most black people did not believe in working on Sunday and would rarely do it.

Later over in the afternoon, here comes somebody else. He said, "You heard what the boss say, didn't you? Everybody not here in the morning won't have no job. What you goin' to do?"

"Oh," I said, "I'll be at Sunday School."

Someone must have gone back and told the boss because after awhile, I saw him coming stepping. "Preacher," he said, "you not coming to work tomorrow, are you?"

I said, "No, I always go to church and Sunday School on Sunday."

"Well, go on and hush your mouth and come on back on Monday."

And so when payday came, I got paid for Sunday too—though I had been at church.

Of course the Negro didn't feel the impact of the Depression in the same way as whites. Many of us already lived from hand to mouth, sometimes without two pennies to rub together. We were already pretty far down the economic ladder, so we didn't have as far to step back.

The upper-crust whites who had never had to do without the basic things they denied us daily were getting crazy and wanting to kill themselves, but we just started preparing to survive without money. Fortunately in this instance, we had had more than adequate training and had developed some expertise in this area. Slavery had left us with some special survival instincts that helped us adapt better during the Depression. We set up a self-help league, meeting from one house to another. We would have cannings (putting up fruits and vegetables from our gardens in jars for the winter) and mattress makings and other programs to help each other out. A few blacks who owned farms lost them during the Depression, but mostly we stayed put and dealt with whatever came along.

There was a community spirit that remained from our African background that didn't seem to exist in the white community. We mostly stayed right around where we grew up and we did most things together, so all our neighbors seemed like family. But that was not to say that we didn't feed both black and white as they wandered through the area looking for something to eat. Sometimes we even provided temporary shelter to black strangers who had found themselves homeless during the Depression. They were adopted right into the family as newfound "cousins." Just being black provided an automatic connection, because educated or uneducated, light-skinned or dark, southern or northern, there were certain daily struggles that only black people in America experienced or understood. We were the only race of people in the whole world that America had defined by law as being so different that we needed to be kept segregated from all other races, cradle to grave.

The Depression finally ended, but many people continued to have it rough. To help the people out, Governor Long came up with this idea about spreading the wealth from the rich to the rest of the people. He called it a "Share the Wealth" movement, and his slogan was "Every man a king but no one wears a crown." He said every man deserved to have a house, a job, and a decent education, all of which sounded good to black people, especially since Negroes were even allowed to form their own "Share the Wealth" clubs. Clubs sprung up not only in Louisiana but all over the United States.

Long started the free lunch and free textbook programs for school children. This made a tremendous difference in the underfunded black schools throughout the state, because many parents hadn't been able to afford schoolbooks for their children. He even opened some free hospitals and clinics so that poor people weren't automatically condemned to die from whatever deadly diseases that happened to come along.

Personally, I held Huey Long in high esteem because at the time, I didn't have knowledge to understand that the occasional bone he threw the Negro was just a decoy to keep us from seeing what was really happening. It was only later, when I did some reading and studying, that I realized how much we had been hurt by Long's term in office. The gap between salaries of black and white teachers increased. The amount spent per white student was almost six times what was spent on black students. Black prisoners at the state penitentiary at Angola were treated inhumanely, including frequent beatings, in response to complaints by whites that prisoners were being "coddled." The number of blacks on the voter registration rolls for the whole state fell below a thousand, out of a adult voting population of about three-quarters of a million people. But the worse thing that happened during the Long years was that the great divide between the races was set in motion.

Huey Long's campaign was based on class issues, and he had won a lot of votes by accusing his opponent of being sympathetic to blacks. In the end, what really came out of the Long years was a notion on the part of poor whites that blacks were largely responsible for poor white folks' poverty, lack of jobs, and whatever else might have been bothering them. And from that point on, it appeared that the poor whites could always be easily manipulated into doing the dirty deeds the richer whites wanted done against blacks. The poor whites would do things to us and think it had been their own idea. But all the time, it was the rich man orchestrating the whole thing, because as long as poor people were focused on keeping each other down, we wouldn't take the time to figure out who really had us in our condition. Poor people were just being used to perpetuate their own bad circumstances.

But I didn't know these things at the time, so when Huey Long was gunned down in 1935, I couldn't help but shed a few tears. He had seemed a little Christian-like to me when he was encouraging people to "Share the Wealth." I admired his ambition. I admired his climbing high. I admired his nerve in the things he would say and get away with, like telling white people "You can feed all the 'pure whites' in Louisiana with a nickel's worth of red beans and a dime's worth of rice." And most of all, I admired how he took on the upper-crust whites and won. He made a lot of Negroes believe that if a change could come for poor whites, a change could come for us too.

# EIGHT

# New Deal/Bad Deal

In spite of the class separation promoted by the Long administration in the early 1930s, things continued to creep forward for blacks in East Carroll. We were over two-thirds of the parish population, and there were enough progressive-minded people in the parish to start making some changes. The organizations we had at that time weren't all about socializing, but about teaching the people how to do better. We were only sixty or so years out of slavery, so we had the seemingly impossible challenge of overcoming the effects of more than two centuries of slavery.

Sometimes whites and other people who had never lived under slavery would come to try to help us, but they seemed unable to fathom the amount of damage that could be done to a people forced to practice things wrong for two hundred years—two hundred years of depending on other people for food and shelter, two hundred years of families not being allowed to live as families, and all that time not being allowed to learn to read, write, or do math. And it seemed even harder for our visitors to understand what it was like to have to deal with people who had for two hundred years been taught that blacks were apes or coons, dim-witted because it was in our genes, and just plain incapable of learning and taking care of ourselves. They couldn't understand the depth of the white supremacy we struggled against. So often the people who wanted to help us offered us the wrong kind of help.

We looked at our situation like a runner just starting to train for a race against an opponent who is already in great physical condition. It meant our training had to be different just to make up for lost time. So we had classes on everything from current issues such as school equality all the way to how to can food, take care of children, and protect our homes from the cold. We had black history classes and forums to discuss what we needed to do to advance the race.

I was still working as a tenant farmer for the Abston, Crump & Wynne Company after the Depression ended, working on the half.

My cotton crop came in at about $375, but by the time the agent deducted gin charges and his half and what I owed on my account, I only cleared about $100 for the whole year. There were too many other tenant farmers like me, except many of them had families to feed. Day hands were working ten hours a day for only 80¢ pay when salt pork cost them 23¢ a pound, sugar 65¢, a bag of meal 60¢, and a twenty-four-pound bag of flour $1.25. There was a hunger among the people to do better, except most of them just didn't know how.

So we had much to learn about how to get better jobs in spite of Jim Crow segregation laws and how to survive without money in the meantime. I was in my early thirties and was thinking a lot about what I should do to help my community. I became increasingly involved with the programs that had been started, because I could see the community changing and getting better as the months passed. In the process, I learned a lot about how people think and what it took to motivate them.

A Democrat had been elected president in 1933. Although I wasn't allowed to vote, I was still a Republican at heart because of the terrible things the Democrats had done to blacks during Reconstruction. Most blacks in the south in the 1930s considered the Democratic Party just too awful to even want to belong to it. In fact, every time something would go bad, the people would comment, "It's gone Democrat." So I really hated to see a Democrat elected, but by reading the *Pittsburgh Courier* before the election, I slowly began to consider Franklin Roosevelt as a Democrat who might not be *all* bad. He actually seemed concerned about regular people and promised a new deal for the common man. Then, after he began his term in office and began trying to rehabilitate the country from the Depression with all of his different alphabets—the WPA, the CCC, the PWA, and the FSA, why, I began to look at him in a totally different way.

I started seeing Negroes out cleaning up the bayous and laying new streets, roads, and highways under WPA (Work Progress Administration) projects. Some of our young men were going to the CCC (Civilian Conservation Corps) camps established to provide work for and restore pride in jobless men ages eighteen to twenty-five. Occasionally the government would even have a surplus food program to help the people.

All this was so new to us because government programs in the past had pretty much disregarded the existence of black people. The southern states always pushed for states' rights, but we knew well what that term meant. That meant that certain states wanted to be free of anyone checking behind them because they were using the money and the laws to the exclusion of certain citizens. So under the Roosevelt administration, we started to see more fairness when the federal government administered the programs than when the states did.

I started to feel hopeful again. There were still a few bad incidents from time to time, like when some Negroes from Lake Providence were hired to work at night on a WPA project over in Oak Grove just west of Lake Providence. They were to help speed up the construction of the new white high school auditorium and gym over there. When the white day workers found out the Negroes had been hired, they decided to visit the site and confront the bossman and the Negro workers. "To hell with you niggers," they said. "We ain't gonna sweat all day while they let these black niggers work in the cool." So they threatened to quit if the Negroes weren't fired.

In spite of the occasional bad incidents, we didn't spend too much time dwelling on the bad. We were focused on the good things coming out of Washington. I just wanted to live long enough to get to vote.

From one election to another, I'd wonder, "Will I live long enough to see the next one?" I was anxious to see what would happen next. Roosevelt inspired my admiration in those early years, and if I could have voted, I would have voted for him when he ran for his second term.

Although many of Roosevelt's New Deal programs impressed me, it was actually something I didn't like during the Roosevelt administration that caused me to first enter the civil rights fight. The federal government started the Farm Security Administration, an agency that was supposed to buy up surplus land and other land where taxes had not been paid and resell it to poor families who wanted to start family farms. The families who could qualify would pay a small sum annually and would own their land in either twenty or forty years, depending on the program they were in.

Transylvania, where I lived at the time, was the richest farming area in the parish. In fact, it was actually one of the richest farming areas in the entire state. Good rainfall and a long growing season gave us a very high yield of cotton to the acre. The Memphis company that owned the 10,000 acres where I lived mostly left the farming to the black families that had lived in the area for almost a hundred years, back before the end of slavery. The agents hired by the owners to run the place didn't interfere with us too much, and over time the six-mile strip of property had turned into a thriving, progressive, and thickly settled almost all-black community with its own church, Rosenwald school, and stores.

Most families had lived there so long that some people had started to think of the land as theirs, especially the independent farmers. They had developed over the years thriving farms, and even in the 1930s some black farmers already used mechanical equipment and had built nice homes for their families on land they didn't even own. Many children from the area had been able to go away for their high school education and some had even gone on to college.

Some residents of the Transylvania area had moved to other places, making a name for themselves and for the area. S. W. Green had become Supreme Chancellor of the Knights of Pythias, the secret society Papa Charley had belonged to, which in the early 1920s owned cash and property valued at over $3.5 million. His brother S. J. Green was principal of Thomy Lafon Public School in New Orleans. A. H. Atkins had served as treasurer of the Liberty Industrial Life Insurance Company in New Orleans. Overall, we felt that our little Transylvania community was moving in the right direction.

So I was really surprised when a white man told me one day that the Farm Security Administration now had possession of the Abston, Crump, & Wynne land. Plans had already been laid to move out all the blacks, about 250 families at that time in 1938, and resell the property to mostly poor whites. He said that the local administrator and certain white people already living in the Transylvania area had had a meeting and decided our land was too rich for black folks to have. The local Farm Security office had already sent out land applications to poor whites both in East Carroll and in other north Louisiana parishes.

For years, people had been promised that if the land was ever sold, they would be given the first chance to buy. Now we were finding out that no blacks would be given an opportunity to buy any Farm Security land in East Carroll. Farm Security representatives had already brought some of the Transylvania residents papers to sign. Some of the people were illiterate, and others who could read had signed the papers without reading them or had signed them because they misunderstood the legal wording in the document. They told me that the man who brought the papers had implied that if they signed them, they could continue living where they were. Actually, they were signing away all their good farmland and at the same time agreeing to transfer to the Thomastown project, a resettlement project some twenty-five miles south of Transylvania in Madison Parish.

I checked around and found out a plan had already been put in place. After they got all the blacks out of Transylvania, they were going to move in white families. Then they were going to build up the community by putting in a meat-curing plant, a canning plant, a cooperative store, and a cooperative selling plan so that the farmers would be able to get the full share of their crops.

We didn't have an NAACP branch in Transylvania at that time, but I remembered what my pastor had said about how they worked to help Negroes in trouble. So we decided to write the national office of the NAACP in New York. They advised me that we'd better get organized fast. They said they would contact the Farm Security Administration in Washington about our situation and see what they could do to help us get some land.

In August 1938, a young man named Samuel Whitney, local reporter for the *Pittsburgh Courier* and the *Southern Broadcast,* joined me in a house-to-house canvass for NAACP members, trying to kindle the fire in the Negroes to fight this move. The first house I stopped at was Charley Coleman's house. I told him the plan and what would happen to us if we didn't stop it. He said, "No, that can't happen to us. We've been here too long."

I went on to the house of another man, Mr. Sherman Tillman. This man Tillman told me, "Now son, listen, I'm from Mississippi and I know how white folks feel about these things. Two young men over there tried to start something like this and they found those two fellows swinging from a limb."

A couple of days later, I was in front of the general store when I overhead two men talking about me. One was saying to the other,

"We can't do that foolish thing Scott wants done. We got to live here among these white people."

So I didn't get too much encouragement, but I went all across the place trying to drum up support. People were scared to take a stand, though we did gain enough support to get our NAACP branch started.

By the time of our organizational meeting, over a hundred people had pledged but only fourteen had actually paid their money. The national office sent up four men from New Orleans to our organizational meeting—Mr. A. P. Tureaud, attorney for the Louisiana NAACP, Mr. G. J. McDemond, representing the National Negro Congress, Mr. O. C. W. Taylor, Louisiana correspondent for the *Pittsburgh Courier*, and Mr. Leon Lewis, representing the Associated Negro Press (ANP), which was like the Associated Press wire service except for black news. This interest from the national office and the national press was quite encouraging. I was elected president, Clarence Shields vice president, Samuel Whitney secretary, and my father treasurer.

Mr. Tureaud and our new secretary, Mr. Whitney, and a few others went out that night canvassing the local white merchants, trying to get them to sign a petition against the move. The white merchants told them they thought the move must have been coming from someone outside the area because it wasn't their idea. They didn't want us to move. They said that outside people had come in before and hadn't stayed long, leaving them high and dry. They liked our stable community because we had lived in that one area for three generations. Almost all of the white merchants signed the petition Mr. Tureaud had designed to be sent to President Roosevelt.

I began to feel hopeful until I found out that the local Farm Security office had already advised the regional office that no Negroes wanted to buy any of the land. I was upset but not surprised that the local office would stoop to trickery. We decided that since the local officers didn't want to do right, we'd bypass them and write Washington directly and ask them to give Negroes a chance to buy.

One day after we had sent the letter, I was standing around minding my own business when this unfamiliar white fellow walks up to me. "You John Henry Scott?" he asked.

"I am."

"Well, you're wanted down at the Farm Security office. They want to talk to you."

I wasn't exactly sure what to do since I was so new at this. Should I get some of the other officers to go with me to help me deal with these people? I decided that me and the Lord could handle it, so I went on down to the Farm Security office by myself.

One of the local officers invited me into his office. He wasted no time getting right to the point. "Did you write a letter to Washington?"

"I did," replying as confidently as my nerves would allow. The man behind the table was obviously not too happy to be hearing from Washington about us.

"Who told you to do that?"

"The people told me."

"What people?" he said, and looked at me like I had just given a stupid answer. "You all have yourselves some kind of organization?"

"We do."

"I thought you was one of those d—— smart Negroes. We had said that we didn't want no Negroes like you around here."

When we first organized our NAACP branch, we had operated almost like an underground organization, meeting and operating in secret. But now that the national NAACP was involved and the Negro press was letting the world know what was going on, people were willing to come out in the open. When they read in the papers how the NAACP was gathering support from so many people, writing the president of the United States and getting an audience with the national director of the Farm Security Administration, then all of a sudden they wanted to be a part of it. By the end of October, we had over two hundred paid members.

We inquired around and listened to all the white folks' gossip, but we still couldn't figure out this proposal to move us all out of Transylvania. No one seemed to know the origin of the plan or who was behind it, or at least no one was telling us. If the local merchants and other local whites didn't support it, then we wondered whose idea could it be.

Our first clue came from Dr. Charles Houston's visit with Dr. Will Alexander, the national FSA director. Dr. Houston, the NAACP's national attorney, had gone to Washington to try to get our concerns addressed. In Washington, he was told that the blacks in Transylvania would be moved about twenty-five miles south to Thomastown, where lots of good land was available and there were better facilities for blacks. But when the NAACP conducted its own investigation, they found out Dr. Alexander had overstated the amount of land by some 6,000 acres, and the land wasn't nearly as fertile as the land we already had. There were no schools or churches for blacks in Thomastown. Thomastown had less than 6,000 acres total, with 34% of its population white. What they planned to do was move those few whites to the 9,000 acres of developed farmland up in Transylvania and move the 250 black families to the smaller project, making Thomastown all black.

The crops were about finished and the winter cold was just starting to roll in when we got our first evidence of how bad our lot might actually be. The rumor was that a big plantation owner down in Madison Parish had cooked up the whole plan. The fellow already owned about 30,000 acres in Madison, where Thomastown was located. He had a reputation for treating the tenant farmers on his place just like slaves. We heard that he planned to stuff Madison Parish full of black tenant farmers who would be under his beck and call, especially since he already controlled most of the land, the jobs, and the cotton gins.

When the whites already living in Thomastown got wind of the plan, they started their own protest petition, which they sent to the Louisiana legislature. They didn't want to move to Transylvania and we didn't want to move to Thomastown.

I had to go down to Baton Rouge to help put together a program for the upcoming statewide Baptist Training Union Convention. After I got there, I found out that the Minister's Institute was being held at the same time. I liked attending their training classes, but I didn't have any extra money to pay for the registration. I went by the Institute anyway, only to find out that the Lord had already worked it out. The man I spoke to, Dr. Bacons, told me to forget about the registration fees and just stay on at the school—he would take care of it. So I ended up staying in Baton Rouge much longer than I had planned.

The day after I returned from Baton Rouge, I was on my way to the store when I saw a white fellow I knew. He usually joked around a lot, laughing and slapping me on the back as he talked. But today he seemed particularly serious. He beckoned me down a side alley, looking from side to side as if someone might be watching him. I followed him into the alley.

"I thought you ought to know that they had a meeting about you and this Farm Security thing. They even discussed how they could dispose of you. I asked them what had you done so bad that they should want to kill you, but I never got a straight answer. They never could quite agree on what to do with you, but I wanted you to know that they have been looking all over the place for you but nobody seemed to know where you were. You better watch out for yourself." And with that, he darted around the back of the store and was out of sight.

I thought about what he had said. Could he really be serious? Were people really planning to kill me? It was a good thing that the Lord had kept me in Baton Rouge those extra days. Maybe they had had a little time to cool off and regain some good sense.

Someone must have told them I was back, because it wasn't long before a truck arrived at my house. The white driver told me he had been sent to bring me to the Farm Administration office.

My heart pounded as I entered the office, but as usual, I was getting myself mentally prepared for a confrontation. I had not forgotten what I had learned from the animals and I had also learned how to pray. I took the seat they offered facing the small gathering of white men.

The director, in a southern drawl, began, "John Heen-ry," dragging out the Henry part. "We meet again. They tell me you the one causing all these troubles."

After he had elaborated on what troubles I had caused him, referring to the NAACP meeting in Washington, I said, "Yes, but they told me that white people were too intelligent to follow-up hearsay."

That sort of knocked him off his feet. He hesitated, trying to recover because his intelligence had been attacked. Then he started again, shaking his finger at me, "Let me tell you, you are going to get beat up. You going to get run away from here. You are going to get yourself killed."

I thought to myself. So *I'll* be the one getting myself killed. Like he would have no responsibility in the matter.

I looked him straight in the eye. This in itself was probably intimidating, because black people weren't supposed to ever look white people directly in the eye. White people considered this to be disrespectful, and Negroes were taught from the time they were very young to never do this.

I spoke as calmly as I could muster. "Sir, I've taken under consideration all that you say. I might get run away from here, but I feel if I do, that the Lord has a better place for me. And I took under consideration getting beat up, but I think it is a sorry man who would not take a beating for what he believes is right. I even took under consideration I might get killed, but my coffin is already paid for." Pointing toward the graveyard, I said, "And my people are buried. I am not afraid to die."

He turned red. "Now listen, John Heen-ry, you must not be such a radical. Much of your life is in front of you. You're mighty young to be pursuing this course. Now you don't need to be working yourself up over this. I want you all to know that we white folks are going to do all we can for you."

"That's what I thought," I said. "That's what I was thinking all the time, but if you were going to do all you can for us, I think we should do something for ourselves."

So they let me go unharmed.

After the Washington meeting with the FSA director and after all the articles in the newspapers, finally in mid-November, the Farm Security Administration sent a Negro lady down from Washington to try to settle the matter. A group of us drove down to New Orleans, where state NAACP attorney Tureaud and members of the press were meeting with her. We informed her about threats of bodily harm against me and the acts of intimidation and threats against other people on the project.

The FSA lady had brought a compromise. She said that if the Negroes moved from Transylvania, they could have four other projects with churches, cotton gins, canning works, barns, and modern homes. She also promised new schools and a school bus to carry the children.

"Wouldn't that be good for the children to finally have a bus?" she asked.

She told us that they would help everybody find a place to live who couldn't qualify for project land, and those who qualified would not have to move until good places had been provided for them. Any people who owed debts would be given a long time to pay them off. When she had finished her proposal, Attorney Tureaud bluntly informed her that the compromise was outrageous and unacceptable. We wanted a chance to buy the land where we already lived. The woman was sent back to Washington without a settlement.

The local officers were outraged that we had the nerve to reject the compromise and make further demands. Time was running out for them, and they needed us to move soon because the white families were making ready to move in. They would have to force us out.

So they made their move. The next thing we knew Mr. Brady, community manager at Transylvania, fired our plantation manager. Then he posted tenant removal notices all over Transylvania: ". . . must vacate the property by January 1st. Vacated properties will be thoroughly inspected and any damages charged against the tenants. Tenants will be prosecuted by the government through the courts for payment if any damages found."

Chaos. That's all you could call it. Families scrambling to find out where they were supposed to go. Mr. Brady calling people in claiming they owed this and that for cotton seed and poison, and rent and blacksmithing and whatever else he could charge the people for, robbing the people not only of their land but what little cash they might have had. He ordered the Rosenwald school closed, saying it was no time for colored children to be going to classes.

Everything was happening too fast, and it was everything we could do to try to keep the people calm. Joining the NAACP suddenly became important to everybody, including the ones who had been scared to earlier. They wanted help figuring out their accounts, help figuring out why they were being charged so much, help trying to get qualified for other project land. And all the time Mr. Brady was promising qualifications to those who did what he wanted done and threatening bodily harm against people just trying to help their neighbors out. Somebody who wanted us out set up a plan to kill our NAACP secretary, Mr. Samuel Whitney, but one of the prominent whites got word to him just hours before the roadside ambush was scheduled to take place.

We had tried to warn the people that they were going to be put off their land, but they hadn't wanted to hear us then, partially because certain preachers and teachers, whom they respected, weren't backing us up. So they hadn't considered our warnings to be credible. Besides, they were used to waiting to see what the boss had to say about everything. Now they got to see just what could happen, but it was too late to try to stand up now.

In December 1938, the 250 black families began to move from Transylvania, some to the incomplete projects we had rejected in the compromise offer. Some people waited right up until the deadline only to come from church and find all their belongings piled up on their porches with notes to vacate the premises by morning. The Farm Security people worked day and night, weekdays, and Sundays to put us out. They brought in wagons and charged the people four dollars a load, really big money back then. The people were running all around because they weren't told where they were supposed to move to until the morning before the deadline. Some were just left stranded with no place to go.

There was no rhyme and reason to the move. Both the qualified and unqualified were often sent to the same place. Some families were sent to farm land on privately owned projects that hadn't been tilled in years. Others were assigned to private plantations without being told what arrangements had been made for them. On one farm, Holland Delta plantation, every house on the place was unfit for people to live in. The roofs leaked and everything going on outside could be seen through the large cracks between the wallboards. In many instances, there was no water. Farmers who had had to move their corn from Transylvania didn't even have a barn or a corn crib on this plantation, so they had to store everything inside their overcrowded houses.

The Transylvania community was torn apart, and family and friends were scattered to the north and south. We left confused because we weren't sure who qualified for project land and who didn't. We didn't even know what constituted qualification. We were put out of the place where most of us had been born, where many of our fathers and mothers had been born, back before the Civil War. Many people had to leave behind houses and barns they had built and the fine crop-growing land they had developed. They even took our Rosenwald school, with its blackboards and separate classrooms, our school that had been built especially for the Negro children by money donated by the owners of Sears & Roebuck. They took the children's desks and all our school equipment and turned it over to the new white settlers, while the children displaced from Transylvania had to start attending classes all in one room at a church, with church benches instead of desks. They even took Seven Stars, the first black Baptist church in East Carroll, the church my great grandfather had founded, and sold it to the new white settlers.

Just when things looked their worst, we got some news of hope. Back on the final day of evictions, the *Pittsburgh Courier* had sent a reporter down to take pictures. These pictures of wagons loaded down with possessions moved some readers to try to help us. We got word from New Orleans that President Roosevelt had received more than three hundred letters asking him to conduct a formal investigation of our situation. Support came from the National Baptist Convention, the Knights of Peter Claver, the Fraternal Council of Negro Churches, the presidents of Southern, Leland, and Dillard Universities, the presidents of all the major black insurance companies, and the Louisiana Teacher's Association, just to name a few.

In February, we found out that President Roosevelt had ordered the FSA head, Dr. Alexander, to look into the situation. Dr. Alexander was going to launch a formal investigation into the whole affair.

The investigation was under way by the third week in February. Federal investigators came down to interview us in Transylvania, and Mr. Taylor of the *Pittsburgh Courier* in New Orleans. After their investigation, they issued a contract to build 147 five-room houses consisting of three bedrooms, living room, modern kitchen, and screened back porch on several projects. Mr. Thurgood Marshall, Special Council for the NAACP, came down at the end of March to make sure that the new homes were started and that the forty-acre plots were actually being made available to Negro families.

Many people ended up getting forty-acre homesteads on one of several Negro resettlement projects. One project, the Henderson Project, was built just south of Transylvania. The land was also fairly rich, but it was so close to the Mississippi River that whenever the river rose high, what we call seepage water would come up from underground, pushing through the water table with such pressure that it boiled up through the soil. It would get bad enough that the farmers couldn't work the land all the time. They built the Henderson School for the children who settled on the project. On the north side of Lake Providence, on the other side of the lake, we got Lakeview Project. Some people got homesteads in Blue Front and Fortune Fork on land down below Transylvania, right outside the town of Tallulah, but the bulk of the people settled on the new Thomastown project in Madison Parish. This land was fairly rich too, but Thomastown land was nothing like Transylvania with its rich loam soil, real delta land, the richest farmland around.

After all the blacks moved out of the Transylvania area, the poor whites moved in from all over. The area was resettled by men who later became some of our bigger farmers with familiar family names, such as the Harveys, Fortenberrys, Thorntons, Harpers, Fletchers, and others. Because each family received such large plots of land, these new landowners were in great need of laborers. In the summer they needed people to chop the weeds out of the fields, and in the fall they needed farm hands to manually pick the cotton. Every day they sent their trucks up to the Lake Providence area to pick up black laborers, some of them displaced from Transylvania.

For a while, some blacks were glad they were there, because they paid better wages than the original whites in the area and they also treated them better. But later, when they began to mechanize their farms, they didn't have much need for black laborers and they began to turn. Even the upper-crust whites later regretted they had turned over all this good land to the poorer whites because after they moved in, they began to exert some political power. The upper-crust whites felt that if they had let the blacks stay, we would have been submissive and would not have had any political ambition.

Many blacks who qualified for project land did well over time, doubling and tripling the acreage they owned. They left Transylvania with a spirit of militancy that would produce many outstanding leaders in the struggle for civil rights in the 1960s, both in Lake Providence and down the road in Tallulah. During the boycotts and picketing in the Tallulah campaign of the '60s, the Negroes who had once lived in Transylvania were right there in the march helping to carry on. So everywhere they went, they carried a fighting spirit. The Transylvania situation taught the Negroes that if they stood together, even people in small country towns could get some attention. The NAACP and the black press had gotten us a chance to buy. If they hadn't gotten involved, nobody black would have gotten an opportunity to buy, and we would have ended up under semi-slavery on privately owned farms all over Madison and East Carroll Parishes.

# NINE

# Life after Transylvania

Since I couldn't qualify for project land, in January 1939, I moved north about nine miles up U.S. Highway 65 to the town of Lake Providence, the northeasternmost town in Louisiana. It had been originally named the Town of Lake Providence to distinguish its name from that of the lake, but over time, the "Town of" part was dropped and everyone just called the place Lake Providence, which was sometimes confusing since the lake was called the same thing.

Lake Providence had sprung up at the foot of the lake, an eight-mile bow-shaped body of water that had once been part of the Mississippi River but had gotten cut off from the original channel. I had always considered Lake Providence to be a pretty town, mainly because it was filled with the beauty of God's nature, the shimmering waters, the abundance of flowers, the fragrance of the flowering bushes and trees.

Along the lakefront were large plantation houses that faced private boat piers and towering cypresses that grew along the water's edge. On Lake Street, from the lake's end to the levee, a space of about three short blocks, was the main shopping district. On the south side of Lake Street were the Lake Theater, several saloons, the Fischer Hotel, a five-and-ten store, a drugstore, and a clothing store. On the north side was the *Banner Democrat* newspaper office, which published a paper each Friday, and the City Hall and the fire department.

Most of the stores were new, because breaks in the levee had caused the town to be moved twice. A new levee system was being built that was supposed to solve the flooding problems, but the new structure had been built so close to the town that it actually loomed up directly in front of the houses that faced it on Levee Street. People could walk out their houses, walk across the street, and be at the base of the levee.

About 19,000 people lived in Lake Providence at that time, with blacks representing about 10,000 of that total. Since about a fourth of the parish's acreage was under cultivation, everybody's job in some way related to farming, with a few exceptions. A few blacks had jobs with the Missouri-Pacific Railroad, which had a stop in Lake Providence, but there was no factory work in the parish unless you counted the two cotton gins. Or maybe you could count the jobs at the sawmills as factory work. Some men found jobs there harvesting and milling the large cypress, oak, hickory, and sycamore trees that seemed to grow larger in East Carroll than in any of the surrounding parishes.

Those first few years after I was forced out of Transylvania were really rough for me. Money was always tight. I worked from farm to farm, wherever I could find a job, but farm work was becoming increasingly scarce. All kinds of new farm equipment was coming out that could do the work faster than people could—tractors, combines, corn and cotton pickers. The new tractors could plow, plant, and cultivate as many as twelve rows at once, and workers were being turned off plantations all the time. One big farmer with over 3,000 acres eliminated all the jobs driving his 110 plowing mules and kept only the seven men he needed to drive his seven new tractors.

The second year I lived in Lake Providence was unusually rainy. It rained some nearly every day for more than forty days. The ground was so soaked that hardly any farming could be done. The standing water generated a crop of mosquitoes so big it was rumored that they were big enough to whip a dog.

I found a job with a white friend. The farm work was sporadic, but when I didn't have any farm work to do, he would pay me to ride around with him. Wages were around $1.00 a day then, but he'd pay me $1.50 just to ride with him and keep him company. We'd go to Monroe, a city about seventy miles west of Lake Providence, and sometimes other places around the area. If it were an overnight trip, he would go to the white hotel and give me my fare to the colored hotel, and come back to pick me up later.

We had some interesting discussions during those road trips. We talked about common problems and even discussed race issues, a subject seldom discussed between blacks and whites. He wanted to know what I thought about the white man. Although he was white, he didn't seem to have a very high opinion of the behavior of his race.

One day while we were out riding, he asked me to start working on Sundays. When I refused for religious reasons, he tried to show me where there was nothing to religion. He named off some white farmers who were supposed to be big Christians and pointed out some of the things they had done. "I'm not a Christian and I wouldn't treat people like that," he said. "I wouldn't treat anybody like they treat their work hands. So there can't be nothing to religion if it won't make you act any better than that."

Of course I didn't agree with the "nothing-to-religion" part, but it did seem to me that he had a better understanding of Christian living than some people who went to church every Sunday.

I struggled through the rest of 1940, and by the time 1941 rolled around, I had about made up my mind to move, probably to some place out west. Work was just too scarce. I went by my cousin's house to see if I could store some of my things there until I could get settled in another state. I would send for my things later.

Rev. Mansel Mason, a good friend of mine who owned a big farm outside of town, happened to stop by while I was visiting my cousin. We talked about my decision and he tried to convince me not to give up on Lake Providence. He drove me out to his farm, and by the time I left, he had talked me into staying and helping him out around his place. So I decided to stay a while longer and give Lake Providence another chance.

I was visiting my cousins again later that year when I heard them talking about a young woman visiting her cousin at the house next door. She sounded interesting, like someone I would want to meet, so I decided to go visiting that night.

I arrived at the front door dressed in my suit and tie and polished shoes, my normal attire for when I wasn't working in the fields. Sitting across in the front room on a couch was a medium-brown-skinned, slender young woman with thick, shoulder-length hair. Well sir, I thought. I know this girl. I've even talked to her a couple of times. She was someone I was used to seeing uptown on Saturday evenings, the time when most black people went to town to conduct their business. The stores would stay open until about eight or nine at night, and after the stores closed, people who liked those kinds of things would go around to Levee Street for drinking and dancing at the various jook joints. Mostly I would stand on the corner and talk to all the people as they passed by. Yes, I remembered her. She would always be looking real nice and walking like she owned the world.

We sat and talked a long time that evening. And could she talk—she was definitely not shy. She was downright feisty, full of energy, and I could tell right off she was smart. Her name was Alease Juanita Truley and she was twenty-three years old, about seventeen years younger than me. She already knew some things about me since I was fairly well known all over East Carroll due to the Transylvania project and my missionary work, which took me from farm to farm and church to church.

We talked about all kinds of things. We talked about how her mother had died when she was young, and we talked about what it was like growing up without our mothers. She had been raised by her father, Thomas "Bus" Truley, and her oldest sister, Rosie Lee, and later a stepmother. She still lived with her father up on Lakeview Project.

We talked about farming, which she seemed to know a lot about. She had worked most of her life along side her father on the farm after her brother had drowned. In fact, she had attended school until she was twenty, not being able to attend enough days some years to be able to pass. She could operate any of the farm equipment—at least according to her—and she talked as if she could take care of any type of farm animal.

I also found out we shared a love of poetry. I collected poems that I cut out from magazines and newspapers and had even bought several volumes of poems by black authors, one of my favorites being Paul Laurence Dunbar. We also both shared an interest in teaching, in one form or another. She taught school at the church school at Jerusalem Baptist Church. I found out that she had two boys, Leotis and Leon, an infant and a two-year-old. Sometime during the conversation, she offhandedly mentioned how she would appreciate having a good husband.

I was so impressed by her that as I headed home, I found myself wondering—I never thought of myself—who could I tell that she would probably make them a good wife. She had a lot to offer. She was smart, with knowledge far exceeding her formal education. Every subject I brought up, she could converse on. She wrote and delivered plays and speeches and didn't seem to mind hard work. She wasn't like the other farm girls I had met, whose minds seemed limited to their circumstances. She had dreams and plans.

A long time back, I had been in a play about a rich widow who was looking for a husband. In the play, I was supposed to help the widow find a suitable beau but I couldn't think of any man who seemed right. At the end of the play, I ended up marrying the widow myself. This play just popped into my mind that night and it set me to thinking. I had been thinking about somebody else, but now I was thinking of myself. Didn't she have what I needed? Didn't she not only have the physical characteristics but also qualities that would support and complement the things I dreamed of doing? And hadn't people been saying that it wasn't "proper" for a preacher to be around without a wife? I decided I would propose to her myself.

When I saw her the next time, I told her, "I know a fellow that might make you a husband if you're willing to take the chance on him. He doesn't have a long time to be sitting around saying a lot of sweet things, but if you can take that kind of chance, why I might tell you who he is."

She was definitely curious and insisted that I tell her who the fellow was. Finally I said, "Well, it's me."

She was quite excited because all the women had figured I would never take a wife. After all, I was almost forty, and although I was popular with the women and had courted quite a few, I hadn't shown any particular inclination toward trying marriage again.

Later that week, we met again, and she said that she would marry me, but I would have to come up to her house and ask her father's permission first. I told her that there was one thing that we would have to agree to before that, and that was how the children would be raised. I told her that I wanted to be a father to Leon and Leotis, but I wanted to be fully the father, not the stepfather. I wanted to have authority and be responsible for them as though they were my own. She agreed, and that was the role I assumed from the time we married.

Mr. Truley was a rather harsh, somewhat mean-looking man who didn't hide his surprise when I asked to marry his daughter. After he had thought it over, though, he must have adjusted to the idea, because he later sent for me and gave me permission. We were married about a month later on February 1, 1942. Rev. Mason performed the ceremony and another good friend, Rev. Camp Butler, stood with me as my best man.

My wife had to make many, many sacrifices because of her decision to marry me. Not only did she have to do without a lot of things, but my causes and fights later put her in the position of having to raise our children under very dangerous conditions. When we first married, I promised her we would probably be out of our bad financial situation in a year or two. I found us a place to stay near the land I was farming with Rev. Mason, land Rev. Mason had rented from the Baptist Association for raising cotton. We moved into an old, unpainted double-family tenant house just south of Lake Providence with another couple, John Russell and his wife, Alberta, who was Rev. Mason's sister.

We lived in the three rooms on the left side—a front room, a bedroom, and a kitchen. Both families shared the porch that stretched the entire length of the front of the house. The house wasn't in the best condition and was certainly a step down from the Farm Security project house Alease had lived in on forty acres with her father and stepmother. We had no electricity or running water, and the floorboards didn't exactly come together. Through the gaps we could see the chickens under the house scratching around in the dirt for food. There was no ceiling, so when you looked up, you were looking at the tin roof, which also leaked during heavy rains. When the cold winds blew in, we tacked up wallpaper of pages from the Sears catalog, hoping to block out some of the winter chill and keep the children warm, but it didn't help much. Because the house was set high on blocks about two and a half feet off the ground, the cold air would still whip under the house and find its way up through the big cracks in the floorboards.

My new wife didn't want to live in the Lake Providence area, and that didn't make matters any easier. She had dreams of a nice house and pretty clothes, and a lifestyle that couldn't be found in a country farming town. I believe when she married me, she thought I would give her these things, maybe because of the way I dressed whenever I was out in public or maybe because I always talked about doing the kinds of things that a black man wasn't allowed to do in the South. Besides, I sort of wanted to move away too.

Ever since World War II had started, shortly after my involvement in Transylvania, the situation for black people seemed to change yearly.

We didn't know what to expect next. After the Japanese bombed Pearl Harbor, we started hearing about these internment camps where they locked up Japanese Americans because somebody had decided they were too dangerous to be left free. I read in the paper that the local white farmers had decided to build a prison camp in Lake Providence, big enough to hold about 350 Japanese. They were going to pitch in $35 apiece for each Japanese American they planned to put to work in their fields.

So now we had something else to worry about. Would the farming jobs now go to the practically free Japanese laborer? It seemed we would have to leave town to get decent wages. All the time, somebody would be standing with a tied-up suitcase and maybe a greasy brown bag containing some fried chicken and bread, waiting for a bus to take them up north or out west to any place where they might make a living. We'd all heard about the big wages people were getting in places like California, where jobs making ships and tanks and other such things associated with the war were plentiful.

My wife and I would discuss moving from time to time, up until we had our first baby together in 1944. We named our little girl Johnita, John for my first name, and "nita" after Alease's middle name, Juanita. Everybody wanted to take a peek at her because she was a Negro baby born with blue eyes, but after a few days, her eyes started to darken up some. A few years after Johnita was born, we had Elsie and then Sharolyn.

So we settled in. My wife stayed at home and cooked (and she was a very good cook) and looked after the children. Later she got involved in the civil rights movement and in church activities, teaching and delivering and writing speeches. Those were her talents. Pretty soon, she was nearly as active as I was. After she got so involved in the civil rights movement, she didn't talk so much about moving anymore. I'd like to think she found meeting the needs of the community to be more satisfying than acquiring material goods. I believe she realized how important our work was to Northeast Louisiana and forgot about how poor she was living and how many things she didn't have that others had.

Her two sisters, Rosie Lee and Cleo, had moved to California, one to Oakland and the other to Berkeley. Later, Cleo moved to Oakland too, into a huge house on the side of a hill, with fancy French furniture and lots of nice things. Her living room and den together exceeded our whole living space. We hardly saw indoor plumbing in the rural area where we lived, but at Cleo's house, I could go into the restroom and into the washroom and see myself in mirrors everywhere I looked. I knew my wife thought about these kinds of things and was disappointed we couldn't afford them, but I think over time she readjusted herself and reacted extremely well under the circumstances under which we lived.

The Bible says "the just shall live by faith," and that's the way I lived. I just don't think my wife found that faith method of living to be very satisfactory. I never knew what I might get or how I was going to get it, but I knew if I trusted in the Lord, he'd build a bridge across every problem. Every need would be met, and about that I never had to worry. Sometimes I couldn't see a bridge in the distance, but it was always there by the time I got to the problem. Still, I don't think my wife ever felt entirely secure with not knowing where things would come from until the things arrived.

In spite of all we had to go through, I never regretted remaining in Lake Providence or rearing my family here. I couldn't consider myself poor when I was blessed with the things more important than money, like a very nice family. I told my wife I thought where we lived was the best spot we could have been, out in God's great outdoors. We were blessed in the early 1950s to be able to move into a nicer house on the sixty acres owned by the Baptist Association, after I became caretaker of the property. This is where Louis and two more girls, Cleo and Harriet, were born. We now had four rooms and electricity and ample space for recreation, both for our children and the children of the community.

The whole family attended Sunday School and church together, and sometimes some of the children would go with me to the fishing hole. Occasionally Johnita and Louis would go hunting with me too. For a long time, until about 1963, we didn't own a television. Those that came up without television made mostly A's and B's in school because they didn't have anything to distract their minds and they could study without confusion. Actually, that wasn't really true, because all the children did well in school, and we had two valedictorians and two salutatorians out of the group. I guess I just said that because I hadn't wanted a television in my house, but my sister Annie B. had decided to give my wife her old one anyway. I think she and my wife cooked the whole thing up.

Actually, my wife was a big part of why the children made such good grades. When the older children got old enough to go to school, the younger ones wanted to go too, so she decided to start having school at home. They didn't have preschool or kindergarten back then, so children started right in the first grade, some just starting to learn to write their alphabets and numbers. We didn't have a lot of extra paper, so my wife would use the S & H green stamp books and print the alphabets in the blocks for the children to copy. They would practice their lessons while she cooked. Most could already read well before they started school.

My wife was good in all subjects, especially math, and as the children got older, she could assist them if they needed help with their homework. She tended the house and fed the children fresh fruit and vegetables, which kept them healthy and away from the doctor. So I have to give my wife great credit. I sensed that she always wanted more nice things, but she didn't complain. And with all the pressure I was later under, if I had had to live under pressure from her too, I don't think I could have made it.

During the time I was first settling in with a new wife and two little boys to raise, I was also trying to salvage something from what was left of our Transylvania branch of the NAACP. After the people from Transylvania had scattered in every direction, our organization had pretty much fallen apart. Even the Lake Providence branch, which had been organized over ten years before we started in Transylvania, was floundering. We decided it was best to merge the remnants of the two branches into a new organization. We called it the East Carroll Parish Branch, and I was elected its president.

In June 1943, the national NAACP called an emergency conference in Detroit, Michigan. I really wanted to attend, but our new branch didn't have enough money in its treasury to send me. We were already struggling to get back on our feet, especially since most of the ministers and teachers did not support the organization. Some of the members got together anyway and raised the cost of my bus fare, with six dollars over. So I left for Detroit for a week-long conference with only six dollars spending change in my pocket.

This was my first trip north, and I arrived in Detroit realizing how poor I was. I had made arrangements to stay with a friend, a lady who had been my neighbor before she moved north. When she and her husband left for work that first day, I walked down to the neighborhood store and bought some bologna sausage and a loaf of white bread. When the white clerk gave me my change, I noticed how she handed it to me, unlike the whites back home who would slide my change across the counter to avoid touching me.

I came back to the house and made me some sandwiches since I didn't have enough money to buy lunch at the conference. After eating, I took the bologna sausage and tried to hide it towards the back of the icebox. Then I dressed and went on down to the conference.

The church was full of delegates—hundreds of men and women from all over the United States. After I had lived in a rural area all my life, this assembly of black people looked especially distinguished and well-off to me. Most of the men were dressed in wide-lapel suits and narrow ties with white handkerchiefs folded up to make four white points sticking up out of tops of their suit pockets. And hardly any men wore their hair parted down the center like I liked to wear mine. I decided that there must be something to what the people said about a better living in the north, because I rarely saw black men dressed this well back home.

After the conference ended for the day, I came back to my friend's house. We were sitting at the kitchen table talking about the speakers and the people I had met that day, when she got up to get something out of the icebox. She started moving things around like she couldn't find what she was looking for. Then she came across the bologna sausage. Pulling it out, she said, "Who put bologna sausage in the icebox?"

She knew full well that it was me who put it there. Embarrassed, I said, "I did."

"You aren't supposed to eat bologna sausage in Detroit. You eat that stuff back down in Louisiana. Now don't let me catch you with any more bologna sausage. You know you don't have to buy anything here. Whatever you see, you can eat it and you can cook anything you want. We can't have you coming up here living like a hobo."

I enjoyed the conference sessions, which were moderated by attorney Channing Tobias. I asked several questions, this being my first time at a national NAACP meeting. I made a plea to them to help the Negro stay in the South. I told them we needed protection so we could feel safe and secure. I tried to explain to the northern delegates what it was like living under the threat of daily violence, never knowing what would set a white person off or when we or our male children might get caught on the streets when the white law enforcement officers decided it was time to "teach some coloreds a lesson." I tried to make them understand the helplessness of people living in an area where only whites elected the legislature that made the laws and appointed the judges who protected the sheriffs who brutalized and sometimes lynched black people.

I asked them to insist to the president that the black man be allowed to hold better jobs in the Southland and that the plantation bosses be forced to give the Negro a fair deal for his crops. I told them that the only reasons Negroes were leaving the South was because of the different oppressions we had to live under. I even made the statement, "If you don't help us, we're going to all migrate north and bring our cousins with us. We're going to bring our customs and traditions up here and we're going to be 'goin' and you're going to be 'going.' Therefore, we are pleading for your help." I could see delegates from the north smiling to themselves when I said this.

I posed another question in the conference. "On the basis of the World Baptist Alliance in Atlanta, Georgia, when they took the segregation signs down and they all lived as brothers for one week," I said, "don't you think that the churches, if they wanted to, could do away with segregation in a year's time?" That generated a big laugh.

They thought it was funny, but in a way I was serious. I believed the church had the moral responsibility to stamp out injustices. If the white American Baptists wanted to hide their prejudices from the rest of the world, then surely that meant they knew that what they were doing was wrong and they should stop doing it. It seemed simple enough to me.

I stayed there at the conference all week. That Saturday evening after the conference ended, several friends from Detroit who used to live in Lake Providence came by to see me. It was interesting listening to their stories about the better living in the north. They even gave me a dollar or two to help out on my trip. Many of them had read about the Transylvania situation in the *Pittsburgh Courier,* and they encouraged me to keep pushing on.

This was to be the first of many trips up north. Although I didn't get to see very much of Detroit because of the conference sessions, the part I saw didn't impress me too much. I went to Belle Isle and other places of interest, but quite a few of the streets I went on were very rough. I saw that some blacks lived poor in the north too. Everybody wasn't living as well as the people whose houses I had visited earlier in the week. Something that did impress me, though, was the want ads in the paper where companies offered good wages for good jobs that were available to black people. But still I didn't have the inclination to leave my hometown. I was glad for the experience—and I came back home with more than six dollars!

World War II continued to rage on, and many black men from East Carroll Parish were drafted. Two of my brothers from my father's second marriage received their draft notices. Baker was sent to the Pacific and J. W. (John William) was sent to East Africa and later to Germany.

It was hard to say in general how blacks felt about the war, since it depended on who you asked. Some people who weren't drafted were glad about the war because of all the new jobs it created. It was the first time many good-paying jobs were available to blacks, because there were more job openings than white people to fill them. During the war, whites in the South even seemed to adjust themselves somewhat to the changes, seemed to almost start seeing black people as Americans first, Negroes second. War seemed to cause white people to act that way, but as the war started winding down, it became evident that they expected everybody to return to their former roles. In Lake Providence, they seemed to take particular offense from any sign of a black person earning a decent living.

There were several gas stations on the main highway that ran through Lake Providence where the attendants made a game of hassling blacks who happened to stop for gas. A relative of mine had driven over from California in a shiny new Cadillac. When he went to the filling station and pulled up to the pump, the young white attendant sauntered over, staring at the new car.

"Whose car that you driving, boy?" he drawled.

"This is my car."

"Now you know ain't none of y'all got a car like this. Whose car you done stole? I'd better get the sheriff out here now to see about this."

Needless to say, that visit was cut short.

Some of the soldiers sent oversees said they did not regret going. They were glad for the chance to have traveled and to have seen so many places outside the United States, or shall I say outside Lake Providence. But even though some of them liked the traveling, I think that for the most part, they were kind of bitter about the war. They had risked their lives in service to America and they thought that should count for something. Even those of us who didn't serve thought that the valiant service of black soldiers would make a difference in our plight. Most people had heard about the lynchings and race riots that followed the return of the soldiers after World War I, but we all expected something different after this war. After all, something should have changed in over twenty years. Surely if white America could feel sympathy and concern over the way the Jews were mistreated in Germany, they should be able to see that their own house was not in order.

But such was not the case. Every week when I got my *Pittsburgh Courier*, I'd read some article about a returning soldier getting into a fight over some racial matter or a soldier being beat without provocation, mostly by police. Sometimes soldiers were even lynched.

We had our fair share of soldier problems in Lake Providence too. One such incident happened in the early months of 1946. Private Oliver Harris, Jr., son of a local minister, had come home on furlough from Fort Dix, New Jersey. Before Harris had gone into the army, he had operated a radio repair shop in Tallulah, about thirty miles south of Lake Providence. While he was home visiting, he decided to do some repair work. He went by the local hardware store to pick up some materials and while there, he and the Negro helper at the store got into a dispute. When the white manager saw what was happening, he came over and kicked Harris while delivering a barrage of racial slurs. A fight broke out, and Harris got the best of the fight. They had to carry the store manager off to the hospital and Harris was thrown in jail.

The soldier's mother, Mrs. Harris, asked me if there was anything I could do to help, so I wrote the State Conference of Branches of the NAACP and requested that they furnish legal counsel for Harris. They told me I would need to get a copy of his court record. So another minister, Rev. Cooper, and Mrs. Harris, and I drove down to Tallulah to see if we could get the records. We walked the streets trying to find someone from Tallulah who would go down to the court with us, but we couldn't find anyone willing to go.

I had known Mr. Hester, the sheriff down there, for some time, so I decided to go by his office and see if he could do anything to help us. Sheriff Hester told us we would need to go to the clerk of court's office to get the court records. He showed us where the office was, and we went down there and requested the papers we needed.

"Oh, you can't just come in here and get whatever you want right on the spot. You'll have to wait at least two days before I can have them ready."

The clerk of court told us how much the records would cost us, and we left and came back home. We waited the two days, and Mrs. Harris and I went back down to Tallulah to see if the records were ready. When we got there, the clerk of court asked, "What you want with these records? You ain't going to try to get him out, are you?"

"I think so," I said.

The clerk looked at me as if I was the craziest thing he had ever seen. He said, "You must don't know. Why, he hit a white man! He should be dead. He's getting off light just getting a sentence like that."

The papers he gave us showed that Harris had already pleaded guilty to the charges. Whatever proceeding had taken place had been conducted secretly. Of course, if he had pleaded innocent and there had been a trial, it would have been before an all-white jury, because blacks weren't allowed to sit on juries. None of his family had been able to see him after his arrest, and none of them knew a hearing had been held. Harris had already been sentenced to ten years in Angola, the notorious Louisiana state penitentiary, a hard-labor work camp where blacks, many of them innocent of any crime, were sometimes beaten and tortured and often killed, all in the name of rehabilitation and turning a profit for the state.

I sent the information to the state NAACP office, which forwarded it to Thurgood Marshall, special counsel for the NAACP. They probably could have helped Harris, but as it turned out, there was nothing they could do because the town officials claimed that Harris had already pleaded guilty.

Later there was another incident involving Private Willie Osborne, who was in Lake Providence on furlough. Private Osborne decided to go to the picture show one Saturday night. We had a little theater in town, the Lake Theater, where only whites were allowed to enter through the front and watch the movie downstairs. Blacks could enter through the colored entrance, pass through the roped-off colored section of the main lobby, and proceed up the stairs to the balcony.

Before the show started, Osborne met up with some white girls in front of the theater and started flirting with them. The night marshal happened to drive by at the time. The night marshal position had just been created by the police department and someone from out of town, a John Sullivan, had been hired to fill the position. He got out of his car and confronted Osborne. An argument ensured, ending with Sullivan shooting and killing Osborne right there in front of all those people at the theater.

We protested, and Sullivan was dismissed from the police force. The army and the FBI also sent people down to investigate but nothing seemed to ever come out of it. Life went on as it always had, but a seed of discontentment had been planted in the minds of the Negro people and was beginning to take root.

*Rev. John Henry Scott and his wife, Alease, in the late 1970s*

*Elder Granderson Conn of Transylvania, Louisiana, John H. Scott's maternal grandfather, was born in 1835 and died in yellow fever epidemic in 1905.*

Seven Stars, the first Baptist Church in East Carroll Parish, was organized in 1867 by Rev. Louis Taylor, John H. Scott's great grandfather on his mother's side. The church (pictured here in the early 1920s) was moved in 1913 after the Mississippi River began to take over the land on which it was situated; the building burned in 1931, and a smaller one was built on the same site. The building was later sold to white settlers when blacks were forced out of the area under Franklin D. Roosevelt's New Deal program.

John H. Scott (far left) and his father, John Scott, Sr. (second from left), outside Seven Stars Baptist Church with other church members, 1920s

Faculty members from East Carroll Training School, 1930s. Front row (left to right): seated, George Washinton Griffin; standing, Mary Coleman, Fannie Butler, Mary Ballard, Myrdice Jefferson. Middle row: Hilda P. Jones, Florence Jones Simmons, Thelma Mershon, Fannie Dyson Coleman, John Henry Scott. Back row: Mary Mershon, Henry O. Simmons.

John H. Scott, 1935

*The Minister's School at Southern University, Baton Rouge (shown here in 1944), was established when male attendance dropped during World War II.*

*John H. Scott, 1950s*

*Thomas Truley (d. 1952),
father of Alease Truley Scott*

*The North Star Baptist Church of Lake Providence, Louisiana, pastored
by Rev. John H. Scott for twenty-five years starting in 1947, was organized by his great-grandfather, Louis Taylor, in approximately 1870.*

*Pastors and officers of the East Carroll Baptist Association, late 1950s. Back row, left to right: Rev. Newson, Percy Knighten, Rev. Francis J. Atlas, Rev. Handy Jackson, Genevieve Shorter, R. B. Stevenson, Rev. N. B. McCall. Front row, left to right: Rev. Spencer Hall, Rev. Freddie Green, Rev. J. H. Moore, Rev. Mansel Mason, Rev. O. L Virgil, Rev. H. T. James, Rev. Percy H. Henderson, Rev. John H. Scott*

*NAACP youth group from Monroe, Louisiana (and canine friend) along with the younger Scott children (front row) at Christmas celebration given for Scott family after shooting, December 1962*

*Baptist Center, Lake Providence, Louisiana, prior to 1964 arson*

*Arsonists destroyed the Baptist Center in summer 1964.*

*Rev. Scott standing on the side porch, one of the only remaining portions of the Baptist Center after a fire in 1964*

*Rev. Scott with dogs Black
Eyes (left) and Joe in the
yard of his family's home
in Lake Providence*

*Rev. Scott loved his grandchildren; he is shown here with granddaughter
Nicholy (daughter of Johnita) in the early 1970s.*

*Daughters of John H. and Alease Scott (from left): Johnita, Cleo, Amatullah (Sharolyn), Harriet, and Elsie*

*Sons of John H. and Alease Scott (from left): Louis, Leon, and Tyrone (Leotis), with Aunt Azzena Scott Thomas (seated)*

*Rev. John H. Scott, mid-1970s*

# I. L. A. REGISTRATION SCHOOL

## COMPLIMENTARY SAMPLE APPLICATION

Sponsored by
Locals
1419 - 1800 - 854
I. L. A.
Portio's No. 1-2

### APPLICATION FOR REGISTRATION
### Office of Registrar of Voters
### Parish of Orleans, State of Louisiana

Date _____
Ward No. _____
Prect. No. _____

_(Residence Address)_

I am a citizen of the United States and of the State of Louisiana and have not been disfranchised by any provisions of the constitution of this State.

My name is _____ (Mr.—Mrs.—Miss)    _____ (First)    _____ (Middle Name or Initial)    _____ (Last)

My sex is (circle one)   Male   Female

I live at _____ (House No.) (Apt. No.)    _____ (Street)    _____ (City or Town)

Have you been a resident of this state for more than one year, of this parish for over six months, and lived at your present address for more than three months, immediately preceding this date. (Check one) Yes ☐ No. ☐

The place of my birth is _____ (City or Town)    _____ (State or Foreign Country)    _____ (Parish or County or Province)

I am over 21 years of age and the date of my birth is _____ (Month)    _____ (Day)    _____ (Year)    I was last registered as a voter

in _____ (leave blank if none)    _____ (Parish or County)    _____ (State)

I hereby declare my party affiliation to be (circle one) Democrat - Republican - States Rights - None - Other _____

(Indicate your answers to the following questions in the spaces provided. All questions must be answered).

Have you been convicted of a felony without receiving a full pardon and restoration of franchise? Yes ☐ No ☐

Have you been convicted of two or more misdemeanors and sentenced to a term of ninety (90) days or more in jail for each such conviction, other than traffic and/or game law violations, within five years before the date of making this application for registration as an elector?
Yes ☐ No ☐

Have you been convicted of any misdemeanor and sentenced to a term of six (6) months or more in jail, other than traffic and/or game law violations, within one year before the date of making this application for registration as an elector? Yes ☐ No ☐

Have you lived with another in "common law" marriage within five years before the date of making this application for registration as an elector? Yes ☐ No ☐

Have you given birth to an illegitimate child within five years before the date of making this application for registration as an elector? (The provisions hereof shall not apply to the birth of any illegitimate child conceived as a consequence of rape or forced carnal knowledge.) Yes ☐ No ☐

Have you acknowledged yourself to be the father of an illegitimate child within five years before the date of making this application for registration as an elector? Yes ☐ No ☐

TURN CARD OVER

_Sample Application for Voter Registration (front)_

Under Louisiana Revised Statutes 18:222, no person shall register falsely or illegally as a voter, or make a false statement in an affidavit or other document that he presents for the purpose of procuring himself to be registered or to be retained as a registrant. No person shall knowingly present, for any purpose within the purview of this Chapter, an affidavit or other document containing a false statement.

Whoever violates this Section shall be fined not less than five hundred nor more than one thousand dollars, or imprisoned for not less than six months nor more than one year, or both. The penalties shall be doubled for the second or any succeeding offense of the same character. I have read the statements above. Yes ☐ No ☐

"Applicant shall demonstrate his ability to read and write from dictation by the Registrar of Voters from the Preamble to the Constitution of the United States of America."

## PREAMBLE

We, the people of the United States, in order to form a more perfect union, establish justice, insure domestic tranquility, provide for the common defense, promote the general welfare, and secure the blessings of liberty to ourselves and our posterity, do ordain and establish, this Constitution for the United States of America. (Article VIII, 1 (c) (7) La. Constitution)

## CITIZENSHIP TEST FOR REGISTRATION

Question Form Selected: (circle one)

1  2  3  4  5  6  7  8  9  10

Circle letter indicating your answers to the six (6) numbered questions you have chosen.

| | | | | |
|---|---|---|---|---|
| 1 — a  b  c | 3 — a  b  c | 5 — a  b  c |
| 2 — a  b  c | 4 — a  b  c | 6 — a  b  c |

Sworn to and subscribed before me this _____ day of _____, 196__

I do solemnly swear that I will faithfully and fully abide by the laws of this State and that I am well disposed to the good order and happiness thereof.

_____
(Deputy) Registrar

_____
Applicant's Signature

### The Following Information About The Applicant To Be Completed By The Registrar:

My race is _____ The color of my eyes is _____ My mother's maiden name is _____

My occupation is _____ My employer is _____

Change of address:
Date _____ Address _____ Wd ____ Pct ____ Date _____ Address _____ Wd ____ Pct ____

Change of address:
Date _____ Address _____ Wd ____ Pct ____ Remarks: _____

Change of name: Date _____ I am now Mr. – Mrs. – Miss _____

*Sample Application for Voter Registration (back)*

## INSTRUCTIONS TO REGISTRARS

### STEPS OF PROCEDURE TO BE FOLLOWED BY REGISTRARS
### AND THEIR DEPUTIES ACCORDING TO LOUISIANA LAW

1. The Registrar or Deputy Registrar shall interview and give examinations to only one applicant at a time. Applicants should not be near each other, in order to keep one from interfering with another during registration and examination. No other person shall be present for any purpose except the authorized representative of the State Board of Registration. During these examinations, no applicants except those being registered by the Registrar or his deputy should be permitted in the Registrar's office.

2. Have applicant properly identified.

3. If applicant has been registered in another parish of the state, take up registration card or certificate from previous parish or have applicant sign affidavit to be returned to his former parish for cancellation.

4. Registrar shall furnish applicant with card (identified as Form 11), so applicant can do the following:

   A. Execute affidavit.

   B. Read and write a portion of the preamble to the United States Constitution from dictation by the Registrar.

   C. Take citizenship test for registration.

       In order to have applicant complete his citizenship test, the Registrar must have applicant select one of ten cards numbered Form No. 1 through Form No. 10, which cards contain the questions for such test. Cards for selection should be displayed, face-down, to the applicant. After applicant selects his card, the Registrar, for identification, immediately circles in ink the number of the card selected by applicant, in the space provided on Form No. 11 entitled (Question Form Selected).

   D. Complete balance of Form No. 11 which includes parish, date, signature of applicant, ward, precinct and address.

5. Registrar shall choose at random one of the five LR-1 cards; and after filling out applicant's home address, ward and precinct the registrar hands the form to applicant for completion. In the case of a married woman, Registrar should instruct her to write her first name, maiden name or initial, and married name.

6. Applicant should not be qualified or rejected by the Registrar or Deputy until all forms are completed.

7. If applicant fails the citizenship test on Form No. 11 or fails to properly fill out Form LR-1, both cards should be attached and filed alphabetically as provided by law.

*Registration Instructions (front)*

8.  If applicant correctly fills out application (Form LR-1) and passes
    the citizenship test appearing on Form No. 11, Form No. 11 is to be
    attached to Form LR-1 for permanent filing. Applicant should then
    sign permanent registration voting certificate in duplicate, in case
    of permanent registration, or, where four year registration is in
    effect, the applicant must sign the proper precinct register, and the
    Registrar or Deputy must write out a registration certificate and give
    same to applicant. (In case of permanent registration, the confirma-
    tion post card notice is filled in later by the Registration Office
    and mailed to the address as shown on the registration application).

*gistration Instructions (back)*

## DO NOT WRITE ON THIS CARD

Form No. 5

Applicant must correctly answer any four of the following six questions so as to evidence an elemental knowledge of the Constitution and Government, an attachment thereto, and a simple understanding of the obligations of citizenship under a republican form of government.

1. The legislative branch of the State government—
   a. makes the laws for the State.
   b. tries cases in the courts.
   c. explains the laws.

2. Limits are placed on the right to vote by the—
   a. National Government.
   b. States.
   c. courts.

3. The powers granted to the National Government in the Constitution are called—
   a. delegated powers.
   b. denied powers.
   c. the final authority.

4. The name of our first President was—
   a. John Adams.
   b. George Washington.
   c. Alexander Hamilton.

5. The Constitution of the United States places the final authority in our Nation in the hands of—
   a. the national courts.
   b. the States.
   c. the people.

6. Each State has as many Presidential electors as it has—
   a. Senators.
   b. Representatives.
   c. Senators and Representatives.

Applicant's answers must be provided on Form No. 11 furnished by the Registrar for permanent records.

**This card must be returned to the Registrar**

*Citizenship Tests required for Voter Registration (version 5)*

# DO NOT WRITE ON THIS CARD

Applicant must correctly answer any four of the following six questions so as to evidence an elemental knowledge of the Constitution and Government, an attachment thereto, and a simple understanding of the obligations of citizenship under a republican form of government.

1. In case of impeachment of the President, the officer who would preside at the trial is—
   a. the Vice President.
   b. the Speaker of the House of Representatives.
   c. Chief Justice of the United States.

2. Money is coined by—
   a. the States.
   b. the people.
   c. the National Government.

3. Our 'Constitution has been changed—
   a. by the President.
   b. by the Congress and the people.
   c. by the Supreme Court.

4. Limits are placed on the right to vote by the—
   a. National Government.
   b. States.
   c. courts.

5. The Constitution of the United States places the final authority in our Nation in the hands of—
   a. the national courts.
   b. the States.
   c. the people.

6. The name of our first President was—
   a. John Adams.
   b. George Washington.
   c. Alexander Hamilton.

Applicant's answers must be provided on Form No. 11 furnished by the Registrar for permanent records.

**This card must be returned to the Registrar**

*Citizenship Tests required for Voter Registration (version 6)*

# FREEDOM
## BUS
### TO
# WASHINGTON, D. C.
### Or
## ANY OTHER CITY IN THE NORTH

Free Transportation plus $5.00 for Expenses to any Negro Man or Woman, or Family (no limit to size) who desire to migrate to the Nation's Capitol, or any city in the north of their choosing. Please send your name and address to Phone 1497, Lake Providence, La. You will be notified at an early date by the transportation company when you will leave.

On the back of this page you will find the names and addresses of the organizations who will help you when you arrive at any of the cities listed.

*Citizens Council Flyer (front)*

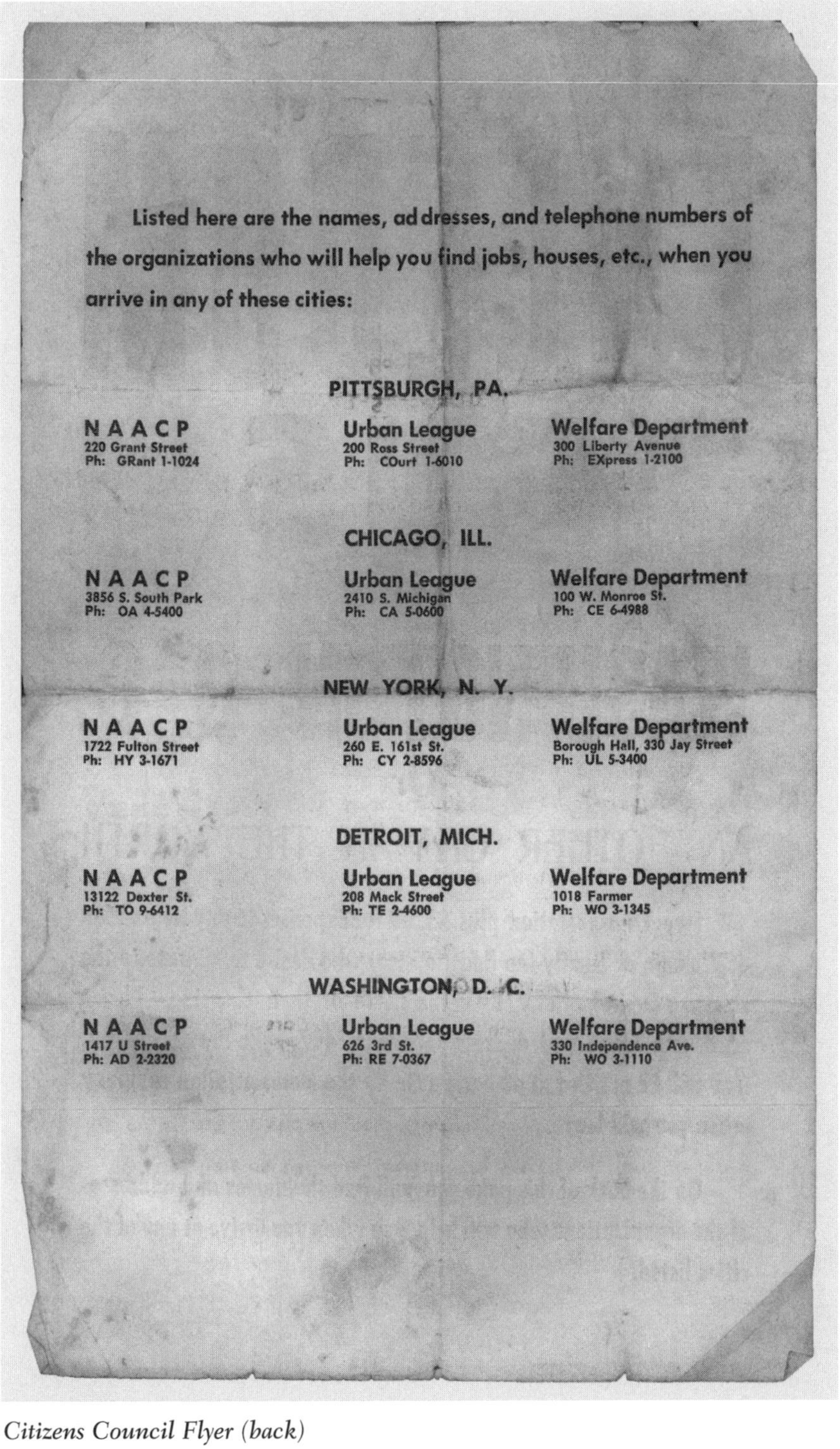

Listed here are the names, addresses, and telephone numbers of the organizations who will help you find jobs, houses, etc., when you arrive in any of these cities:

## PITTSBURGH, PA.

**N A A C P**
220 Grant Street
Ph: GRant 1-1024

**Urban League**
200 Ross Street
Ph: COurt 1-6010

**Welfare Department**
300 Liberty Avenue
Ph: EXpress 1-2100

## CHICAGO, ILL.

**N A A C P**
3856 S. South Park
Ph: OA 4-5400

**Urban League**
2410 S. Michigan
Ph: CA 5-0600

**Welfare Department**
100 W. Monroe St.
Ph: CE 6-4988

## NEW YORK, N. Y.

**N A A C P**
1722 Fulton Street
Ph: HY 3-1671

**Urban League**
260 E. 161st St.
Ph: CY 2-8596

**Welfare Department**
Borough Hall, 330 Jay Street
Ph: UL 5-3400

## DETROIT, MICH.

**N A A C P**
13122 Dexter St.
Ph: TO 9-6412

**Urban League**
208 Mack Street
Ph: TE 2-4600

**Welfare Department**
1018 Farmer
Ph: WO 3-1345

## WASHINGTON, D. C.

**N A A C P**
1417 U Street
Ph: AD 2-2320

**Urban League**
626 3rd St.
Ph: RE 7-0367

**Welfare Department**
330 Independence Ave.
Ph: WO 3-1110

*Citizens Council Flyer (back)*

# PUBLIC KLAN RALLY

*Featuring*

## JACK M. HELM

*Grand Dragon - State of Louisiana*

# CROSS LIGHTING CEREMONY

2:30 P.M., Sunday Afternoon

Oct. 2, 1966

LAKE PROVIDENCE, LA.

2½ Miles South on Hwy. 65

*Sponsored By*

# UNITED KLANS OF AMERICA, INC

For Information Write: P. O. Box 489, Lake Providence, La

*Klan Rally Flyer*

# TEN

# Am I Not a Citizen Too?

Since 1922, not one black person had been allowed on the voter registration rolls in East Carroll Parish. It had been even longer since any black person had voted; in fact, it had been since Reconstruction. This really bothered me. I thought it was so unfair for us to still be denied our basic American rights almost eighty years after we were supposed to have been freed. It didn't seem right to me that there should be laws controlling our lives, made by people we didn't have a chance to select and in many cases, by people who thought we were subhuman and wished we didn't exist, except when it was economically advantageous to them to have us around.

Our voting problems had actually started in 1898 when 96% of the black people on the voter registration rolls were wiped off by a new Louisiana constitution. Ex-slaveholders just regaining their power at the end of Reconstruction had written this constitution as payback.

There had been a few Negroes here and there registered as Republicans to keep the party in the state, but by 1936, the state attorney general had ruled that the white Republican Party was the only legally constituted Republican Party, and blacks were banned from the nominating process. By 1940, there were fewer than a thousand black people registered to vote in the entire state. Prior to Roosevelt's election, I don't think it ever crossed our minds to become Democrats. And of course the Democratic Party had no desire for the Negro to be actively involved in it either, so we really had no party we could turn to. This made the black man's hopes somewhat low, but once in a while someone would bring some positive news and start a fire to burning.

For a long time, we couldn't even find out what we had to do to meet the voter registration requirements. It was like a big secret that all white people in East Carroll had been sworn to keep. It wasn't until 1946 that we finally got our hands on some sample registration forms so we would know what to expect if we went to the registrar's office. A member of the NAACP in New Orleans, through a labor union called the International Longshoreman's Association, had gotten the forms for us. Rev. Paul Taylor, a young fellow who was vice president of our NAACP branch and also my pastor at the time, went down to the ILA Registration School in New Orleans to be trained how to fill out the registration forms. We both practiced, and when we felt we could fill them out correctly, we decided it was time to go try to register.

None of the black people we asked knew exactly where the registrar's office was. After all, no blacks had been registered for many years. So we went uptown and asked around until somebody finally told us that the registrar's office was in the courthouse building.

We parked in front of the courthouse and walked up the steps that led into the front of the two-story gray stone building. A long corridor ran the entire length of the courthouse, with offices on either side. We walked down the hall, glancing nervously right and left, trying not to draw too much attention to ourselves.

When we didn't see anything that looked like the right place downstairs, we decided to check upstairs. I spied a door marked "Registrar's Office," and I told Rev. Taylor, "Here is the door."

The lady behind the desk looked up from her work as we walked in.

"What office y'all looking for?" she asked, naturally assuming we must be looking for a different one.

"We're looking for the registrar's office."

She looked surprised as she pointed. "Y'all will need to go on down to that next door."

We went the way she had pointed only to find out there was no other door. By the time we came back up the hall, the first door, which actually was the Registrar of Voters office, was closed and locked, and we decided it best not to knock on the door to try to get the woman to come out. So we left and didn't go back for a long time.

The next time I went with my close friend, Rev. Mansel Mason. The same registrar who had misdirected us before was still there, but this time she allowed us to complete a registration card. She told Rev. Mason his was correct, well, nearly correct, but his address wasn't right. So we didn't get registered that time either.

During the 1940s, I increased my involvement in the NAACP. I was appointed to the executive committee of the Louisiana State Conference of Branches, helping make decisions about NAACP projects throughout the state. Money was always short, but whenever a special case or situation would come up, all the branches would chip in a portion of the cost so that the work for the entire state could go on.

Most of our projects centered around voting rights, equal pay for equal work, and equal educational facilities, all topics of great interest to me. We still had a serious problem with unequal education in East Carroll. While the parish provided two accredited high schools and nine elementary schools for the small population of white children, it provided only a training school for Negroes that took children through the tenth grade and provided another thirty short-term schools for the rest of the children.

Our executive committee meetings were held at various locations across the state, which sometimes made travel difficult. We couldn't stay in the "white only" motels so we would leave out after midnight and take turns driving through the night in order to arrive at our meeting destination by morning. But driving at night also had its particular problems. There was always the danger of being stopped by policemen in a mood to harass black travelers passing through their towns.

The work we did required unusual personal commitment. The racial pressure would sometimes come so strong that it was not unusual for a branch leader to just up and leave the South from one meeting to the next. I remember one man, a Mr. Jones, whom the state conference had assigned to organize the teachers. He was with us one meeting, but by the time we met again, he was dead. He had taken some blacks to register to vote in Lebeau, Louisiana, but when they got to the registrar's office, a mob of whites led by several police officers attacked them. The police slugged him in the ribs with the butt of a gun and knocked a hole in the side of his head with a pair of brass knuckles. He died of complications from the beating.

People in Lake Providence were pretty responsive to the NAACP programs. I believe it gave them some consolation to know there was an organization to turn to whenever troubles arose—like when one of our members got pushed and kicked off the bus because the driver said he didn't move fast enough getting behind the black curtain that separated the colored and white sections of the bus. The driver threw him off and didn't refund his fare and left him stranded far from home. Incidents like these were common, but now we could turn our complaints over to people like Thurgood Marshall, and sometimes our cases were heard.

The NAACP was most successful with the programs that focused on educating the people about their rights as citizens. We were trying to apply some of the teachings of Carter Woodson (the man who started Black History Week) to East Carroll Parish to see how they would work. The things Mr. Woodson wrote made a great deal of sense to me when I observed the people. One thing in particular he said stuck out in my mind as being the absolute truth. He said that if you can control a man's thoughts, you didn't have to worry about his actions. If you could make a man feel he was inferior, you didn't have to compel him to accept an inferior status, because he would seek it for himself. He said if you could make a man think he was justly out-cast, then you wouldn't have to order him to the back door, he would go without being told, and if there was no back door, his very nature would demand one. So this was what we were up against—too many people trained from birth to accept and pursue an inferior status.

So we had to teach the people not only that they should have a right to go through the front door but that they *deserved* to go through the front door. Of course, it's really hard to change people's thinking when they've been thinking the same way all their lives. Besides, there wasn't much evidence around Lake Providence to make them think otherwise, and you couldn't get most of them to buy a *Pittsburgh Courier* so they could see black folks doing something different. They based their attitudes on the evidence they could see and feel—"White Only" signs on public bathroom doors, separate and sparsely fur-nished waiting rooms in the back of the bus station or in the doctor's office (but no difference in the price of the bus ticket or the doctor's bill), "colored" back door entrances into the drug store, a "colored" side window from which to order ice cream from the Dairy Bar, black and white schools dismissed at different times for the specific purpose of making sure black and white children did not have a chance to mingle on the streets, being expected to step off the sidewalk when approaching a white person, like you had some kind of contagious disease. This was the world that was real to them.

I would speak at the PTA meetings at the high school, which of course was still segregated at that time. I would talk about the true meaning of citizenship, what it was supposed to mean. I'd talk about voting and taking part in the government and the meaning and impact of international events on our lives. I'd speak to the young people, encouraging them to study and try to be somebody when they grew up. When I spoke, I'd watch the young people, looking for a sign that they could see what I was saying—see it, not just hear it. More often than not, I would see what I was looking for. The young people seemed to be able to catch on to a vision of a new kind of future, while their parents seemed stuck with seeing the world only as it already was. And I knew that each young person we won could break the cycle of submission in the next generation for that whole family, but every child we missed, we would have to wait another generation to try again. It could take hundreds of years to reach everyone since the slave bond had to be broken family by family.

The NAACP tried to get the ministers involved in the organization, but many of them refused. Some would pay their NAACP dues but then they wouldn't come to any of the meetings or promote the organization to their church members. They were afraid to speak out about civil rights. So we started concentrating on the youth, and the NAACP youth membership grew. We held our meetings at the First Baptist Church. We taught the youth how to fill out the voter registration cards, and then they taught the adults how to do them correctly, including how to calculate their ages down to the number of months and days as required on the registration form.

But I still didn't feel that we had enough members in East Carroll to make a successful push for our voting rights. So we decided to put on a big NAACP membership drive.

We invited Mr. Daniel Byrd, the first president of our state conference and a very energetic worker, to come up from New Orleans and speak to kick off our membership drive. The rally was set for Monday night, May 6, 1946, at the Parish Training School. We set the meeting for 8:00 P.M. to give the people time to get in from the fields.

Mr. Byrd accepted our invitation and arrived in Lake Providence midmorning on the day of the rally. He met with the vice president of our branch, Rev. Taylor, and they went over to the school to set up the sound equipment. After they finished, Mr. Byrd decided he'd go try to get some rest before time for the meeting that night.

As soon as Mr. Byrd settled in for his nap, he received a call from the principal of the training school. He said the superintendent of schools had just called him, and now there might be a problem with using the school. The superintendent wanted to meet with Mr. Byrd down at the courthouse to discuss the matter.

I don't know what had gotten the local officials all worked up at the last minute. Maybe it was something they had heard from one of the black stoolies they regularly paid for reports on happenings in the black community. Or maybe it was something passed on to them by a telephone operator. Back then, we had to go through a phone operator to get connected to another party. So the operators always knew who we were calling, and we believed they listened to our conversations. But whatever the case, the officials had obviously heard something they didn't like.

After Mr. Byrd called me about the problem, I called Rev. Taylor, Rev. Cooper, and Rev. Green. We decided we'd all go down together, because obviously there was going to be trouble.

When we arrived at the courthouse, we were told to go to the school board office instead. The superintendent was to meet us over there, but when we got to the school board office, we were told that the superintendent was in a meeting. We sat a half hour, then an hour, and the superintendent still hadn't come out. Annoyed, we decided to leave and told the receptionist we'd check back later. When we returned about forty-five minutes later, the receptionist told us that the superintendent was still in the meeting but she would go and get him out for us since we had already waited so long.

Mr. Byrd had just completed a study on the inequities in the East Carroll Parish educational system, so he saw this meeting as an opportunity rather than a potential problem. He looked forward to speaking to the superintendent—and the superintendent had certainly asked for more than he bargained for.

Mr. Byrd, a light-skinned, bespectacled man with a thin mustache, was not your ordinary Negro of the 1940s. He had spent his teen years in the North, where he had started in his youth taking a stand against injustices. He was an attorney for the NAACP's Legal Defense Fund and he had had his share of confrontations, particularly on the subject of education. He had enough courage for several people and wasn't afraid to argue a point with anybody. He was also tall in stature, and his demeanor showed he was not to be intimidated.

The superintendent finally came out, apologizing for the long wait. We all sat down and, after a brief exchange of niceties, Mr. Byrd maneuvered his way into controlling the direction of the meeting.

He started in on the long list of concerns the NAACP had accumulated about the East Carroll schools. He talked to the superintendent very cordially, questioning him about the secondhand textbooks at the black schools, books the black children received after the white children finished with them, when they were practically worn out and the information was out of date. Mr. Byrd knew that the state provided funds for textbooks for all students, and he also knew that our children's money had been spent at the white school, but he decided to ask the superintendent anyway.

"Where is all the money going that you receive for the Negro students?" Mr. Byrd asked. Then he commented on the nice new two-story brick high school with its gymnasium and auditorium and new desks for the white students, and the sad condition of the over-crowded wood-frame Parish Training School for Negro children he had just visited.

"How can you be building new schools for white children while the Negro children go to school in such overcrowded classrooms? And why are the Negro schools getting only discarded desks from the white schools? And since there are about a third more black students than white, this means that many Negro children don't even get a desk."

One word led to another, but Mr. Byrd was on a roll and did not intend to stop. He asked why the school board still required a split session for Negro children and how the children could ever get an equal chance when they got fewer months of schooling than the white children.

"Why are Negro children in East Carroll required to stop school at the end of April to chop weeds and grass out the cotton?" he asked. "Then they have to go back to school in July and August when it's too hot inside for the children to work, and by the time they get used to being back in school, your school board makes them stop again in September for cotton picking. How will Negro children ever have an opportunity to better themselves if the school board members put picking and chopping cotton on their plantations ahead of learning?"

Then they got into it about the school buses. Negroes didn't have a single bus. Black children had to walk to school no matter how far away they lived. Many children who lived in the rural areas outside of Lake Providence never attended high school because of the distance, and they had no other options for transportation. Some parents moved their children in with people in Lake Providence during the school months just so their children could attend high school.

"Why don't the Negro students have any buses?" Mr. Byrd asked the superintendent of schools.

"Why—why—we don't have the money to buy any more buses."

Mr. Byrd continued. "How many buses do you already have?"

"Well, we have five buses in operation now."

"Five? Then why can't the Negro school have one of those? I don't understand how you could have the money for five buses for the white students when you don't have any for the Negro." Mr. Byrd pulled out his notes. "That seems a bit one-sided since there are 34% more Negro students than white." He looked up from his notes and smiled. "Don't you agree?"

The superintendent was very apologetic. He acknowledged that the school board had not done what it should have done for the Negro schools but went on to say that they hadn't done right by the white schools either. He said that there just wasn't enough money and, in fact, that was what they were meeting about just that afternoon. They were trying to figure out how to get more money from the state to put into education.

Mr. Byrd's offensive attack had thrown the superintendent off track from his original agenda, but he finally got around to why he had called us over in the first place. He said, switching the subject, "We just found out what kind of meeting you all are having. We don't let anyone use the school for political purposes, white nor Negro."

"The NAACP isn't a political organization. It is a civil rights organization," responded Mr. Byrd.

The superintendent still insisted that we move the meeting to another location. It was now late afternoon and we had to do something soon if we had to move. "Let's go," Rev. Cooper said, rising and heading toward the door looking agitated. "We'll just find another place to meet."

As we left the building, we ran into the high sheriff. "John Henry," he said, "I want you to come down to my office and," glancing over at Mr. Byrd, "don't bring anybody but yourself."

I thought to myself, they've already taken away our meeting place. Wonder what they want now.

I walked the short distance from the school board office back to the courthouse, leaving Mr. Byrd with Rev. Cooper and Rev. Green.

I was directed into a small room where four people sat around a table talking. When they looked up and saw me standing there, they all stopped and turned to stare in my direction.

I'd have to say that this was quite a little assembly for my benefit—the high sheriff, the deputy, the collector of court, and the jailer. There was one empty seat at the table, directly across from the collector of the court, apparently left for me.

In the South, policemen were often judge, jury, and executioner and creator of new laws as they saw fit. I knew that the assembling of this particular group—the sheriff, the deputies, and the jailer—was meant to inspire fear. But I had learned long ago that if people thought they were upsetting your mind or doing you some harm, they would go further. So over time, I developed a technique for dealing with serious confrontations. I could slip into my "you-can't-scare-me" manner of speaking and put on a straight, smiling face, no matter how upset I might have actually felt inside. I slipped on my other face.

I took a seat, wondering what they were up to today.

The high sheriff said, "John Henry, what kind of meeting that y'all having here tonight? People been calling me all day, and they say some white man coming here to teach you all about voting or something. But now I understand that there is a colored man here that got here about 10:30 this morning."

*So that's what this is all about,* I thought to myself. "Oh, we're just having an NAACP meeting and that's nothing more than the president of our state conference of branches. We invited him here for our membership drive."

"Well, what's he going to talk about?" continued the sheriff.

"I don't know what his speech is about, but I believe he is going to talk about the Hall vs. Nagel decision."

The sheriff looked at me blankly, so the collector of the court said, "You know, that's the decision that practically gives coloreds the right to vote." Then he turned my direction and out came the most overused line in the South. "If you don't like our way of doing things here, why don't you just leave?"

Well, at least he didn't ask why I didn't just go back to Africa and I didn't have to ask him why he didn't go back to Europe. I don't suppose he really expected an answer at all, but I felt obliged to give him one anyway.

"Well I was born here," I said politely, "and where I go, I might not be satisfied there either, so I decided to stay here and try to help correct the things at home."

They talked around and around, fishing for information about the meeting. After a while, I guess they got tired of asking me the same questions in different ways and receiving uninformative answers, because they finally told me I could leave. As I stood up to go, the sheriff said, "Well, you tell that fellow to be d——ed sure he don't say nothing about voting."

I don't know why I didn't just say okay and leave but at that moment, I just felt compelled to let them know that they were already too late to stop us from learning how to register to vote. During the meeting I had sensed that their fear of what they perceived we could do was greater than my concern for what they could do to us. The nervous tapping on the table, the same questions phrased and rephrased, the way the sheriff leaned forward rather than leaning way back in his chair the way he normally did when he knew he was in control, were all telltale signs.

I said, "He doesn't have to say anything about voting. I already have somebody in every ward who knows how to fill out those registration forms and figure out age and everything." Standing in the doorway, I added, "I've been to school for that myself. So we didn't send for him to come here to say nothing about voting."

I came out the sheriff's office, but before I left, I invited the sheriff to come over to the meeting if he wanted to see for himself what it was all about.

They had wasted another precious hour, leaving us with very little time to find another place to meet and inform the people about the change. We also had to go back over to the schoolhouse to take the sound equipment down.

By the time we got permission to set up at First Baptist Church, there was no time left to get word to the public about the change. We had a good group of young people working with us at the time, so we got three of them, Audefine Williams, Bobby Webb, and James Reed, to bike over to the school and turn the people back to the church.

The church was packed, and, as usual, Mr. Byrd gave a dynamic speech. He started off discussing the school system. He asked the people, "Have you seen the new white school? Do you wonder why there is so much money that their schools can look like that and so little money that yours has to look like it does? Well I'm here to tell you why." And that is how he began to open the people's eyes to the truth, by giving them the information he had learned in his research on the East Carroll schools.

He explained to the people how the education money coming into East Carroll was divided. He explained how the state allocated education money to the parishes based on the number of students. Much of the allocations for black students was actually spent on white children. Since there were about twice as many black school-age children as whites, this allowed the white students to get a significant advantage off the black children's allocations. He told them how the education money was actually being spent in East Carroll—$109 for each white student, while only $20 went for each black student.

He asked, pounding his hand on the pulpit, "Is this fair?"

The people yelled, "No!"

I looked across the church. Although it was around 9:00 P.M. and most people had worked all day, nobody looked tired or sleepy tonight. They were listening to Mr. Byrd's every word.

He asked them how their children would ever be able to stand up beside white children for jobs if they went to school two months less than white children did. "Is it fair for your children to be on the split session system just because it's convenient to the big farmers? Do you want your children working in the fields all their lives?"

Some people were now on their feet.

"No," the people yelled.

He talked about how there were five school buses for whites and no buses for Negroes. He asked them whether they realized this was being done to keep black enrollment down.

"Children without transportation most times never make it to school. And when you've only got one Negro high school in the whole parish, then most Negro children are being denied access to a high school education. If rural children never go to school, then won't they always be available to do field work? Is this your plan for your children?"

He pointed out that the whites had seven libraries in East Carroll and the Negroes had access to none. "Don't we want to read books too?" he bellowed. "Don't our children want to read?"

Mr. Byrd continued to present the kind of information most people in East Carroll never heard. Since we weren't allowed to vote, and no Negroes held positions in parish offices where they might get access to this kind of information, we could only assume we were being cheated. We just didn't know how badly. Here was a man standing before us with the facts, and the people were getting about as mad as they could get.

Then he spoke to the teachers in the audience. He pointed out that they worked as hard as any white teacher, even harder since their average class size was forty-five students while the white teacher only had to deal with about thirty students per class. Then he said, "And guess how much they are paid to teach these smaller classes with nice desks and new textbooks? Their pay is an average of $1,500 a year compared to a $400 average salary for you."

The people were so upset now that they were whispering in the pews. The time was right for Mr. Byrd to plant seeds about voter registration. He had their attention.

Mr. Byrd explained the new court rulings on voting. He made the people see how when they couldn't vote, they had no say-so in the decisions that affected their daily lives. He explained why white people were so afraid of blacks registering, since in East Carroll Parish, we so outnumbered whites. If we voted, we would have an impact on local and congressional elections and everything else that went on in Lake Providence. Then he closed with information about things the NAACP was doing to improve education throughout the United States.

Before Mr. Byrd finished, I knew that the meeting was a success. The people were finally mad enough to move to action. That night at the reception following the meeting, we signed up many new members and raised $78 to support the NAACP work. That was a lot of money for a rural community, in 1946, made up mostly of day laborers.

The next day I was walking down the road when I saw the high sheriff's patrol car coming toward me. It came to a stop.

"Get in the car," he demanded. "What'd that fellow talk about last night?" he asked as I slid into the seat.

I figured he'd already spent most of the morning gathering information. In fact, we had noticed one of his known snitches snooping around the church that night, trying to see who was there. White bosses across town were probably already hard at work, picking their maids and yard hands for information.

"I don't remember what he talked about. I was presiding. But I invited you out, and you could have been there to hear for yourself if you had wanted to."

"Well I was wondering about something," he said. "Yesterday you said something about you had folks trained in all wards as leaders in this voter's movement. Will you tell me their names?"

I said, "Is this strictly confidential, between you and me and nobody else?"

"No, I'm not going to promise you that."

"Well, I'm not going to tell you the names either."

The sheriff cut me an angry look, as if he had actually thought I would give him the names. He said, "I want you to realize that I'm the sheriff here and that I have to furnish protection and I can't be putting up with this fool stuff here. You liable to start a riot. There are new white folks coming here, and they're not as tolerant about these kinds of things as the old ones."

I said, "Well, I've associated with some of the new people and I think that some of them are not as bad as some of you all."

He ignored my comment and went back to his questions. "Who are those people around talking about voting?"

"Now you don't have to worry about those people. You have me. I'm the president. If there's anybody done wrong, arrest me. But I'll take the same position Jesus took that night when the mob came to get him. I will feel no need to defend myself or my actions. So if you want to find anybody guilty, you just go ahead and kill me and just forget about those others."

After we finished our conversation, and I had given the sheriff no satisfaction about stopping, he decided to take up the matter with another minister. He went to see an older preacher, one of the ministers who took no part in the onward movement. The sheriff talked him into calling a meeting of the people to discuss the matter of voting.

The meeting was held at Rev. Taylor's church. Of course I wasn't invited, so I can only relate what I was told, since I wasn't there. I was told that the sheriff lined up several preachers to make speeches to the people. He knew if he could influence the ministers, the ministers would in turn influence the people.

Rev. Taylor had opened up the meeting that night, and the high sheriff presented his case. He told the people what he had said to me and what I had said to him. He had brought with him a preacher who had been living in East Carroll for many years, who got along well with white people. The high sheriff felt like this man would be able to convince the people to stop their movement toward voter registration, so he asked the man to take the pulpit and speak to the people.

"Why, I can't see what y'all worryin' about voting for. I lived here all my days and I have not voted, and my father lived here and we got along fine with these white people. We don't want to make enemies of them now. What good is voting going to do anyway?"

When he finished, the Methodist preacher got up and went to the podium. "Yes, I used to be a member of that NAACP organization but the young Negroes, they have it now and they are radical. I got out because there's some who just want to show themselves and want to push things too fast."

Somebody else got up to talk and made reference to me in their speech. So when Rev. Taylor got his chance to speak, he said, "Rev. Scott is the NAACP president, and I don't think that anyone should make any reference to him when he's not here to defend himself. But I want to speak in defense of the NAACP."

"That preacher got up here and said—'What we want to vote for?' What do white people want to vote for? Nobody asks us what we want to pay taxes for and nobody asks what we want to go to war for. We want to vote because we are citizens and that's what we plan to do. We plan to vote."

"When you all coming?" the sheriff asked him.

"I don't know exactly when we're coming, but we will be there."

It wasn't long after this meeting that the whites put Rev. Taylor under pressure, and he left Lake Providence and moved to St. Louis, Missouri, never to live in this area again.

After the meeting ended, word spread swiftly about the speeches made by the ministers, how they were supporting the old way of life, of not voting. All on the streets the next day, the people were cursing about what the preacher had said about colored people not needing to vote. They were saying, "I put money in the church collection on Sunday that takes care of him. I won't put any more in there, not as long as he's the pastor."

The reaction to the meeting was quite unfavorable for the sheriff. His plan backfired because it influenced more people to want to vote, after some of the ministers spoke out against it. In some churches, the pastor wouldn't even let voting be mentioned, but even in those churches, there were people in the congregation, including church officers, who were getting active in the movement.

So we kept pressing on. When the Baptist Association election came up shortly after the Byrd meeting, I was nominated to run for president against Rev. Owens, who had held the office for twenty years. I won the election, the first non-pastor to ever be elected president. I found myself in the bad situation of serving as president with all the old officers who had supported the previous president. Most of the ministers involved in the Byrd situation belonged to the association, so I decided it was best to act as if I didn't know what they had said (since I wasn't at the meeting) and never bring up the adverse side of it. I never responded to their snide remarks during association meetings, and I never talked about them behind their backs. And that's the way I got along with them.

I had learned that there simply was no purpose in getting mad and talking bad about people who didn't want to stand up. Talking about them generally made them act worse, so it was just better to keep putting out the information in hopes that one day, they would catch on. So I went ahead and put in a recommendation for the Baptist Association to press hard for the right to vote. One minister actually pulled his church out of the association, saying we were making a church association into a political organization.

The rumors about black people potentially voting created nearly as much excitement as someone dropping a bomb on the town. All kinds of tactics were used to dissuade us from our course, but the more the white people and the preachers talked against it, the more the people wanted to vote. So by the end of 1946, our NAACP membership had exploded and was so active that we were asked to host the Louisiana State Conference the following year.

In the summer of 1946, I went again to try to register with two other men I knew, Jack Gibson and Jack Hubbard, but when we got to the registrar's office, nobody was there. We waited a while then decided to look for the registrar in some of the other offices, yet we still couldn't find her anywhere in the courthouse building. We figured someone in one of the other offices, probably the sheriff's office, had seen us coming in and tipped her off not to come back to her office. The sheriff's office had been on high alert since the big meeting, so we concluded she was hiding out, waiting for us to leave.

We left the courthouse and met later that afternoon to decide what to do. We devised a plan to catch her. We would put our plan into effect the following day.

The next day we put on two watches, one for the morning and one for the afternoon. The people on the morning shift watched for her until lunchtime, but she never showed up at the courthouse. I was on the afternoon watch, the only man with a group of women. Over in the afternoon, we finally caught sight of her going into the courthouse. Nobody had even seen her drive up.

We moved in quickly, because we didn't want to take the chance of her slipping off again. When we walked in, she gave our little group the once-over and then looked straight at me.

"What do you want?" she demanded.

"We want to fill out a form to get registered," I answered politely.

She gave each of us a form to complete. When we finished filling them out, she quickly scanned each one and said blankly, "They are all wrong." No explanation about what was wrong, just they were all wrong.

Then she turned and spoke directly to me, "I want you to stay a minute. I want to talk to you." Feeling uneasy about not having witnesses, I told the ladies who were with me, "Don't leave that door. When you go out, you stay right at the door until I come out. I don't know what she wants."

After the ladies had gone into the hall, the registrar said, "Your registration card is all right. If you can get some white people, two electors, to identify and sign for you, why then you will get registered."

I left the office feeling hopeful that I could finally register to vote. I had one or two friends among the whites that I thought I would probably ask. But then I found out from a white friend on the police jury that the whites had called a special meeting about the matter and agreed not to sign for anyone. So I didn't have the confidence to even ask them.

Later another minister, Rev. Percy Henderson, and I decided that we should go back to the registrar's office to see if Rev. Henderson could get registered. Rev. Henderson was a very polite fellow, and he had known Mrs. Beard, the registrar, for a long time. He talked to her a while, saying a lot of complimentary things to her. She gave him the form to fill out, which I had already taught him how to complete. When he finished, she reviewed it and told him it was okay, but he still had to get two white people to identify him before he could get registered.

Rev. Henderson came out the registrar's office grinning. He was elated. "Well, I'm going to finally get registered."

"How?" I asked.

"Well, you know I can get white people to identify me. They all know me. I've been working for so many of them."

"Well, I tell you this much, you'll sure play the devil getting them."

So he went and finally got a white fellow to go back with him to the registrar's office. This fellow apparently had not been briefed on the plan to keep us from registering, so when he got there, the registrar called him off into the back and whispered something to him. He came back out looking flustered. "Well, I-I tell you Percy, I can't fool with anything like that. I-I'd rather not be involved."

So Rev. Henderson couldn't get anyone.

In June 1947, I was asked to be on program at the national NAACP convention in Washington, D.C. This was exciting but ironic for me because here I couldn't even vote, but I was going to be on the same platform with the president of the United States. President Harry S. Truman was giving the closing address of the convention.

When President Roosevelt had died and President Truman took office, I had been fearful that black people would be set back. So it was really a surprise to me when President Truman went to the podium and began to speak to the thousands of people gathered at the Lincoln Memorial about his commitment to civil rights. He said that America had to put its own house in order first before democracy could be strengthened abroad. He said that the nation couldn't wait any longer for the slowest state or the most backward community to get a will to change their ways. He told the audience that everyone should have the freedom from fear. The crowd roared with approval.

He presented his nine-point program for civil rights, which gave me encouragement. In fact, I left Washington a Truman man, not just because of what he said but because he was sort of a little man from a little town—like me. It gave me hope and courage for the people from the small towns. So I came back home with a new fire to keep the struggle going.

It was almost time for our annual Baptist Association meeting when I got back from Washington, and I needed to prepare my speech to end my first year as president. The ministers were still divided over my election and the fallout after the Byrd incident, so I decided to speak on the topic of unity. At the First Baptist Church, I spoke to the gathering about how the Bible told us that a house divided against itself could not stand. I reminded the ministers that men God had raised up were to use their power to challenge the world, united in love, not splitting into factions.

But of course unity was not what we had. All the old officers were opposed to me as president, and they had decided to make a big effort to unseat me. Two other ministers were nominated to run for president—Rev. O. L. Virgil, my father-in-law's pastor, and Rev. Owens, the former president. When the votes were counted, Rev. Virgil and I had a tie. There was no one to break the tie, so another election was called for the following night. The gossip mill must have worked night and day because the next night, we had a huge turnout, and I won the election along with a new set of officers.

So over time, we settled into a somewhat peaceful coexistence, trying to act like God would have us act. Of course, some still weren't happy with me, but they seemed to learn to tolerate me after a while. In 1948 the election went without conflict or opposition. That year we got the State Department of Christian Education to come in and train workers. The same year we paid a worker from Nashville to come in to do a Vacation Bible School workshop, and we created our own program of Christian Education. Things were progressing well as the people learned more about what they needed to do. I firmly believed what the Bible said, that "the people are destroyed for lack of knowledge." I didn't want them to have that excuse again.

Through the end of the 1940s, we continued to try to register. Rev. Mason, Sam Shorter, and some others went back to the registrar of voters, and some of them filled out the forms again. Mrs. Beard, the registrar, reviewed Rev. Mason's form and said it was perfect, but just like with Rev. Henderson, she said he would have to get somebody to identify him. Rev. Mason was actually able to find someone willing to sign for him, but for some reason, the registrar said that she couldn't accept it.

At some point, for some foolish reason, I came up with this idea that my trying to be a Democrat must have been making it difficult for me to register. I decided to go try to register again along with another acquaintance, Francis Joseph Atlas. When the registrar gave me my card, I decided to write in "Republican" as my chosen political party. The only other party I could think of was "Communist" and I wasn't about to put that down. People were already starting to get nervous about a communist takeover.

I completed the card and gave it to the registrar. She looked it over and then went over to her file where she pulled out a registration card I had filled out during a previous visit. Looking at the other card, she said, "On this card, you said you were Democrat and on *this* card," shaking the new card at me, "you're saying you are a Republican. What are you?"

I said, "Well, actually I'm not anything until you register me."

Well you know how things can just fly out your mouth before you give them much thought. This was one of those times. I could see by the color coming in her face that my humor and great wit hadn't been fully appreciated.

She snapped, "Well, don't you know you can't change your party that fast?" So I had to go out again.

We tried everything we knew to try to get around the identification problem. We tried going often, hoping to aggravate Mrs. Beard into letting us register. We tried taking different people, hoping that maybe somebody might be able to get through. We had Mr. Simmons, the professor at our school, to go by. He had a bachelor's degree from Southern University and a master's degree from what was supposed to be a good college, Columbia University in New York City. So we figured he should be able to register, especially since he was more educated than most of the whites already on the rolls. When that didn't work, we sent the Methodist minister, Rev. S. S. Obee. The registrar was a Methodist too, so she talked very nicely to Rev. Obee, all about church and all. She handed him the forms to fill out, but in the end we were still right where we started.

# ELEVEN

# Worse Than You Can Imagine

The 1950s began with lots of promise, both personally and politically. I was still the president of the local branch of the NAACP and was continuing my statewide work through the state executive committee. I was also one of the vice presidents of the Louisiana State Baptist Convention. I had even managed to maintain my position as president of the local Baptist association after another big push to unseat me in 1949.

In 1950, a dream of mine was realized when my recommendation was approved to take three acres of association land to start a Baptist Center. We started construction in 1951 by adding a new building across the front of the old high school building, creating a T-shaped layout. Pretty soon, we had our own place for association and other community meetings, with a dining hall and big kitchen in what had once been the old high school.

In the late 1940s, black people had really gotten into baseball after blacks were finally allowed to play in the major leagues. We were all Brooklyn Dodger fans to support Jackie Robinson and Dan Bankhead. We decided that the Baptist Association should put together some softball teams so that the children from the community could get together and learn the game. The teams competed against each other, but I was the pitcher for all the teams. The association provided the gloves and bats for the boys.

I didn't like basketball all that much and sure didn't like to play, but the young people did, so I recommended to the association that we also put up some basketball goals so that the boys from town could have a recreational area they could walk to. It was approved, and I was excited to see all the young people down there enjoying themselves.

I was in my late forties and early fifties when we really got everything going, but as I got older, I stopped pitching for the softball teams and just came out to the games to keep the peace. So as time passed on, our youth department grew, and we added more activities for them such as wiener roasts, Valentine get-togethers, and contests like corn totes and Bible quizzes with prizes.

I was still farming in the early 1950s with the boys, which required long hours. Often we would be in the fields until seven o'clock at night and then would have to come home and do other chores like cutting and bringing in the wood, feeding the pigs, and moving the cows around. Although we were busy, I still tried to make time for a few games of checkers and dominoes with the boys. Everybody in the family loved playing games, and my wife was the most competitive of them all. Her favorite game was Chinese checkers, and she dared anyone to try to beat her.

We had a battery-operated radio that I only used to listen to the news in order to preserve the battery, but after we got so wrapped up in baseball, I had to start letting the boys listen to the games when we'd come in from the fields for lunch and sometimes at night. Pretty soon, we were listening to boxing matches too.

I still hunted and trapped in the cold months. I had perfected my trapping skills, and some of my mink and fox furs even won awards for their fine quality at the fur shows. I was also blessed with my first car in April 1950, when the people of East Carroll got together and presented me with a 1941 Pontiac in appreciation for my services to the community. I was feeling very blessed indeed.

Much of my attention was going to my new responsibilities at North Star Baptist Church, where I had been elected pastor in 1947 after Rev. Taylor had been "persuaded" to leave town following the Byrd incident. North Star was one of the churches my great-grandfather, Daddy Lou, had organized about three years before he died. Although I had been an ordained minister since 1937, this was my first time pastoring, and as any Baptist preacher will tell you, pastoring is no easy job. I was also going to school, trying to earn my bachelor's degree in theology. It was a very busy time, but I was satisfied with the direction my life was taking.

Politically, we could see things starting to change in Louisiana. Louisiana was already the most diverse southern state, with its French, Indian, African, and Spanish backgrounds and its higher degree of race mixing. So it was not surprising that Louisiana might move forward before some of the other southern states.

In 1950, LSU's graduate school became the first Deep South college to admit a black student, and a few towns had even hired a black or two on their police forces. The federal government was even starting to show some inclination toward getting involved in crimes against blacks, such as lynchings.

Most parishes were bending under the pressure of NAACP lawsuits and were starting to let blacks vote, but unfortunately, East Carroll was not one of those parishes. The local whites we dealt with were taking an even harder line against us, seemingly more determined than ever to keep us off the voter registration rolls.

The registrar continued to demand that a voter already on the East Carroll rolls, all of whom were white, identify us. And of course that was the one thing we couldn't get, because they had made up their minds not to register anyone. The few white people who would even talk to us about voting told us that the system was set up strictly not to register any blacks. Some who were supposed to be our friends would just shake their heads and say their hands were tied. There was always an excuse—they couldn't do anything because of the position they held, or because of politics, or because they were afraid they'd get in trouble. After a while we came to the conclusion, that all the white adults in East Carroll fell into two categories—the ones that strictly didn't want us to vote, and the ones who could be intimidated by the ones who didn't want us to vote.

We decided that the only way we would ever get registered would be to file a lawsuit against the registrar of voters for refusing to register us. So in the fall of 1950, we got some of the people who had tried to register to write up their complaints, and we sent them in to the state NAACP. The NAACP said they would consider filing a suit on our behalf, but they would have to first send some of their lawyers up to Lake Providence to make an investigation.

Two young attorneys came up from New Orleans and met us at the Baptist Center to discuss the complaints. Mr. A. P. Tureaud, who had worked with us in organizing our NAACP chapter back in 1938, was in charge of the investigation. After the meeting, one of the lawyers went around from house to house verifying the remaining complaints from the people who had not attended the meeting. He interviewed several people, but it seemed, in his opinion, they were too afraid or they would not make good plaintiffs. He said they would probably back out if things got too hot, so he decided not to include them in the suit. The attorneys continued to tell me that I should stay on the sidelines and let them take care of things. They thought it would be better if somebody else got up front in the suit, since I had been working on the voting thing for such a long time.

The attorneys drew up the legal papers and brought them back to Lake Providence for the people to sign. When the people didn't see my name as a plaintiff, they said, "No, I can't do this, I'm not going to sign. I don't see Scott's name on there." Rev. Mason came down to the house. "I ain't going to move a peg until I see your name on there," he said.

The young lawyers apparently took this refusal to sign to mean that we wouldn't stand up, so they didn't even file the suit.

When I went back to the NAACP conference the following year, I raised cane with them about not being able to get our suit filed. So the president of the state conference at that time, Dr. E. A. Johnson, decided that we could bypass Mr. Tureaud and get another attorney, a Mr. Louis Berry.

I got with a couple of friends, James Levi and Watson Sanders from the Henderson Project, and we drove the five and a half hours down to New Orleans to meet with Mr. Berry, a little fellow from Alexandria, Louisiana. We brought along $300 our local organization had raised to file the suit, and we put our complaints before Mr. Berry and Dr. Johnson, who was connected in through a two-way phone.

We told them about people going to register and being turned away because the registrar said there were too many people in the office. We read to them accounts from people who were told they had to recite the preamble from memory and read and explain the constitution of the United States in order to register. Another person was asked to give the name of the president and the secretary of war and recite the Bill of Rights.

Watson Sanders recounted the story of the time he and Levi and a group of people had gone to meet the registrar at a store in Ward I. They had been told that the registrar was coming to the store to register people who lived in that rural area.

"When the registrar got there and saw a group of Negroes waiting for her, she went straight through the store into a private room in the back. We waited around about an hour and a half, then we decided it was time to do something because she obviously wasn't coming out. So we asked the owner of the store if we could see the registrar. He told us that the registrar wasn't even back there, said she had left a message that she had to go back to town.

"We decided we'd wait around awhile longer to see if she came back. We waited another hour, and in the meantime white people kept coming in the store, going in and out of this back room. We knew she had to be back there, so we asked the store owner again whether we could see the registrar. He let us in this time, and when we went in, the registrar was sitting there registering white people. I believe she had been there the whole time.

"We told her we wanted to register to vote. She gave us the registration cards to fill out, and I know we filled them out correctly because we been practicing how to do them for a long time. But the registrar said mine was wrong because I made contradictory statements and that Levi here just didn't pass. Then she picked up her registration book and left the room. Just like that, she just left the room. Left us standing there and a whole room of Negroes out there waiting to see her."

Mr. Berry and Dr. Johnson decided we had a worthwhile case. They prepared some affidavits or complaints for us to sign and we drove back home.

It wasn't long before we received the suit papers, charging that the registration practices in East Carroll were discriminatory to Negroes. To our three names were added Henry Scott, C. B. Prentise, Rev. Mansel Mason, Percy Knighten, Mary Eliza Jakes, James Sanders, Rev. Otis Virgil, Anderson Lee, and Francis Joseph Atlas. I was told that my name would be listed last on the complaint, but when Mr. Berry filed the suit, he moved my name from the bottom and brought it to the top. That made me the main plaintiff in the vote suit, so in December 1951, when the story came out in the newspapers, it said "John Henry Scott vs. Mrs. C. E. Beard."

I continued my work with the state NAACP, which at the time was filing and winning many lawsuits relating to voting, equal pay for teachers, and equal access to education. When I attended the national NAACP conference in St. Louis in 1953, they were even talking about

school desegregation. Here I was working to get school buses and trying to get black children in school the same number of months as
white children, and here they were actually talking about integration.
I thought Mr. Thurgood Marshall was talking about something that
would never happen, something he shouldn't even be trying to tackle.
We hadn't even worked out the little things yet.

As time passed and the people began to see the results of the
NAACP work, they started joining the organization in increasing numbers. Louisiana had more than 13,000 members in those early years
of the 1950s, and blacks were beginning to register in large numbers
in other parts of the state. Enough blacks were registered in some
towns to swing an election. For the most part, things seemed to be
progressing in the right direction, that is, until the Supreme Court
handed down the Brown decision in 1954.

When the highest court in the land made segregated schools illegal, life for black people in the South changed almost overnight. As
usual, the newspapers interpreted the meaning of the decision for the
people, telling them that integration meant the destruction of the
white race and the loss of the Southern way of life. This propaganda
got the white community worried and all worked up, since many white
people thought they were entitled to have things stay the way they
were. After all, they had been living under the Jim Crow laws since the
early 1900s, a system of legal separation of the races that had worked
quite well for them, especially economically. All of a sudden they were
expected to put their children in close contact with a race of people
they considered to be subhuman or at a minimum slow-minded.

I had never seen so many bad things printed about black people in
all my fifty years. There were newspaper articles, books, and pam-
phlets that called black men things like baboons, mongrels, apes, and
coons. I saw cartoons of Negro men, jet-black with oversized droop-
ing lips, popped eyes, hair going in all directions, either saying something stupid or shown in hot pursuit of a white woman. A seed of fear
was being planted in the minds of people who had been without a
unifying cause. Now they had one—the defending of white girls and
women—and nothing was spared in the fight against integration. Anything was acceptable. It was as if the South was fighting another Civil
War by trying to beat the federal government on the integration issue.

In the 1930s and '40s, we had had problems with the local police coming down hard on black men and boys, but now they started to press even harder. One night after the junior-senior prom at the black high school, a group of black boys, including one of my neighbor's sons, were headed toward town when they passed some white girls in a car headed in the opposite direction. The girls, the daughters of a local car dealer, turned around and caught up with the boys. They pulled up beside them, calling out to them to stop, telling them they looked good in their prom clothes. The boys kept driving and went on up town and parked at the Dairy Bar, a local hamburger place where youngsters liked to congregate. The girls pulled into the parking lot behind them and they started playing around with each other. When someone came up and made an issue about them messing with black boys, to save face, the girls said the black boys were bothering them.

Somebody called the sheriff, and all the black boys who happened to be around at the time, ten in all, were hauled off to jail and charged with stealing. They dragged the boys, all dressed in their fine prom clothes they had worked so hard to pay for, and threw them into a filthy jail cell. They clubbed the boys with flashlights and billy clubs and knocked them around, trying to force them to sign confessions. They beat some of them badly. One boy ended up with a knot on his head that I believe never went down.

They made the parents put up cash to get their children out of jail, told them they couldn't accept property bonds like they usually did. Even after I talked to attorney James Sharp, Jr., over in Monroe and found out this was illegal, they were slow about giving the parents their money back and taking the property bond in place of the cash. The sheriff said he would have to take the boys back into custody if the cash bonds were withdrawn.

About three months after the beating incident in Lake Providence, right over in Money, Mississippi, a fourteen-year-old boy named Emmett Till was kidnaped and lynched. They say that a group of white men made him strip down naked and then they tortured him. They beat him about the head so much until his forehead was crushed in. Then they gouged out his eyes for looking at a white woman. And if that wasn't enough, they shot him in the head and threw him in the river with a seventy-five-pound cotton gin fan hung around his neck.

Emmett Till was just a naive boy visiting down south from Chicago. He didn't even know what he was doing, because children up north didn't get murdered for what he did. They said he was killed because he said, "'Bye baby" to a white female storekeeper on a bet he made with some boys he had met down south. By the time they found his mangled body in the Tallahatchie River three days later, he was so bloated and his face so messed up that he was unrecognizable. And this is what they used to acquit the men who did it, after only a little over an hour's deliberation. The jury said that although the two men on trial admitted to abducting the boy, they couldn't convict them of murder because the body couldn't be positively identified. They said they couldn't even say for sure that the boy was actually dead. But when you came right down to the truth, they just didn't want to say because the prevailing sentiment of the white community was that he deserved everything he got for getting out of his place, and they raised $10,000 for the accused's defense to make sure they got off. They wanted us to be clear on how far they would go to maintain their new cause.

There was a growing uneasiness in our community when we saw on television and read in the papers how proud of the killers the local people seemed to be. This inspired fear in black children, as they discovered that many white people could justify killing them over little or nothing. The dead boy's mother had an open-casket funeral so that the whole nation could see what they had done to her boy, and *Jet*, a national magazine, carried a picture of the boy's grotesquely disfigured face. It was a graphic picture that increased the children's fears and made black mothers afraid for their sons to be away from the house, afraid something said might be taken the wrong way and their sons end up taken from them too.

Mothers, fathers, and grandparents tried to school the boys on the roles they had to assume to stay alive or to stay out of jail, while all the boys really wanted was just to be teenagers and free to do at least some of what white boys their age did. Little did I know that less than three years later I would be sending my own son Leon off to California over threats behind something so insignificant. Leon had come home for the summer from Grambling College, where he was attending school on an agriculture scholarship. He had run into Leon Minsky, a white boy he had known and worked with at White's Restaurant and Motel since they were both thirteen. They were side by side in the two lines on either side of the velvet rope that separated blacks and whites entering the lobby of the movie theater. My Leon said, "Hi, Leon" to Leon Minsky, who in turn informed my Leon that he should be addressed as Mr. Minsky. Of course, my Leon, who never held back on his opinions, proceeded to inform the Minsky boy in no uncertain terms of the foolishness of his request. The Minsky boy must have gone home and told his parents, because the threats against Leon started that same night, and the calls continued over the next few days. The threats worried my wife so much that she talked me into agreeing with her to send Leon to California to live with her sister.

When the trial date finally came around for the local boys who had been arrested and beaten after the prom, I told the people to come out to the courthouse. The boys' classmates turned out in such numbers that we jammed the courthouse out. No one else could get in. People were all outside in the courthouse yard.

We stayed there all day, and finally someone called the boys over in the evening and told them they could go home. They told the boys that if they needed them any more, they would send for them. But even after that, when the parents had been told there was no case against their sons, the court was still slow about giving the parents their bond money back.

We continued working on our various suits and causes, trying not to get caught up in the fear already moving through the community. One family had already decided to leave town and move to Buffalo, New York, after their son's beating and arrest. They had left me in charge of selling their property. Others were talking about moving too, just to keep their sons safe.

We had started a new project, preparing to sue the local school board to try to end the split school term. This was the system under which the school schedule for black children was based on the farming seasons. School would close twice during the year—once for cotton hoeing time and again in the fall for cotton-picking time. This schedule caused the black children to only get eight months of school, and sometimes as little as seven, although the law required nine months per school term.

We were very busy those early months of 1955, oblivious to meet-ings being held all across the South where plans to destroy the NAACP, its leaders, and its supporters were being mapped out. A new organization was quietly being put together called the Citizens' Coun-cil, and we had no idea how this organization would change our lives.

This new organization was everywhere across the South at once. They held rallies and ran newspaper articles about their stance on white supremacy and states' rights. They had a regular publication that we managed to get our hands on from time to time, either through the cooks or maids or through whites who did not agree with the position of the new organization. In their speeches and publica-tions, they talked about how resourceless we were, how they had taken care of us for hundreds of years. Recognizing that we still owned very little capital, they threatened us with economic blackmail. They warned us through their publications that they could basically cut us off economically, and where would we be? They proclaimed that if integration were allowed, the next thing would be the commingling of the races and the total loss of America's greatness. Their children were in grave danger, they said, and had to be protected by every means.

The NAACP provided bits and pieces of information about this organization, but we had no idea at the time what we were dealing with. We were expecting this new organization to operate like the Klan, except maybe the members would do their dirt in ties rather than in work pants, but we figured wrong. This new organization didn't have a secret agenda like the Klan, and sometimes they pub-lished the names of their members, especially their officers. They openly and boldly professed their position on keeping the Negro "in his place" and maintaining segregation through legal and economic means. They operated under carefully laid out plans—none of the emotion-driven, spur-of-the-moment stuff the Klan usually did.

Citizens' Councils targeted the leading white citizens of each town as its members, especially lawmakers and large business owners and bankers. When they had them on board, the organization controlled a town. They could then exert power over jobs, the courts, lawmakers, and the flow of money and goods in and out of a town.

Although the Citizens' Councils professed to use only lawful means for their cause, their rhetoric moved many to violence, much of which was directed at NAACP leaders. Before the end of 1955, Rev. George Washington Lee was shot to death, and Lamar Smith, another NAACP leader, was lynched right in the courthouse yard over in Mississippi. This happened just two weeks before they killed the Till boy from Chicago. And whatever craziness was going on over in Mississippi seemed to always spill across the Mississippi River into our part of Louisiana.

I kept up with the news and the times as much as I could, regularly reading local and national papers and listening to radio stations that didn't expect a black audience. The Citizens' Council media campaign was extensive, as they were always trying to influence public opinion to increase their ranks. During the first four months of 1956, there were regular inflammatory articles in the *Monroe Morning World*, the daily paper from the largest city near Lake Providence. One editorial said the NAACP had manipulated some weak and inexperienced Supreme Court justices into a desegregation decision, but the South wasn't going to take it lying down. I thought it amazing that they'd give the NAACP credit for having that kind of power.

When Rosa Parks was arrested for refusing to give up her seat for a white passenger who was just getting on the bus and the Montgomery bus boycott started, the *Monroe Morning World* issued another editorial blasting "men of God" (preachers) and the NAACP. The editor marveled at how Negroes had the gall to be using economic pressure on them when whites controlled their jobs, their economic security, their credit, and their education. They posed the question and veiled threat that struck fear in the hearts of Negroes—can the NAACP be your employer if we stop employing you?

The editorial concluded that Negroes' sticking together on the bus boycott showed our "slavish" nature, how we were incapable of individual thought. They said we were still governed by witch doctors and we hadn't come very far from being the uncouth African savages they had brought over. We were warned that we should be careful, since the white people had done so much for us.

I used to sometimes sit for hours after reading the paper trying to fathom the mysteries of this manner of thinking, and why the reading public seemed to want to believe this senseless rhetoric. Were not all black people in the South subject to the same humiliation of having to get up to give their seat to a white person? Were not all black people in the South being educated in underfunded, inferior schools? Were we not the only race, by law and by practice, not allowed to eat in restaurants, to use public bathrooms, and attend the same schools? Then why would anyone consider that we shouldn't act as a group? Were they not speaking of problems that arose simply from our being born nonwhite? Their own articles proved they considered all black people as a group instead of individuals. We had a group problem that required group action. We didn't have the luxury of exerting our individualism. I wondered if the people in power were really that simpleminded and actually believed the propaganda they printed, or whether they were as usual just trying to arouse the emotions of the poor and working-class people whose support they needed to maintain their own power and wealth.

East Carroll was one of only four parishes remaining in the whole state of Louisiana that still would not let any black people register to vote and one of only five parishes that still had a split school session for black children to work the fields. So of course Lake Providence was a Citizens' Council kind of town. In early March 1956, I read in the paper that Lake Providence had formed its own council, organized at the white high school, with the sixth judicial district judge as moderator. They got 224 paid memberships that first night out of the 300 people attending. Members included some of the best known and well-off people in town—the kind of people generally classified as the "upstanding" members of the community—bankers, store and gin owners, policemen, large farmers, educators, landlords, lawyers, legislators, and local and district judges—people with economic, political, and legal control over the community.

The members were people we did business with. Some of them we had even considered to be our friends. But we soon found out that in integration matters, there were few friends and no rules of human decency. Because the council members controlled almost all the jobs, the financing, the services, and the court system, they were able to create a climate of fear and reprisal in which few whites and even fewer blacks dared to challenge council actions and edicts.

Before the Citizens' Council was organized, those of us whose names were on the voter registration suit were being intimidated. But after the formation of the council, intimidations increased, especially against people who they suspected might be involved in the NAACP or people who appeared sympathetic to our cause. If we needed to borrow money, they'd make sure we didn't get a loan. This tactic was especially effective on farmers who borrowed every year before planting time and repaid debts after the crops came in. Anybody in debt, who was as little as one day late on their payment or a little short one month, why, they would press for immediate foreclosure.

They made it hard for some people to hold on to a job. Some people were told they had to sign a paper that they wouldn't get involved in "that NAACP mess." Those who refused were turned off their jobs. They starved the people into submission or into leaving town, because people had to be able to feed their families.

After the Citizens' Council had organized in many towns across Louisiana, they, along with the joint legislative committee on segregation, put into action the first phase of their plan, which was to destroy the NAACP. What was so ironic about the plan put into effect in the spring of 1956 was that a 1924 law originally passed to break up the Ku Klux Klan was now used to break up the NAACP. The law, which really wasn't enforced anymore, required every organization, except churches and the National Guard, to file a complete membership listing with the secretary of the state by the end of each year.

The attorney general filed a lawsuit on behalf of Louisiana asking to shut down all NAACP operations in the state until the membership lists were produced. Twelve state NAACP officers were charged with breaking the 1924 law. By the end of March, the state attorney, who was also an executive in the Citizens' Council, had seized the NAACP's state bank account, and the judge who heard the case had put an injunction against the NAACP, banning all meetings in the state until we all produced our membership lists.

The newspapers that supported segregation were filled with victory stories. They called the NAACP ban a turning point "in maintaining the social and economic status of the Negro." The president of the newly formed Association of Citizens' Councils of Louisiana, who was also a state senator, advised us to be looking for some surprises beginning with the May legislature.

Our local branch received a letter from the state NAACP headquarters advising us not to meet any more, because if we did, we would be in violation of the new law and could be arrested. They told us to secure our records and withdraw our branch's money from the bank to try to keep the state from taking it. In the meantime, they said, the national NAACP was trying to work something out.

Many of our members didn't want their names made public because of the retributions they could suffer, so we refused to provide our membership list. But the work had to go on, so we just organized something else under another name and kept on conducting business.

The second phase of the Citizens' Council's plan was to remove from the registration rolls every black registered voter in Louisiana. Louisiana had a law that allowed two registered voters to challenge the legality of another registered voter simply by filing an affidavit. Members of the Citizens' Councils went down through the registration rolls all over the state, identifying black registered voters. They filed affidavits challenging their legality based on any error they could find on the applications, no matter how trivial.

Once a voter was challenged, they weren't allowed to file a counteraffidavit to help anyone else who had been challenged. Since blacks couldn't help each other and whites wouldn't vouch for them, it didn't take long to purge the rolls. Over in Monroe, the city nearest to Lake Providence, members of the Citizens' Councils were at the registrar's office, telling the registrar whom to purge. In just fourteen days, 90% of the 5,000 Negroes registered there were removed from the rolls.

Thirty miles down Highway 65 in Tallulah, all the Negro teachers were told they would have to fill out a form before they could teach the fall semester. The form asked if they were members of the NAACP, if they had ever been a member, or if they intended to join. Over in Shreveport, teachers were told they would lose their jobs if they allowed students to ever mention the word integration. In Minden, things turned violent, and they blow-torched a man to death.

It was like watching an avalanche grow larger and larger, destroying everything in its path that we had worked for. Tensions rose as the Citizens' Councils continued to set us back in every part of the state. Every week, legislators who led the councils or who were directed by the council, issued another proposal, another law, another slanderous news story, aimed at putting us in a worse condition than we were before.

Although the NAACP injunction had cut us off from a lot of information, I still read a lot and traveled enough to get information anyway. The state legislature was fairly well controlled by people who openly professed to be segregationists, and it seemed they spent night and day coming up with new ways to dehumanize black people. The legislators called us colored bugaboos. They made insulting statements to their constituents (which of course didn't include black people) that if they didn't take a stand, that their children would end up sitting in school by "filthy, runny nosed, ragged, ugly, little niggers." We were called "the great menace" for wanting to get into LSU or other white state-supported schools.

To show how far the legislators would go, they even proposed a law that would have made it unlawful for blacks to be in any television role that would show them equal to whites. They only wanted us portrayed in the roles of maids and butlers or in the roles of grinning, shuffling, dancing buffoons, roles reserved for black men. The only reason the law didn't pass was because they couldn't figure out a way to control the television studios. I learned from this and from my studies of how Hitler got away with killing so many Jews that image is everything. The media could make a whole group of people look good or make them look bad, but once a people's image was destroyed, any kind of injustice could be heaped upon them and the masses would rationalize that the cruelty and injustices were somehow justified. This new proposal also helped me understand just how far whites in power would go to control not only what other whites thought about blacks but also what blacks thought about themselves.

Most of the segregationist bills proposed in 1956 did pass, even though the legislators had to know that some of them were unconstitutional or illegal and some downright impractical. They were just trying to buy time until they could figure out what to do with us. One law required blacks and whites working for the same company to start eating in separate areas. Another law required the state's permission before someone could sue the state or any local agency. This was aimed at preventing further NAACP lawsuits.

The state legislature was given the power to decide which schools could be used by which race, to head off the discrimination suit filed by the NAACP against the New Orleans school district. They even legalized children not going to school if a school was forced to integrate. Interracial games, sports, and contests were banned, and teachers would be fired if they belonged to or contributed to any organization that promoted integration. They could even be fired for saying they agreed with integration. That meant that all our teachers had to withdraw their memberships from the NAACP, which was working on their behalf to get them pay equal to white teachers. All over the state, people canceled their memberships and resigned their positions so that their names wouldn't be on the list at year-end—especially since the lists already submitted had managed to get into the hands of the Citizens' Council and the names had been printed in the papers. To be on a membership list meant instant trouble.

Intimidations were not just reserved for blacks. Across Louisiana, whites who tried to speak out against the works of the Citizens' Councils put themselves in jeopardy. Throughout the spring and summer of 1956, white preachers were run out of the pulpit, college professors were fired, store owners were boycotted out of business for saying that the way blacks were treated in the South was wrong. Policemen set up roadblocks to some sympathizers' businesses, making blacks afraid to continue to do business with them. Newspaper owners who had enough nerve to run articles about crimes and injustices against blacks were dealt with through economic boycotts (through their advertisers or subscribers) or through lawsuits. It didn't take long to convince the sympathetic whites that they couldn't afford to help us.

Toward the end of August 1956, the schools ended their eight-week session for Negroes so that the children could go work in the fields until the end of October. Soon after the children got out, I left for Denver to attend the National Baptist Convention. After a great week of worship, I arrived back in Lake Providence feeling good about the sessions but worn out because I had been up most of the night. Bus rides could really wear you out. I was looking forward to getting home and getting some rest.

The bus driver let me off at the end of my road, and I started the quarter-mile walk to the house. Leotis and Johnita were out in the yard, and when they saw me coming, they came running, not like they normally would when they wanted to see what I had brought them, but like something was wrong.

"Daddy!" Leotis called. They were about out of breath.

"Sheriff Gilbert and Deputy Ragus came here and took Mama away in the police car! She told him she was waiting on you, but the sheriff said she had to go with him right then. We asked the sheriff where he was taking Mama but all he said was 'she'll be back.'"

"Where are the rest of the children?" I asked as I hurried down the dirt road toward home. "Who's minding the baby?" Cleo wasn't even two years old at the time.

"She's in the house sleeping. She's with Elsie and Louis because Leon had already left for work before they came and got Mama. Mama wanted to call somebody to come watch us, but they wouldn't even let her use the telephone, so when she left, we went over to Mr. Green's, but they were gone, so we didn't know what else to do. Mama told us to just go in the house and pray, but we were outside watching for you. She said for you to come down to the courthouse just as soon as you get here!"

I told them to get my suitcase and to go get our other neighbor, Mrs. Shorter, to come over, and I hurried the rest of the way home. I jumped in my '52 Dodge and headed for the courthouse, speeding up Highway 65. With all the craziness I had read about in the newspapers lately, they could have been doing anything to my wife by now, and she was seven months pregnant. They had no right. If they wanted to know something about me or what I was doing, they should have come to me. And they didn't even have the decency to let her see about the children. I suspected my wife's arrest had something to do with the NAACP injunction, and making their move while I was out of town had hardly been coincidental.

They were obviously expecting me. As soon as I set foot in the courthouse yard, a state trooper walked up and handed me some papers. I stopped to scan down the document before I went inside— dated September 11, 1956 . . . testify before a special grand jury on NAACP affairs . . . provide instantly copies of all NAACP memberships lists, meeting minutes, bank statements, anything that would reflect NAACP activities for the last six months . . . Sixth District Judge Frank Voelker. Judge Voelker was behind the whole thing.

I went on into the courthouse, thinking all the time that we were supposed to have had until the end of the year to turn in our membership lists and here they were trying to force us to give them the lists already.

The officer escorted me into a room where several other people sat. I looked around and I saw our PTA president, Francis Atlas, who lived out in the rural area west of town. He was responsible for publicity for our NAACP branch. Eric Armstrong, owner of a local dry cleaners and gas station, was also there along with two other ministers, Rev. J. H. Moore and Rev. O. L. Virgil. I had been out of town for a while, so I started waving and speaking to everyone I knew.

"You're not supposed to talk to anybody in here!" a police officer shouted from the side of the room. He was making his way across the room as if to subdue me. I muttered under my breath, "I wasn't talking. I was just speaking."

I inquired into my wife's whereabouts and found out that she was already being interrogated about NAACP branch records in another room. She had been our branch secretary before the state closed us down. When it was my turn to go in, as I entered the room, I caught a glimpse of her being taken out through another door. She was wearing a blue flowered dress, one that she would never have worn away from the house. My wife took care of her appearance and she always made sure she was just so whenever she left the house, so I got mad at the police all over again—no time for the children, certainly no time for fixing up so you wouldn't look bad in court.

I was told that it is unlawful to tell what goes on in a grand jury, so I can't say what they said to me, but in my estimation, it was just a Citizens' Council gathering, folks prying for information. And they pried all day, because we didn't get back home until late that evening, and by that time, the children were really worried that they had put us in jail.

I found out later we had been brought before the grand jury all because of an untruth. A paid informant had reported to a Citizens' Council leader that he had seen me collecting money for the NAACP. What he had seen was me accepting some donations to go to Denver to the National Baptist Convention.

They thought for sure that they had caught us disobeying the ban on NAACP meetings, which carried a prison term of up to six months. With all the officers in jail, they figured they could easily break the organization. And if they had proven we were meeting, they could have sent all the members to prison too and fined them up to $500. They had sent out policemen simultaneously to pick up each person because they thought we would need to get together to get our stories straight. But we were ready. We didn't have a warning or legal advice or legal representation. But through God's help, we made it through the test anyway. I refused to identify any former members, and I didn't admit anything, because I wasn't guilty of anything. I just kept repeating, "We have not been meeting and we are not in violation of the law."

We found out later that they also wanted our membership lists and minutes so they could compare them to their list of Negro teachers, bus drivers, or other employees of the Board of Education. They planned to fire any of them who were NAACP members based on the new law that forbade school employees to be in an organization advocating integration. We also found out they had planted paid informers among the teachers, who reported back to them everything the teachers said or did.

By the end of 1956, we were beaten down. The Citizens' Councils and their supporters had practically destroyed the NAACP in Louisiana, reducing state membership from more than 13,000 to fewer than 1,700 members in less than one year, leaving the people with no one to defend them. The NAACP never regained the power in the community it had held before 1956. The Citizens' Council managed to disqualify most of the black voters in the entire state, and we now had more segregated rules and regulations than ever before.

Many people in Lake Providence, both black and white, now lived in fear. The white folks were scared, mostly because there were so many of us. They could someday lose their political power to a group of people they had treated really badly. Some were even afraid that all the anger and conflict might lead to a race war. Black folks were scared that white folks were going to kill them for taking a stand, or scared that their taking a stand might result in their killing a white person in self-defense. Blacks and whites who had maintained friendships for years were afraid to speak to one another.

With every little act—a large gathering of black people for church, reading a black paper, buying a decent car—something was read into it. It could be considered a plot, or the black person was trying to act equal to a white man, which for now was a grievous crime. People walked around expecting trouble, looking for trouble, and causing trouble.

Certain white men hung around on the streets uptown, and when they'd see a black person coming up the sidewalk, they'd move toward them until they forced them off the sidewalk, into the street. Police officers would see a black man on the streets and say "Show me a dollar in your pocket." If the man didn't come up with a dollar, they'd arrest him under a charge of vagrancy.

The *Monroe Morning World* even ran a couple of editorials about me in 1957, and of course some people actually believed that everything printed in a newspaper was true. They didn't realize that the news people printed what they wanted us to know and often slanted articles according to what their owners wanted us to believe.

I was the first NAACP leader in north Louisiana to be publicly identified in the papers, which made me somewhat of a celebrity. The editorial said that whites had come to realize that the Negro population had been neglected too long and that they were working on plans "that would make us the envy of our northern brothers, if we didn't let the NAACP upset the apple cart." The paper said that southerners wanted to work things out peacefully, but I was just being used and manipulated by the communists, who were out to destroy the United States by bringing confusion between the races.

The fear of a communist takeover was the big scare at the time, with towns building bomb and fallout shelters, and I was as much against communism as the next person. But many white folks were just as scared of integration as they were of communism, so the leading segregationists figured out a way to link the two fears. Anyone pushing for integration could be accused of being involved in subversive communist activities, and that would be the end of them.

After the article ran in the paper, black people began avoiding me, partially because I might be communist, but also because I might be keeping white folks from acting better, and that was something black people wanted more than anything. They wanted white people to finally see the wrongness in the things they did to black people, to feel some guilt about killing us and disrespecting us and stealing our labor.

It took a great deal of energy fighting for dignity and respect each and every day, and many wanted to lay this tiresome burden down. So to have the newspaper say that I was responsible, that I was causing white folks to have second thoughts about being decent and fair, was unsettling to many. They whispered behind my back. They accused me to my face.

"See what you done gone and done. Made the white man mad and now we all got to suffer. You know how crazy and evil white folks are." "Why couldn't you just leave well enough alone? We were making do just fine before you came up with your grand ideas about voting and going to the same schools."

It was like being hung out all by yourself to dry. I had tried to help the people, and now they blamed me for causing them all this trouble. The council had us right where they wanted us. They had broken the organization, and now they were trying to destroy the leadership. Either they could convince the people to turn on me, or I would become so discouraged that I'd quit, or both. Either way, the movement would be destroyed and the council would have achieved their goal.

Some black people knew the articles weren't true in a lot of respects, but they were smart enough to figure out that white people were feeling threatened. It wasn't normal for the white press to dedicate two days' editorials to a small-town black preacher. Nothing we ever did merited that kind of attention in the white world. So there was a rising fear that if certain people felt threatened enough, it wouldn't be long before they moved from economic blackmail to their lynching ways of the 1910s and '20s, like they were already doing over in Mississippi. And most blacks in northeast Louisiana in 1957 seemed to be willing to practically do or accept anything to keep from dying.

# TWELVE

# A Glimmer of Hope

The voter registration suit we had filed dragged on for years due to one technicality after another. First the registrar's attorneys tried to get the suit dismissed because of an error on Mrs. Beard's name. The suit named C. E. Beard, the previous registrar, rather than the current registrar, Myrtle Cole Beard. That took almost all of 1952 to resolve. Then we just kind of lost touch with the suit until 1954 when I found out Mrs. Beard's attorney had filed a motion to dismiss the case. They said the case was a state issue and it shouldn't have been filed in federal court, because the federal government didn't have any jurisdiction in the matter. They contended that we should have to present our case in state court, although it was the state that was now defending the registrar in her efforts to keep us from voting.

The federal district judge did review our case, but he decided he had no jurisdiction to try it. He said it was a three-judge case and sent the suit to the judge for the circuit court of appeals. The circuit court judge refused to appoint a three-judge court and ordered the case back to the district court. In the meantime, we had lost all of 1954 waiting to be heard.

In the spring of 1955, the suit came up on the federal docket to be heard by Judge Ben Dawkins but was pushed off the docket to the fall court sessions because the judge said they ran out of time. They told us it would be the first case they heard when court reconvened in September or October. Then they started pushing the case back and forth between the courts. It seemed no judge wanted to handle such a suit or be put in the position of having to make a decision.

Our case was finally rescheduled in February of 1957, but then the district attorney said he couldn't do it because he had to be at a convention. The next time it was scheduled, our attorney, Mr. Berry, had an important case somewhere else. Finally, after about six years of technicalities, Mr. Berry moved from Louisiana to Los Angeles, California, and I wasn't exactly sure what happened to the suit after that.

The courts eventually lifted the NAACP ban, and in 1958 some NAACP branches started reorganizing. But things weren't the same. We had lost our momentum during the ban, and economic reprisals had caused many of our leaders to resign. Many had permanently left the South. I was invited to serve on the newly reactivated state board to try to revitalize the NAACP in northeast Louisiana. I jumped at the chance to help rebuild the organization, because I didn't want anybody to think they had whipped me.

The extreme behavior of the Citizens' Councils, especially in purging the rolls of black voters, eventually backfired on them. It gained the attention of the national press, which started showing the South as we lived it, not genteel and mannerly, but violent and often barbaric, and our stories pricked the consciousness of some people in high places.

I was always watching for something that might help us, especially since our suit seemed to be going nowhere. After the Civil Rights Act was passed in 1957, I started monitoring closely what was happening in Congress. I heard that the Justice Department was planning to set up a civil rights commission that would formally investigate whether people were actually being deprived of their right to vote just because of their race. I decided that as soon as it was set up, I would contact them to see if they would come down to Lake Providence to help us.

In early 1959, Mrs. Beard, the registrar we filed the suit against, left office through a resignation or retirement, we didn't know which. Mr. Cecil Manning, who owned and operated a country store about five miles north of Lake Providence, was hired to take her place. We thought we might have more success with him because his store up towards the head of the lake catered mostly to the black community. He had also been a substitute mail carrier for Route 3 for about seven years, so he personally knew many people in the area, both black and white. Surely he would let us register without requiring two people to sign for us.

Six of us, Percy Knighten, Bertha Williams, Caroline Wilson Gilliard, Clifton Maxwell, Francis Joseph Atlas, and I decided we'd go down and give the new registrar a try and see if we'd fare any better with him. We met at the Baptist Center and rode up to the registrar's office together.

Mr. Manning was sitting at his desk when we arrived. He was a youngish fellow, looked to be in his thirties. He looked up from his papers and asked, "What can I do for y'all?"

When we told Mr. Manning what we wanted, he inquired as to how long we had been living in East Carroll. Most of us had lived in East Carroll all our lives so he said, "Well," as he showed us these little forms I had never seen before, "You have to get two qualified electors from your ward and precinct to identify you and fill out these forms saying they know you."

When I reached for one of the forms to see what it said, he pulled the form back. "You can't carry the forms out," he said. "You'll have to bring the person here to vouch for you."

He didn't even let us fill out an application, which by now we could fill out in a fraction of the time required by the average new applicant. So we went on out. The new registrar hadn't even let us get as far as the old one.

I was talking to Mrs. Bertha Williams as we came down the courthouse steps. "I know I can get two people to come down here and identify me," she bragged.

"You might think you can, but you can't."

"But I know I can," she said seriously. "I have some white friends and we are all Christians."

Mrs. Williams was a deeply devout Christian woman respected in both the white and black communities for her special relationship with the Lord, but she didn't understand this voting thing.

I told her, "But Christians and this registration business is different. Nobody's a Christian when it comes down to identifying you." But she was convinced otherwise.

She went back to the people she worked for as a domestic and told them she wanted to register to vote, but she needed them to come down to the courthouse to identify her. She came back and told me, "Oh, yes. They say they will go with me on Monday."

But just like I thought, before Monday she was back. "Well, it's just like you said. They told me they couldn't bother with that."

Not long after our visit to the registrar's office, I heard that the members of the Civil Rights Commission had been selected and an office set up. I wrote Mr. Roy Wilkins at the national NAACP office to find out how I could let the commission know about our situation. He sent me the address, and I immediately wrote them requesting that they investigate the Lake Providence registrar. Their reply said they would give my letter due consideration, and as soon as the hearing on voting rights abuses in Louisiana was scheduled, they would notify me.

When I sent in my NAACP membership dues to the national office that year, I inquired about the complaints we had turned over to them some years back. They advised me to mail copies of our complaints to the Civil Rights Commission and see what they would do about them.

It turned out to be a good move, because in the early summer of 1959, the commission sent two gentlemen down from Washington to talk to us. From the group assembled at the church, they selected the ones who they thought wouldn't be afraid to speak up and tell the truth. They said there would be a commission hearing held in district court in Shreveport, Louisiana, in July and they might be calling some of us to testify.

Four of us received subpoenas; however, the night before the hearing, I was called and told that the hearing was canceled. Judge Ben Dawkins had issued an injunction to prevent the hearing from taking place. The state attorney general and various registrars of voters had filed a suit challenging the constitutionality of the Civil Rights Act of 1957.

I was sitting around one day when it occurred to me that the complaints we mailed to the Civil Rights Commission were against a registrar who wasn't in office anymore. I discussed this with some of the other ministers, and we decided we would need to gather some evidence specifically about the new registrar.

About twenty of us got together and went down to the courthouse. The registrar's office wasn't very large. At best, you could only squeeze about ten people in there at one time. Since we had so many people with us, we decided that Rev. Mason, Rev. Green, and I would go in and talk to Mr. Manning. The rest of the group would wait outside in the hallway.

When we got inside, Mr. Manning told us the same old thing about needing to be identified. I had found out recently that the registrar was only to ask for identification if he or she had a good reason to believe that we weren't the same people as the names we put on our registration forms. So I told Mr. Manning, "We identify folks at the bank and at the post office and other places. We have come around and signed to get folks out of jail, went on their bonds. We have lived here long enough to be known."

Well, of course those were just wasted words in the wind, and Mr. Manning sent us on our way again, but not before asking us to sign our names to a piece of paper, and he wanted our addresses too. Now we all knew the purpose of this request. One of the men with us said sarcastically, "Oh, sure we will give you our names."

I turned to the group and said, "Let's go. There's no point in writing our names and leaving them here unless we are putting our names on an application card. This could mean intimidation."

I turned back to Mr. Manning. "We didn't come up here to sign up. We came to try to register." I told him my name only and we left.

That afternoon we decided we should write up new complaints and send them to the Justice Department. A young lady who was a student at Grambling College composed a letter for us, and about two months later we received our reply. They said they wanted to help, but their hands were tied in Louisiana until certain legal matters were settled, and the case might go all the way to the Supreme Court.

About this same time, we started to notice that quite a few out-of-town blacks, particularly ministers, had been struck with a sudden interest in our struggle in Lake Providence. They'd show up in town or at out-of-town meetings, expressing great interest in our plans and how things were progressing in Lake Providence. They wanted to talk to those of us who were most active.

One such visit came from a preacher from Little Rock, Arkansas, who called himself Prophet Willett. He was the self-appointed chairman of an organization he had named the Dark Samaritans of America. He even had a couple of churches, one down in Natchez, Mississippi, and another one in Ferriday, Louisiana.

I knew of him before I actually met him because he had a radio show and held big tent revival meetings from town to town throughout the South. Of course, from what I heard, he did more preaching about the values of segregation and the same old patterns of living than he did about saving souls. His message, which was often carried in the white papers, was "Negroes just need to accept their place and stop listening to the outside agitators who are just stirring up trouble in the south."

One afternoon I was out in the yard tending the cows when a late-model Cadillac pulled into the yard. After I had restrained my barking dogs, out stepped a man in an expensive-looking tailored suit, black high-collared shirt, and spit-shined shoes. Smiling broadly, he extended his hand. "How are you doing this afternoon? You may not know me, but I'm Prophet Willett and I need to talk to you a bit, in private."

Of course my private office was the big outdoors, so we stood in the yard and talked. He said he was running a revival in the area and had been talking to the local white folks. He said he had a message for me from "the white people." "They say if you let this voting thing alone, they will take care of you."

He showed me some checks he had and the nice Cadillac he was driving. He had a check from Sheriff Gilbert.

"Now, Negroes don't have anything to give you, and even if they did, they wouldn't let you have it. Look at how hard you have to live."

I could see his eyes behind his wire-framed glasses scanning across the dirt yard, scratched bald by the chickens. I followed his eyes around toward the house with its peeling paint to the big barrel on the side with the tin going up to the roof to catch rain water for cooking and bathing.

"You could be living in a nicer house with gas heat and indoor plumbing. If I was you, I'd just let it alone. Your children here, it will be hard for them to get jobs, and you'll starve to death fooling around with these Negroes."

Of course I sent him on his way unsatisfied. I told him I'd never quit and he could tell that to whoever sent him.

After that incident, a couple of preachers came over from Monroe, about seventy-five miles west of Lake Providence, to visit Rev. Virgil. Rev. Otis Virgil, who had run against me several times in the 1940s and '50s for association president, was pastor of the Mount Calvary and the Jerusalem Baptist churches and also was a big farmer. Although he was in his mid-sixties, he still farmed over 1,400 acres he owned. His farm gave him a pretty good living, and he always drove late model, top-of-the-line automobiles like Lincolns.

The preachers from Monroe claimed they had overheard a disturbing conversation by several white gentlemen at the courthouse in Monroe. They said the men were talking about a preacher over in Lake Providence who owned land and a lot of other property who would likely lose his property if he didn't let this voting thing alone. They were so concerned that they had decided to come over by night as "friends" to warn Rev. Virgil. They suggested it would be wise for Rev. Virgil to get out of the group promoting voting. Rev. Virgil told them, "Well, it's more in it than me and if I get out, it won't help any, because the others can carry on. So maybe you want to talk to all of them."

Rev. Virgil called me, and I arranged for a meeting at the Baptist Association Center building and invited some of the others involved. I opened the meeting and expressed appreciation for our guests' interest and for their taking the time to come all the way from Monroe to talk to us. After introductions, I turned the floor over to them.

The main spokesman recounted what he had overheard about Rev. Virgil losing his property. "You stand to lose something if you don't stop what you're doing," he warned us.

When he finished talking, we discussed the risks we were probably taking and decided we would go on. But the spokesman went on to insist that we shouldn't go on. He said disgustedly, "You remind me of a bunch of boys on the bank of the river and here comes a big steamboat by and you jump in the water."

"Now wait one minute here!" Rev. Mason, who was sitting across from me, jumped up. He pointed his finger at the preacher at the front of the room.

"You come in here saying you want to give us some advice, but you look like you trying to insist on it now. Seems to me you're acting like somebody else sent you here. If we don't want to accept your advice, that's our business. We won't have you coming in here insisting."

We could all guess who might have sent them, and the whole situation was starting to get absurd. They had used the press to try to ruin my reputation, then they tried to use my lack of material possessions as a reason to buy me out, and now they were sending preachers, people who should have been working toward justice, the same as we were. I wondered what their creative minds would come up with next.

I told them, "We appreciate your coming. But now if anybody did send you here, you go back and tell them that we are determined to go on. And I am speaking for myself—if all the blood runs out of my veins, I believe it will cry from the ground for freedom. We are not going to stop."

In the summer of 1960, the Civil Rights Commission hearing on voter registration abuses was finally rescheduled, after having been canceled the summer before. I along with Rev. Mason, Rev. Atlas (who became a minister subsequent to this time), and Watson Sanders received subpoenas for the hearing to be held in New Orleans. Rev. Mason was still a very close friend, although we didn't farm together anymore. Watson owned a small grocery store down on Henderson Project, one of the projects we had gotten back in the 1930s when we were put out of Transylvania. All three men were farmers, owning a fair amount of acreage. I was the only one of the group who wasn't farming at the time, because the farm had gotten to be too much for me after Leon went to college and Leotis went to live in Jersey City, New Jersey, with my sister, Hattie.

The day before the hearing, the four of us rode the five and a half hours to New Orleans, arriving after dark. I felt anxious and jittery because we had been trying to register for so long and now I was going to have my say in front of the United States government.

All night, I tossed about restlessly, filled with anticipation of tomorrow's events and the new future tomorrow's testimony might create. I dreamed of a new day in the South and what I would feel like when I finally had my rights as a man, as a United States citizen. But you know sometimes when you're flying high and things seem to be going your way, you wake up and discover that things are not at all like you expected. If we could have seen what was down the road for us, we might not have ever come to New Orleans that day. But the good Lord kept us blind so we would go and do the job our hands were assigned to do. When we walked into that hearing room bright and early on September 27, 1960, we were prepared and ready to do battle, oblivious to the evil that lurked in the minds of our white acquaintances back home, some who we even considered to be our friends.

# THIRTEEN

# All of One Accord

We arrived at the hearing fairly early that morning. To kill time, I sat observing and scrutinizing the vast assortment of people assembling in the hearing room, trying to figure out who was there and for what reason. There were the obvious ones, the ones with cameras, notebooks, and tape recorders. I recognized one reporter from the *Monroe Morning World*. And then there were the not so obvious, the observers. I decided one fellow must have been sent to gather information because he had that snoop look. The next one, I decided, was definitely a Klansman—he had that hateful, spiteful look. Then there were the men in dark suits and dark glasses, who must have been government people. I spent the rest of my time until they announced the beginning of the hearing figuring out who was for us and who was against us, and which witnesses looked too scared to do a good job and which ones were doing the best job avoiding the cameras.

The commission members finally came in and took their seats around the table. With witnesses from the eleven or so parishes under investigation by the Civil Rights Commission and the variety of news people jockeying for the best positions, the hearing room was quite crowded by the time the hearing started at 8:30 A.M. The meeting was called to order and the head of the commission explained to everyone the purpose of the hearing.

"The purpose of the hearing today is to conduct an investigation that will determine whether certain citizens of the United States are being deprived of their right to vote just by reason of race, color, religion, or national origin," he told the assembly. He went on to explain that their decision would be based on testimonies from witnesses and from research the Commission had already conducted. He explained the rules and told the newsmen how they were expected to behave. "If any witness does not want his or her picture taken or their face shown on television, then you've got to respect their wishes," he reminded them. "We are not going to have the witnesses feeling intimidated."

After the instructions were completed, Mr. Berl Bernhard, deputy staff director, was called up to present background information. He explained that the commissioners needed the information to be able to evaluate our testimonies in the proper context. His charts and graphs showed how from 1888 to 1910, the percentage of black registered voters in Louisiana fell from 53% to 1% and stayed that way until World War II. After the war, the percentage of blacks of voting age who were actually allowed to register had risen to a high of only 28%, although more than 80% of the blacks in the state could read and write. Over 82% of voting-age whites were registered. He ended his presentation with a summary statement: "The charts speak for themselves and suggest that certain forces are operating in the state to perpetuate these conditions."

Just as Mr. Bernhard finished his presentation, the doors swung open, as if on cue, and the state attorney general and his entourage of five assistant attorney generals made their grand entrance into the hearing room. A murmur went across the crowd as people hunched each other and whispered. They had arrived just in time to hear the witnesses, and an atmosphere of discomfort descended over the room. Some of the witnesses looked more frightened than before, if that were possible.

I was called up as the first witness of the day, representing one of the only four parishes left in Louisiana that still wouldn't let a single black person register to vote. They swore me in, and I took my seat. They said I had been selected as the first witness because my testimony would establish the background information on voting problems for the entire hearing. I would also show the kinds of problems encountered when blacks were required to get a registered voter to identify them.

As Mr. Bernhard turned to face me, I smiled broadly, partly to let him know I was up to the job and partly to let the state attorney general know that I was neither afraid nor intimidated. After all, that's why I had been picked to go first. Besides, some of the other witnesses looked like they needed a morale boast, a little encouragement. So I had to set the tone for the rest of them.

Mr. Bernhard started off by telling everyone about East Carroll Parish, about how there were about 4,700 voting-age Negroes, none of whom were registered. He pointed out that this had been the case since 1922. He also pointed out that almost every white person of voting age was registered, 99.7% of the 2,800 eligible. Then the members of the commission started questioning me.

They asked me where I lived and for how long, what kind of work I did, and what my educational background was. I had to tell them in detail about all the many times we had tried to register and how we were denied because we couldn't get two white registered voters to identify us. I even told them about the time I tried to register as a Republican after trying several times to register as a Democrat, how the registrar had demanded to know which party I really belonged to and how I had told her I wasn't in either party until she registered me. That brought a few chuckles and helped to lighten things up a bit. I figured they needed a little humor because everyone was looking just too tense.

They asked me whether anyone had tried to intimidate me because of my activities. I related one incident, but I also told them I had been warned not to say anything. But I wanted to go on record that I was not afraid. I told the commission, "I just go on in spite of the threats, because I feel like I'm right and I know where I'm going, I know what I'm talking about, and I don't care what happens. No matter how I leave here, I'm going to heaven, so if I go for my people or for the right to vote, I will be perfectly satisfied."

Near the end of my testimony, the vice chairman, Mr. Storey, asked me why I wanted to register to vote. This was one question I could easily answer because I had spent so much time thinking about it. With all the conviction I felt, I said, "I have always felt like that was a responsibility that belonged to the citizens—after reading Louisiana history and the Constitution of Louisiana and the United States, it says that the right to vote belongs to the citizens and I noticed, it always gives recognition. I noticed the streets where people voted were fixed. I noticed the roads were graveled where the people who voted lived, and the people who didn't vote had dirt roads. I noticed that the officers of the law respected the people who voted and treated them differently from the people who didn't vote. And after reading Negro newspapers and traveling quite a bit, I felt like it was a responsibility. After my two brothers served in the army in World War II and even before then during World War I, when the president was talking about making the world safe for democracy, and everybody had the right and privilege to participate, it had always been a burning zeal and desire within my heart to vote. I have to fight for this because I will never be able to explain to my children why the Negroes should be treated in such a way or be cast about."

Some of the people at the hearing said I was the only witness that day who had a smile and didn't look scared to death. But they didn't understand. I got to participate in this hearing because I searched the commission out. I asked to be there—not because someone came and convinced me to come. And I felt satisfied that I had finally had my say.

Although four of us from East Carroll were subpoenaed, only two of us were called to testify. If we had known the reaction to our participation would be so great, we would have asked the commission not to call the big farmer, Rev. Atlas, to testify. But the commission selected the ones they wanted to talk, so after I finished, Rev. Atlas was called up to give his testimony.

Rev. Atlas, who had lived in East Carroll all his life, was well respected in the community, the former PTA president and a church superintendent for twenty years. He had been involved in the struggle a long time, serving as secretary of the Voters' League back in the 1940s. His schooling had been at Tuskegee Institute in Tuskegee, Alabama, where he had finished a trade in plastery and brick masonry.

Atlas was fifty-five years old. He owned about 175 acres and about 24 head of cattle, and was a proud man who believed farming was as honorable a profession as medicine or law or teaching. He lived in an eight-room farmhouse in the rural area west of Lake Providence where he had raised twelve children. Eight had graduated from college or were in college at the time and two were in the army. That was quite a feat for a black man in the south at the end of the '50s. Lots of people talked about sending their children to college to get them a better life, but not many had actually been able to do it.

When they put Atlas on the stand, they asked him the same kinds of questions they had asked me, all about his background and what happened when he had tried to register to vote. He recounted his stories, and then we sat to listen to the rest of the witnesses.

After the hearing, we rushed back to Lake Providence because Watson and Rev. Atlas wanted to be able to get into their fields early the next morning. When we arrived that night, we found it had rained, so they wouldn't be able to get into the fields after all. Rev. Atlas went on home, but in a few hours, I was surprised when I heard the dogs barking and looked out to see him driving into the yard. I went out to meet him as I always had to do for visitors, since my dogs, Joe and Black Eyes, wouldn't let anyone out of their car without my permission.

The troubled look on his face told me right away that something had happened to him. He said that not long after he had gotten home, Sheriff Gilbert and someone he didn't recognize had shown up at his house. Sheriff Gilbert was hot mad and had told him that for his smartness, no one was going to gin any of his cotton or do any credit for him in any form—not anyone in the whole parish—and he reminded Rev. Atlas that it wasn't against the law for them not to gin it. Then the sheriff just walked back to his car and left. I told Rev. Atlas, "Well, don't pay Sheriff Gilbert any attention. You take your cotton and put it on the gin lot and let them tell you they're not going to gin it."

Rev. Atlas did as I advised and went the next day to talk to Mr. Mitchiner. Mr. Mitchiner, who was supposed to have been a good friend of Rev. Atlas's daddy, owned the Olivedell Gin where Rev. Atlas normally took his cotton. In fact, Rev. Atlas had had cotton ginned there just three days before the hearing. Mr. Mitchiner told him that as much as he hated not to, he couldn't gin his cotton. It had been decided at a meeting of the Ginner's Association that no one would gin, so he had no choice but to go along with it. He spoke of his friendship with Rev. Atlas's daddy and said he would try to work something out and let Rev. Atlas know. But the next day, Mr. Mitchiner's son-in-law came over and asked Rev. Atlas to please not bring over any more cotton. He said that meetings were being held and there was too much pressure. Rev. Atlas asked him how they could be under so much pressure since they owned their own gin. He said he just couldn't talk about it.

A few days after Rev. Atlas told me what Sheriff Gilbert said, I went into the Feed store to buy a few items. A white clerk who I had considered to be my friend over the years saw me picking up a few items. He walked up to me and said, "I can't sell those things to you."

"Why can't you sell them? This a holiday or something?" I continued to pick up things off the shelf.

He turned me a cold "don't-get-funny-with-me-nigger" stare that definitely was not the look of friendship. "Oh yes, it's a holiday for you," he said.

I still didn't fully realize what he meant, but I didn't argue with him. I put the articles back and went on out the store. I walked down the street, where I met one of my friends, a black man. I said, "I just went over to the feed store and they wouldn't sell me anything over there. Take this money and go see what's wrong."

So he went on over to the feed store and he got what I wanted and brought it back to me. It was only then that I knew for sure what was going on. As it turned out, they had shown part of the hearing on television. They had shown our pictures, then showed us talking. They even ran stories with names in the Monroe and the New Orleans newspapers, so everyone knew exactly who had given evidence before the commission. And after I finally talked to Rev. Atlas again, I really had a better understanding of what they could do to the witnesses.

Mr. Mitchiner never worked anything out about ginning Rev. Atlas's cotton and everywhere Rev. Atlas went, they refused him. He hauled his trailer round from gin to gin, and they'd tell him he'd have to get that cotton off their property. He went to every gin in the parish. He talked to Mr. Hider, another gin owner. Mr. Hider told him that in his judgment, Rev. Atlas had done something not in the best interest of the parish so he was going to have to hustle for himself. He was stuck with a hot potato. Rev. Atlas went to see Mr. Amacker, owner of the Hollybrook Gin. Mr. Amacker said his gin was shut down but even if it was running, he couldn't gin it. Someone had called him and told him not to gin Atlas cotton.

Rev. Atlas even tried a gin in the next parish, over in Oak Grove. They agreed to gin his cotton but when somebody asked for his name and he said "Atlas," the man told him, "Oh, no, we can't gin that." He would always ask the people, "Who told you you can't?" and they would always give the same answer, "We can't say."

I decided I'd go talk about the boycott with one of the white ministers I knew. I figured a Christian minister would be interested in doing what was right, regardless of what the devil might be trying to do. He was a young fellow, and when I tried to talk to him about the situation, he seemed distant. I quickly found out that he and several other ministers in town were strictly controlled by their environment and not by the Holy Spirit. Later on, when this same young man decided to leave Lake Providence, he preached his farewell sermon that showed his true side. He told about a meeting that he attended where all the people were together, blacks and whites, singing and praising God together. He said that seemed more like heaven to him. He even talked about the wrongness of the pattern of segregation, which was really an unusual position for a white person to take at that time. But that was his farewell sermon. He couldn't have said those things if he had planned to continue living in Lake Providence.

From September to November, Rev. Atlas tried to convince someone to gin his cotton while his crops continued to deteriorate in the fields. In November, he talked to a U.S. attorney who told him that he understood the Outpost Gin at Alsatia would gin his cotton. When he called the manager, the manager said he would be glad to gin it. Since the Outpost Gin was about eighteen miles south of town, it was too far to pull a trailer of cotton with a tractor down a main highway, so Rev. Atlas borrowed a truck to take his cotton down to Alsatia.

They had ginned six bales when the manager asked why he brought his cotton so far to be ginned. Rev. Atlas explained that he had had a misunderstanding in Lake Providence and couldn't get it ginned. He told the manager he had about twenty-five bales more, and at the time the manager didn't seem to have a problem with ginning the rest. But when he came back with two more bales to be ginned, the manager told him that some people from Lake Providence had gone over to Mound, Louisiana, and met with the owner of the Outpost, a Mr. Yerger, and the owner had instructed him not to gin any more Atlas cotton.

Because I didn't do a big credit business, they found it much harder to get to me. In fact, my family and I lived largely outside of dependence on the white community. I bought my gas at a black-owned station, had my clothes cleaned at a black-owned cleaners, got my car fixed at a black-owned repair shop, and bought my groceries at the Chinese-owned grocery store. I didn't borrow money from the banks, and I rarely bought anything on credit. I'd save up for whatever I needed. My income came from the church and from what I made hunting and trapping. My wife sold Avon and, seasonally, cleaned house and chopped and picked cotton for the black farmer who lived next door. The older children earned all their own spending change and even bought some of their own clothes with money they made from picking and chopping cotton and picking up pecans for the black farmers in the area.

For food, I raised my cows, chickens, and occasionally pigs, and I could always go fishing and bring home some fish. When I hunted, I brought home rabbits, squirrels, possums, and occasionally duck. So we always had meat, eggs, and milk. I lived rent-free on the sixty acres owned by the Baptist Association, property with plenty of fruit trees— plum, pear, apricot, apple, fig, mulberry, peach, and pecan—trees that would bear with such abundance that the limbs would sometimes break from their burden.

I planted a large garden each year, about a half acre where I grew carrots, peas, beets, corn, watermelons, peanuts, and every variety of beans and greens—you name it, I raised it. To take us through the winter, my wife, with the help of the girls, canned fruits and vegetables, from dewberries in the spring to the cooking pears that came in in late fall. She also made the best jellies and jams, which she sometimes sold. The extra corn I raised would be dried out and shelled for feed for the chickens. We'd dig up sweet potatoes and then rebury them under a dome-shaped pile of dirt to keep them from rotting during the winter months. All winter, we'd go outside and dig out a few as we needed them. Sweet potatoes were my favorite. In fact, my wife and I probably knew more things to do with a potato than George Washington Carver knew to do with a peanut.

We always had a milk cow and maybe another bull cow we were raising to sell. We milked the cows daily and set the milk in the icebox so that the cream could rise to the top. My wife would then skim the cream off and accumulate it in the churn until she had enough to churn out a batch of butter, which she sold to others, along with eggs from our chickens. For the most part, we had more than we needed and plenty to give away. And of course God was always blessing us with all kinds of things the family needed.

Although our diet included few store-bought foods and was limited mostly to fish and what we could raise—fruit, vegetables, and chicken—it was a diet that kept us out the doctor's office. With the help of natural healers I could make from roots and plants I found in the woods, such as mullein and sassafras or sarsaparilla tea, along with a bit of Father John's, Black Draught, and white vermifuge, we were all able to stay quite healthy. In fact, in all the years of raising eight children, I never spent over $100 all together on doctor's bills. Three of my children went all twelve years of school without missing a single day. Elsie was even presented a certificate by the governor for being the first Negro student in the state to never miss a day of school.

The children never had cavities even though none of them ever saw a dentist outside of the dentist who made periodic visits to the school. Polio was also a big concern at the time, and all children were supposed to get their polio shots or be put out of school. I refused to sign my permission for the shots because the doctors disagreed with what I was doing, so I was leery of them giving me or my children shots or medicine. I never knew what they might try to do to us. I figured I was better off letting God keep the polio away. And fortunately, the teachers made no move to put the children out of school.

Although we didn't have a lot of money, my wife knew how to stretch what we had. I turned all the money over to her, and she always found a way to make it last to the next month. It also helped that we didn't have a lot of monthly bills. We didn't have running water and used wood instead of gas for heating and cooking. For water, we used our hand-crank pump or rainwater we diverted from the roof down a piece of tin into a fifty-five-gallon barrel.

My wife was very handy with electrical things, repairing our wiring, radios, and other appliances. She also made most of the children's clothes. They would pick out what they wanted from the Sears catalog, and my wife would cut a pattern out of newspaper, just by looking at the pictures. She used zippers and fancy buttons she found on used clothing donated to the Baptist Association.

It was harder for them to control me because all I had for them to take was my life. It was much easier to get to a farmer who had to borrow money every farm year to make his crop.

So it was Rev. Atlas who felt the full impact of the plan that had been put in place, because he had no options. His livelihood depended almost solely on his white business associations. When Rev. Atlas went to the Farmer's Seed and Feed store, Mr. Norris, the manager, told him that he didn't want his business at his store—he had enough customers without him and would appreciate it if he didn't come back. He also warned Rev. Atlas not to bring his soybean crop to the grain elevator Mr. Norris owned with Mr. Terral. Soon after that Mr. Norris turned Rev. Atlas's account of $580 over to a lawyer for collection, and so did the John Deere dealer. The butane gas companies wouldn't sell him any fuel, so he ran completely out of gas right before Christmas. He had to buy wood stoves to heat his house and cook on. He didn't have gas for his hot water tank.

When he got ready to harvest his soybeans, the black man who was supposed to combine it for him said, "Joe, I can't do it. I am afraid the white people might retaliate against me too if I help you combine your beans."

Another black man agreed to help him, but his combine—a machine used for harvesting soybeans—mysteriously burned up. Rev. Atlas tried to get Warren & Coody Grain Company, the grain elevator company that used to buy his beans, to combine his crop, but they refused. They wouldn't even sell him feed so he could feed his cattle.

Because Rev. Atlas couldn't get his crops sold, he couldn't pay off his farm debts. All his creditors turned his accounts over to lawyers for collection. Everywhere he went, the white people were all of one accord. Either they were a part of the conspiracy to break us, or they said they were under pressure from this mysterious "they" that controlled and directed the activities of not only East Carroll Parish, but apparently could reach out and control other parts of the state too. And what made it even harder was the relatives and close friends who criticized us for agreeing to testify, like Atlas's relatives that were so angry with him for putting in jeopardy all that land handed down from Atlas's father.

Many blacks were so fearful of the white community that they were afraid to be seen with us. They wouldn't even stop on the street to talk to us, afraid that they might be found guilty by association and become subjected to the same mistreatment. Now more than ever, they wanted nothing to do with this voting thing. We were left pretty much out there on our own.

So the struggle really began. Before the hearing, a few whites had reacted to what we were trying to do, but there had been no local organized reaction. The whites had figured they were so established that there would be no way we could break through. They had just counted our lawsuit and us as a joke. But in 1960, they saw something different—people who could not vote had been able to get the ears of people in high places, and they were very unhappy about that. We had come to the place of organized reaction, and I was shocked and unprepared.

# FOURTEEN

# Victory and Defeat

We struggled through the rest of 1960 without much outside help. We had testified before the federal government and we felt like it was their responsibility to help us—but anyone who deals with the government knows that you have to go through a lot of red tape before you get them to move.

When Rev. Atlas first wrote the Justice Department for help, they told him to see a private lawyer and go to court. Sometimes it seemed that the people at the Justice Department were totally out of touch with the reality of being black in the South. I wondered what lawyers or judges and all-white jury did they think was going to deal fairly with this matter when everybody was already operating on one accord. It was like Rev. Atlas said, "That's like a bug going on trial before a courtroom full of ducks. The judge is a duck. The jury is a duck and all the lawyers are ducks. Now what chance has a bug got when you know how ducks love to eat up bugs?"

It would soon be spring planting season again, and the local businesses were still refusing to sell anything to us. Only two of the main businessmen I shopped with refused to go along—Mr. Stapleton, who owned the Dixie dry goods store, and Mr. Jong, one of the Chinese grocers.

We had endured the boycott for almost four months before Mr. Robert Kennedy, the U.S. attorney general, Mr. John Doar, acting assistant attorney general, Mr. Frank M. Dunbaugh III, and other attorneys from the Civil Rights Division of the Justice Department finally made an effort to help us. In January 1961, they filed suit against the sheriff and eleven local businesses that had boycotted Rev. Atlas—the gin owners, the finance company, the grain elevator owners, the butane company, and the two feed and seed stores—all of whom were told to answer for what they had done.

Unfortunately, nature doesn't wait for the slow wheels of justice to turn. Much of Rev. Atlas's crop was ruined, and he had lost a lot of money. The soybeans had been standing in the fields since harvest time in November. By February, they were shelling in the fields, so he lost his whole soybean crop. He had only gotten ten bales of cotton ginned before the word of the boycott reached all the ginners. He had picked another thirteen bales that he had stored since fall in his barn and in two leaky old tenant houses he owned. Since he had run out of storage space, he had had to leave the rest in the fields. Altogether he lost about fifty acres of cotton yielding a bale and a half per acre. In total, he had lost over $5,000 in crop proceeds.

The Justice Department finally broke the boycott in February. Rather than have all the evidence brought out in court, the defendants agreed to settle out of court. None of them admitted to doing any wrong but agreed to gin Rev. Atlas's cotton, buy his soybeans at fair market value, and supply him some butane gas. They also agreed not to intimidate or threaten Rev. Atlas again about voting. But no one was made to pay Rev. Atlas for the crops that had been lost or for the low market price he got for his soybeans due to the crops being held so long. The national NAACP stepped in to help Rev. Atlas make some arrangements to meet his most pressing debts and ended up making him a small loan. But Rev. Atlas still suffered for years afterwards because he couldn't make up for the crops he had lost. Nature doesn't let you play catch-up. He was over $10,000 in debt and ended up having to mortgage his farm and his farm equipment and sell his cattle.

Though Atlas had to know that I was in sympathy with him, the stress of his situation brought out resentment and strained our relationship. For the same actions, Rev. Atlas had received the greater punishment. Nevertheless, he still remained steadfast in the fight.

Although concerns about retribution were at the forefront of everyone's minds, there were still some bold enough to carry on the fight. Besides, we figured they couldn't include too many black people in that retribution thing because there were a whole lot more of us than them, and certain stores needed our trade to stay in business.

Since Mr. Manning, the registrar of voters, had turned us away because he claimed he didn't know us, we decided in March 1961 to go back to his office with some people he definitely should know. That way, if we should ever get a case to court, he wouldn't be able to legitimately say that he needed identification from everyone.

One of the people we took was Mrs. Daisy Hadden. Mr. Manning delivered her mail and had talked to her on numerous occasions about postal matters. When Mrs. Hadden spoke to Mr. Manning about this, he said, "Well, Daisy, I pass your house and I leave your mail there, but that doesn't necessarily make me know you. I don't know any of you, nobody but . . . ," pointing at Frank Nervis, who lived near him and was a regular customer at his store, "I know him. I can talk to Frank, but I don't know whether he is eligible to register or not."

"Like I told you all before, if you get me two registered voters from your precinct, then I'll talk registration with you. Until then, you don't need to come back."

He seemed to be getting angry, and we didn't want to aggravate him, so we decided to go on out. As we left, he called Frank Nervis back in. As it turned out, it wasn't that he wanted to help his neighbor and customer get registered. He just wanted to pick him for information about how we had gotten to see the registration cards and who had given them to us.

Later I was talking to Benjamin Blockwood, a contractor who did a lot of work for Mr. Manning. "Since he knows you so well, you think he might let you register?" I asked him. "And even if he doesn't, we'll have more evidence to use against him in court."

"Well, it's worth a try," Blockwood said.

Mr. Blockwood went on over to the registrar's office and told Mr. Manning that he wanted to get registered and that he had picked Mr. Manning to be the registered voter who identified him. Mr. Manning told him, "I don't know a d—— thing about you."

Sheriff Gilbert must have heard Mr. Manning, as loud as he was talking, because he came over to investigate, with his hand on his gun.

"You best get out this courthouse if you don't want no trouble," he told Mr. Blockwood. His deputies came to stand behind him and back him up. So of course Mr. Blockwood had to leave after that.

So far, our testimony before the Civil Rights Commission seemed to have brought us only trouble instead of help, so we decided to try another approach. We decided to ask the Justice Department to take over the lawsuit we had filed against the registrar more than ten years before. We mailed our complaints to the Justice Department, and to our surprise it wasn't long at all before they sent some men down to talk to us. I guess that after the Atlas case they had just wrapped up and after getting to meet first-hand the fine people we dealt with in Lake Providence, they knew that if anyone needed help, we were the ones.

The men from the Justice Department arrived in an old engine-tapping jalopy. We thought the government must have fallen on some hard times for their agents to have to drive such clunkers, and we were wondering why they were dressed so funny since they were dressed all farmer-like. Later, we found out it was all a disguise so they could move about town without attracting so much attention. They went from house to house, interviewing each person who had attempted to register and vote. Then they went back to Washington and chose a group of us to support the next complaint.

Our new lawsuit was filed in April 1961 in the name of the United States vs. Cecil Manning of East Carroll Parish and the State of Louisiana. The suit asked the courts to throw out the requirement that we had to get two registered voters to identify us before we could get registered, because the requirement was discriminatory. The suit was filed under the names of Robert Kennedy, then attorney general, Burke Marshall, assistant attorney general, John Doar for the Justice Department, and T. Fitzhugh Wilson, U.S. attorney from Shreveport. The defendants were Cecil Manning, the East Carroll registrar of voters, and the state of Louisiana represented by Louisiana's attorney general, Jack Gremillion, and assistant attorney general, Harry Kron, along with the governor's special counselor and the district attorneys for the fourth and sixth districts.

The Justice Department issued a press release through the Associated Press at the same time it filed the suit. Before the Louisiana attorney general and Cecil Manning even knew what the suit said, newsmen were already pressing them for an official response. They were madder than snakes about being put on the spot like that.

They were also mad because a Kennedy was involved. Many southern whites seemed to despise the Kennedy brothers. The newspapers belittled them, and the cooks said white folks were always grumbling around the house about how the Kennedys were trying to destroy the southern way of life, especially Robert Kennedy with all his discrimination suits. They even talked about how somebody needed to take care of "that problem."

The black community heard about the suit through the traditional channel, by word of mouth. It was the only way to get information if you didn't get a black paper or read the *Monroe Morning World* because, as usual, the local Lake Providence paper was silent about the suit. But as the word got out that it was Mr. Manning who wouldn't register black people, blacks who had never tried to register but who shopped at Mr. Manning's store now stopped shopping there, if they could find transportation some place else. Mr. Manning suffered a big drop in his business.

The newspapers had always been a problem for us, because locally we only had the "colored news" section, which was pretty much limited to deaths, births, and church news. Some black people worked for whites, but because blacks rarely, if ever, expressed their real feelings or thoughts around white people, whites had no way to know or did not care to know what was on our minds. Because of uneven newspaper reporting and because so few white people knew black people on a personal basis, we couldn't quite determine how white people formed their opinions about us and the things we did. If they really knew us, would they support the same causes? We didn't know how to respond to or react to what people must have just made up in their heads about us.

Court was set for November 27, seven months from the date our suit was filed, and we were advised that we would all have to give depositions before the actual hearing took place. Mr. Manning's deposition was scheduled first, but when Mr. Dunbaugh and Mr. Sidney Young, the two young attorneys for the Justice Department, went to the registrar's office on June 26, they couldn't find Mr. Manning or his attorneys. Later they finally showed up, but they refused to permit the deposition to be taken.

At the beginning of August, during the peak Louisiana heat, I decided to take a trip out west and visit some of my many friends who had moved out there. I stayed in California almost a month, preaching at least twice a week and teaching the people from Los Angeles,

San Francisco, Oakland, and Berkeley about the struggle back home. Many people made contributions to help our cause. It was a good trip that gave me needed time away from the everyday hostilities of Lake Providence so that I could get mentally prepared for the upcoming trial.

Shortly after I returned from California, I received notice that we would have to give our depositions before the end of the month. They were scheduled for Thursday and Friday, September 21 and 22, 1961, but right before the deposition date, one of our leading witnesses and my closest friend, Rev. Mason, died. He was one of our primary witnesses because he was the only one who had been able to get a white witness to write a letter vouching for him, and he still had not been allowed to register.

His death hit me hard because he was the one person in the struggle I trusted most, and I needed real friends when facing this big lawsuit against the state. We always had to be careful about who we talked to because so many people wanted to stop what we were doing. I hadn't had many occasions for crying in my life, but I shed tears for the loss of my friend. I had lost my only confidant.

Rev. Mason's funeral was scheduled for Friday, the same day I was scheduled to give my deposition. Our lawyer requested that I be allowed to give my deposition on the first day of testimony so that I could attend and participate in the funeral service on Friday. They denied my request, but I just prayed about it, and after some argument they finally came around. This new schedule did not exactly fit in with the state's plan, which I figured was to wait and question me on the second day, using the testimony of others to try to trip me up.

Thursday morning, I came up to the courthouse with the rest of the people scheduled for the first day's testimony. We were taken upstairs and put in a couple of rooms where we were watched by the police on duty like criminals about to escape. Then one by one, Sheriff Gilbert would come in and take a person into the questioning room.

They didn't get to me until almost 1:30 that afternoon. I looked around the questioning room and observed that our side was a little outnumbered. All I saw were the two Justice Department attorneys, but it appeared that any local white person who wanted to come by was free to sit in on the questioning. I counted the people for the other side—seven in all. There was Mr. Thompson Clarke, the district attorney, and Mr. Kron, the assistant attorney general for the state of Louisiana. They were doing the questioning. And then there was Mr. Patrick from the police jury (a town city councilman) and Mr. Manning's attorney, Mr. Frank Voelker, Jr., standing against the wall staring as if his look could strike fear in somebody. Sheriff Gilbert also kept coming in and out, occasionally standing around with his hand on his pistol, as if he might have a mind to use it. Even the person we were making the charges against, Mr. Manning, was allowed to sit in and listen while we were interrogated. Judge Voelker even sat in on part of the depositions.

When Attorney Dunbaugh questioned why all the extra people were present, the district attorney acted insulted.

"What are you insinuating? Has anyone said or done anything that could be considered an act of intimidation or coercion toward any of the witnesses?"

When Mr. Dunbaugh tried to explain how their very presence would affect us, Mr. Clarke just cut him off. "Is it your position that these people," and he swept his hand around the room, "are such un–law-abiding people that they will create an atmosphere of fear toward these people who are witnesses?"

I wanted to tell him that that was exactly our position, but he was already busy explaining away their presence. He claimed that the sheriff was just there to maintain order and that Judge Voelker had come to get a cup of coffee and had stayed a little while.

They started out calm and quiet, asking me general questions. Then they started to ask questions about the lawsuit we had filed against Mrs. Beard. Mr. Kron as much as called me stupid for paying an attorney so much money and never really knowing the outcome of the lawsuit. I told them that I thought Mr. Berry had long since earned that $300. They made it seem like I couldn't be that interested in voting if I hadn't kept up with what was happening with the lawsuit any better than I had.

Then they said I was teaching the people wrong.

"Were you teaching your people they had the right to vote, regardless of the other requirements of good character?" Mr. Kron asked.

"Well, I didn't think all the Negroes in East Carroll had bad character. I thought somebody's character would be good enough to register and vote, based on who I see around here getting registered."

So they changed the subject and started asking me questions about the makeup of the government and the function of the local officials.

"Since you seem to understand these functions so well, do you think a person should be qualified that don't understand these functions?

Mr. Dunbaugh objected. "You are asking him for a legal opinion. I don't understand the purpose."

"Oh, this is the man who is known throughout the United States in teaching people they have the right to register," Mr. Kron said sarcastically. "And we want to know what his understanding is," he snapped back at Mr. Dunbaugh.

The whole mood of the questioning was starting to shift. He was leaning in, too close up in my face. "Would you answer that question, please?" His voice had taken on an icy edge.

I was starting to feel the pressure. My mind was racing. "I . . . I got crossed up, I forgot the question," I managed to stammer out.

"Then I'll repeat the question," Mr. Kron said. "Under a republican form of government, you understand that there are three divisions of that government, legislative. . . ?"

"Yes."

". . . judicial and administrative. Now then my question is if a person applies to register and does not understand the functions of these divisions, would you think he was qualified to be a registered voter?"

My mind searched frantically for a good answer I could give that would be the truth but not mess up the case. What was the motive behind the question? They weren't giving me enough time to think before they fired the next question at me. All I could think of was that white people qualified who didn't know these things. I had to come up with an answer.

"Well, I don't—I don't think these requirements ought to apply to just one group of people. I think they ought to apply to all of the people."

I knew he could hear it in my voice. I was bending under the pressure, and I could tell he knew it. He started off slowly. "So I ask you again, as an ordained minister of the gospel, you believe that two wrongs should make a right?"

What does he mean, two wrongs make a right? What is he talking about? How do I answer this? "Well, I don't believe two wrongs should make a right, and I believe . . . my personal opinion, I believe . . ." I was stammering again because I couldn't think of anything to say to that crazy question.

Mr. Dunbaugh interrupted with an objection that gave me about five whole seconds to collect my thoughts. Mr. Kron didn't even acknowledge Mr. Dunbaugh. He just kept going like Mr. Dunbaugh hadn't said a word.

"So in order to accomplish your purpose, you are willing to teach your people, and you have already testified that you taught your people, that just by their being citizens and by their answering the questions on the application cards correctly, that they would be qualified to vote, when you knew that that was not the only requirement for the privilege of registering to vote. Is that true?"

"I wouldn't say that's true."

"You did that purely and simply because some other people within your knowledge had registered, who had not met those qualifications, is that not correct?"

I decided I wouldn't fight them anymore. I'd just give in.

"Well, I . . . if you want to say it's correct, I'll let it —"

"I'm not trying to say it's correct, I'm asking you whether it is correct!" Mr. Kron was extremely agitated now.

"But I don't want you to get in mind that I'm trying to teach the people wrong," I tried to explain.

"I'm asking you whether you did or not!" He slammed his hand on the table.

"I've tried to teach the people that they should register and vote."

"Well then why didn't you go forward in your teachings and tell them of the other provisions and requirements of the registration law of the State of Louisiana which they would have to fulfill?"

Mr. Dunbaugh objected again and he and Mr. Kron began to argue back and forth about whether I should be asked these kinds of questions. In the end, Mr. Kron said he accepted Mr. Dunbaugh's objections, but he was going to ask the questions anyway. So he asked the question again and I decided to answer the question honestly, regardless of the consequences.

"Well, I've never been able to find out all of the requirements that belongs to a Negro. That's what we've been working at over the years, trying to find out what were the requirements for us, and what we had to do different from the rest of the people."

And so we went back and forth for almost fifteen minutes, Mr. Kron asking question after question about what I told the people and what I should have known since I supposedly kept up with the law and what our attorney, Mr. Berry, should have told me about the registration laws. He tried to make me admit that I had misled the people, like there was nothing the Negro could do to ever be qualified. And the more he badgered, the more defiant I became because I realized he wasn't getting what he wanted or he would have given up. So I dug in my heels, and the last thing I told him was that I thought we had a right to register, and I wanted to know who should determine that right. Finally, Mr. Kron gave in and said, "That's all." An hour and a half of interrogation and I left the courthouse not sure what to think.

The depositions continued into the next day. Afterwards, we met secretly to see what kinds of questions had been asked. Most of the questions seemed to be directed toward finding out who was really leading the push for registering and how involved the NAACP was in the whole matter, or whether the government was pushing us up to file this suit. They wanted to know where everyone worked. Did they work for the school system, or were they on welfare—looking for where they might be able to exert a little economic pressure. They asked where we were meeting and how often. They wanted to know the name of every Justice Department agent we had spoken to. They apparently had decided that I was the leader, since several people said they referred to me as the "brains of the outfit." Of course, since they called me "an instigator" to my face when they questioned me, I was pretty clear where I stood with them.

We had from the end of September until November 27 to prepare for court. On the day of the hearing, a good-sized group of us rode over to the U.S. Courthouse in Monroe. United States District Judge Ben C. Dawkins, Jr., was presiding and would be responsible for making a final decision on the voting issue.

Court was called to order, and all the witnesses were sworn in and sent out of the courtroom. Unfortunately, I had been demoted to the position of spectator. The government had decided not to use me as a witness because of the hard line they had taken with me during the depositions. They felt they couldn't risk putting me on the stand.

The federal government took testimonies all the first day of the hearing. The Justice Department attorneys, Mr. Frank Dunbaugh and Mr. David Norman, had only one purpose, and that was to use the witnesses to show that Mr. Manning required different levels of proof of whites than he required of blacks.

Mr. Hadden, a farmer, Mrs. Caroline Wilson, who owned a lot of residential rental property, and Rev. Atlas took the stand and told about the times they had tried to register. Rev. Atlas testified that he had asked whites with whom he had done business all his life to identify him and they wouldn't.

Then the government called to the stand its first white witness, Robert Earl Hicks, a sharecropper from the farming community of Elmwood. Mr. Hicks testified that he and Mr. Manning did not know each other and he had just walked in and had been given a card without having to show any identification.

Jack Gremillion, the Louisiana attorney general, had apparently confused the Hicks fellow with someone else because during cross-examination, he started asking him questions about his parents and where he worked that didn't seem to make any sense at all to the Hicks fellow.

Mr. Gremillion continued his questioning. "Isn't it a fact you used to drive a truck in Lake Providence?"

"No sir, I didn't drive a truck in Lake Providence." He frowned in confusion. "I drove one on the farm for my boss."

"Is your farm close to Mr. Manning's place?"

"No, sir, I don't know where he lives." Of course anyone from the area would have known that Elwood was southwest of Lake Providence, nowhere near Mr. Manning's place.

"Why do you say Mr. Manning doesn't know you."

"I don't know him. It was the first time I'd ever seen him. He might know me, but I don't know him."

"Do you deny Mr. Manning knows your mother and father and you, and he knew you prior to the time you came to the court house to register?"

As it turned out, the man's mother had left him when he was born. His grandfather had raised him. I wondered how Mr. Manning was supposed to know his mother when the witness didn't even know anything about his own mother. But even after all that came out, Jack Gremillion was determined to make the fellow change his story. He kept pressing with more questions, trying to make the Hicks fellow say that Mr. Manning could have known him.

He asked again, "Can you deny Mr. Manning knew you and knew both your mother and father at the time you came to register?"

"As far as my knowledge, I don't think he knows me." The fellow hesitated. "Well, I don't know. It is possible people could know me and I don't know them."

Mr. Gremillion seemed satisfied that he had finally gotten the fellow to agree with his premise. He smiled and said, "That's exactly what I am getting at."

The next witness up was another white person who had been allowed to register without identification. Then Mr. Dunbaugh called Rev. Virgil and Otis Blockwood (whom Mr. Manning really did know when it was convenient) and finally a white woman, a Mrs. Brzozowske.

I had thought that the attorneys for the other side sounded confused before, but they seemed even more confused now. After Mrs. Brzozowske told the court what had happened when she and her husband went to register, Mr. Gremillion started asking her questions about Mr. Manning's mother. I assume this was to prove that Mr. Manning knew the lady.

"I understand Mrs. Manning, Mr. Manning's mother, has done some baby-sitting at your house or has been to your home."

The lady looked at him funny. "No sir, she hasn't."

"Do you know his mother?"

"No sir, I sure don't."

It turned out that her children were already grown, so they changed their story from baby-sitting to claiming that Mrs. Manning had been to the lady's house to sit with someone sick. When they couldn't pull that story off either, they got her to admit that it was possible that Mr. Manning had known her and her husband through a mutual acquaintance at the Tennessee Gas Company. I thought it was strange that they expected me to know so much about the law of Louisiana, and here they were the highest attorneys in the state and didn't seem to know to check out the witnesses ahead of time.

A pattern was clearly established as black witness after witness took the stand to tell how they had asked lifelong white acquaintances to identify them and how all of them had refused. But I believe the turning point for us was when Mrs. Hadden took the stand.

Mrs. Hadden was sworn in and Mr. Dunbaugh began his questions. "What happened when you went to try to register?"

Mrs. Hadden started off slowly. She had false teeth both top and bottom and always talked with her teeth clinched close together as though she was afraid they might fall out.

"Well, we went in and Mr. Manning was sitting at his desk. Mr. Charlie Leach was there too, sitting at Mr. Manning's desk filling out a registration blank."

"Is Mr. Leach a white man or Negro?"

"He is a white man who runs a grocery and a dry goods store in Lake Providence. When we went in, Mr. Manning asked us what we wanted and we told him that we came to register to vote. He told us just like he told us before, 'I don't know you. I don't know you all.' My husband tried to show him his driver's license but Mr. Manning said 'I can't use that for identification.' So my husband turned to Mr. Leach and said, 'Mr. Charlie, you know me. You can identify me. We been dealing with you two or three years.' When my husband said that, Mr. Charlie jumped up and like to ran over me getting out of there. He ran outside without saying a word."

"Did you say anything to Mr. Manning yourself?"

"Yes sir. I told him, 'Mr. Manning, you know me.' I said, 'I bought money orders from you. I met you down at the road and you filled out the forms for me. I bought stamps from you. I gave you letters to mail.' And he said, 'I know where you live and I put mail in your box. I put mail there today.' I told him, 'I know you did. I saw you.' And yet he said he didn't know me after selling me money orders and different things. He said, 'I still don't know you.'" Her head was shaking from side to side and I could see Mrs. Hadden was getting herself all worked up.

Attorney Dunbaugh showed copies of money orders Mrs. Hadden had bought through the years from Mr. Manning. Mr. Manning had filled them out for Mrs. Hadden and had written her name on them. It was obvious that he knew her from the evidence presented.

Mr. Gremillion rose and tried to tie Mrs. Hadden up under cross-examination, but he couldn't because Mrs. Hadden was a tough witness and wasn't afraid of anybody. Just to let Jack Gremillion know that she wasn't admitting to anything, no matter how much he tried to tie up her words, as she was leaving the witness stand, she looked Mr. Gremillion dead in the face, wagging her finger toward Mr. Manning and shaking her head, "He did know me, regardless of what he says."

It was late by the time Mrs. Hadden finished, so the judge dismissed court until in the next morning when the state would present its witnesses. I rushed home because it was my daughter Sharolyn's thirteenth birthday, and at our house, birthdays were big events. The birthday person always got their favorite ice cream and cake and a present. I wasn't very good at picking presents, so I would usually give some money to my wife or one of the children and tell them to pick a gift. After I picked enough bad presents for my wife (like stuff for the house), I started letting the children do the picking all the time. Of course, they liked picking out presents for me so that they could get me to try something new—like the time they bought me a blue shirt and made me wear it when I had worn white shirts and a tie whenever I left the house, pretty much all my adult life. After I got so many compliments, I decided to get some other colors too. So birthdays were always fun. It was late when I finally got home, but they had saved the ice cream and cake celebration until I could get there.

I was up early the next morning for the drive back to Monroe to hear the state present its witnesses. When they got to Mr. Manning and asked him about being able to identify any of us by name, he answered, "They were just some more Negroes to me."

They asked him why blacks had to be identified by two individuals when whites only had to be identified by one or none. His explanation was that based on his past experience and knowledge of the Negro race, that one Negro was not reliable to identify another Negro without mistake.

I was amazed. Negroes couldn't accurately identify each other when we lived in the same neighborhoods and went to the same schools and churches in a small town, but white people, who we rarely associated with and who didn't bother to even know more than our first names when we were around, were supposed to be better at identifying us. Amazing indeed.

Christmas, my birthday, spring planting, our big annual Easter play, and school closing had all come and gone before Judge Dawkins issued his ruling at the end of May. But when the ruling finally came, it was a day of great rejoicing. Judge Dawkins ruled that there had been a pattern of racial discrimination because Mr. Manning refused to let blacks register unless two white voters identified them. Of the almost 3,000 white registered voters, only fifteen had been required to bring a registered voter to identify them, and no white person had ever been kept from registering because of insufficient identification.

By law, Mr. Manning should have allowed us to use other forms of identification such as our driver's licenses, homestead exemption certificates, hunting licenses, or deeds to our houses. The court papers said that to require us to produce two registered voters was to make black people dependent on the white community for permission to apply, a permission no black person had been able to obtain for forty years. The court ruled that if it did not restrain the defendants, they would continue to engage in the same discriminatory practices.

The court ordered Mr. Manning to file a monthly report to the federal clerk of court listing whom he registered and the names and races of everyone he rejected. And if Mr. Manning rejected our applications, under the Civil Rights Act, we could apply directly to the court for a hearing to determine if we were wrongfully denied and they would have to hear our case within ten days. The registrar was even ordered to pay $1,300 in court proceeding costs, although we figured he was probably acting under the direction and orders of the Louisiana Sovereignty Committee. The court papers said that Mr. Manning seemed to "know" almost all white people but he did not even "know" blacks with whom he had regular contact.

We had a planning meeting that Saturday night, the day after we got word of the ruling. All the next week, we went by the registrar's office, but the door was always locked. On Monday, we had even called Benjamin Blockwood to inquire about Mr. Manning's whereabouts. Blockwood, a black contractor whose specialty was swim piers, boat docks, and seawalls, was building a boathouse on the lake out back of Mr. Manning's house. He told us that Mr. Manning was right at home cutting grass. Manning had even helped him drive in the posts for the boathouse.

On Tuesday afternoon, my friend Eric Armstrong decided to call up to Mr. Manning's store and ask when the office would be open again. Mr. Manning happened to be there at the time but said that the office was closed for the time being and that Eric should check back later in the week.

By Saturday, we had concluded that Mr. Manning wasn't going to reopen the registrar's office, but with election day being so close, we figured he had to be registering people somewhere. There was a law requiring all registered voters to re-register every four years, and if he didn't open the office some time, the majority of the white people wouldn't even be qualified to vote in the upcoming primaries.

So we decided we would just try to catch him in the office. We met every few days to discuss who had been by the registrar's office and what had happened when they went. Every day, I would drive by the front of the courthouse to see if I saw Mr. Manning's little car and then drive around the corner to where I could see through Mr. Manning's double windows on the north side.

The office was rather small and with the blinds up, you could practically see his entire office from the street. Sometimes I'd just drive by slowly, and other times I would sit for a few minutes to see whether anyone would stir inside, whether anyone would come in or out of the registrar's office. Others in our group continued to drop by the office at different times throughout the week, but the door was always locked.

So this is how it went until Mr. Manning officially resigned his position on June 14, 1962, just thirteen days after the ruling. He said he wasn't being paid enough to subject himself to embarrassment and potentially being sent to jail because he didn't understand the words in the court decree or couldn't interpret the law to the federal government's satisfaction. So we had won the court ruling, but we still couldn't vote because there was no registrar available to register us.

# FIFTEEN

# A Cross for Every Voter

After Mr. Manning resigned, the Justice Department began working on how to get us registered without a registrar. The primaries were coming up in little over a month, and it seemed certain we wouldn't get registered in time to vote. I told the men from the Justice Department I was going down to New Orleans for a week but to call Eric Armstrong if they needed anything while I was gone.

The break came while I was still in New Orleans. The Justice Department advised Eric that anyone who wanted to register could get a chance just by sending a letter to the U.S. Clerk of Court in Shreveport within the next three days. The letters had to tell why we thought we were qualified and it had to include a statement that we had been denied the right to vote because the registrar's office was closed. So Eric got as many letters as he could get in two days and drove them over to Shreveport, about 150 miles west of Lake Providence.

By the time I got back home, it was already too late for me to submit my paperwork. I called one of the Justice Department lawyers about it and he said, "That's a shame. You've been in this fight a long time, but the other folks are going to get registered to vote before you."

I was so disappointed, but God worked it out that I got a chance too. Judge Dawkins decided to give us ten more days to file, so I was able to get my request over to Shreveport after all.

This was our big break, but since no one had ever gotten past the application stage of registering, we needed a crash course in voter registration. The NAACP sent a Mr. John Brooks, voter registration director out of Richmond, Virginia, to help us organize a program. In ten days, with the assistance of three young people, Erma and Inez Millikin and Amy Jefferson, we taught everybody who showed up for class how to pronounce and write all the words in the preamble, how to properly fill out the applications, and how to answer the constitutional questions correctly (as best we could interpret them ourselves).

We canvassed the community to try to get more people to sign up before the deadline, but as usual, we ran into the same scared Negroes. "Scott, now you know I can't get involved in no voting. You know I'll lose my job." "Mr. Charlie owns the plantation I live on and he'll put me off the place if I get involved." "Rev, I know you been hearing about all those Freedom Riders getting ambushed and beaten all across the South and about those men getting lynched over in Mississippi. Where the government going to be when they stringing us up a tree? You tell me that!"

Sometimes, it was "What you want to vote for? White folks treat us pretty good around here. At least they not killing nobody." Farmers would say, "I don't want to end up like Atlas."

I tried to make them see that they had to stand up some time. Somebody had to stand up or our children would have to suffer the same humiliations we did. I wondered how they thought it was better for blacks folk to die a little each day and gain nothing, than to stand up and possibly die for a change.

But I knew it was hard for the people when the bad stories kept coming all of 1962. There were stories like the bombing of Dr. Simpkins's home over in Shreveport, or down in New Orleans where the little eleven-year-old girl had been killed by a group of young white men while she was waiting at the bus stop, or the soldier, a military policeman, on the Greyhound bus traveling through Mississippi who refused to move to back of the bus and when the driver called the policemen, the policeman came and shot the soldier in the heart.

But I couldn't let the people or the stories discourage me, because we were too close to turn back. We kept talking to the people who expressed some interest and tried to avoid the known snitches who were trying to gather information for our opponents. By the deadline, we had turned in papers to the courts for seventy-eight people. It wasn't a great showing, but we could have done a lot worse in the atmosphere of fear that was now moving across the South.

About a week and a half after we sent in our paperwork, we received registered letters telling us we had to come back over to Monroe for a hearing on our applications. We didn't get much notice because the hearing was scheduled for Thursday, July 12, 1962, which was just two days away and only one day before the registration books were to close for the July 28 elections.

The morning of the hearing, my wife and I were both up early, partially because of excitement and anticipation, but also because we had to drive the seventy-five or so miles to Monroe and we didn't want to be late for the 10:30 hearing. My wife, who always got up ahead of the rest of the family to get the wood fire going, already had a batch of biscuits coming out of the stove by the time I came through on my way outside. I wandered aimlessly through my outside chores, my mind far away. As usual, all my chickens came running, following me around the yard clucking as I got my pan and scooped up their corn. My wife came out and headed over by the Center building to milk our cow, Daisy Mae. It was still early and I could already tell that it was going to be a repeat of most of the summer days of 1962, a real scorcher.

About 8:30, we met up with some of the others who were going to try to get qualified, and we got on our way. We traveled the back roads past miles and miles of fields of cotton stalks that formed perfectly straight lines as far as the eye could see. The farmers hadn't left a single tree, just an occasional dilapidated house or barn, a reminder of a useful life long since ended. Periodically we passed a tractor, puttering down the highway at the high speed of ten miles per hour. I watched a crop duster swoop down over a field, skimming along close to the tops of the cotton plants, so close it seemed it was riding on the tops of the stalks. The long cloud of poison flowed out, and the foul odor poured into the car through the rolled-down windows.

We traveled on through Epps to Rayville past rows of shotgun houses called that because they only had three rooms in a row, front to back. You could shoot through the front door and the bullet could past through the middle door opening and straight out the back door. We turned onto Highway 80, the main east-west highway across the top of the state, leading into Monroe. Every now and then, I'd see a gang of field hands off in the distance, their straw sun hats bobbing down the rows as they tried to make haste and chop the weeds out of the cotton before the hot July sun got too high up over head—adults trying to make that $3 a day to put some food on the table and children trying to save money for school clothes and shoes. They reminded me of the possibilities before us and the trials that lay behind us. For so long, picking and chopping cotton had been almost our only choice for work, but here today, Negroes had a chance to make a change—yet how many of them had chosen the field that morning rather than the trip to Monroe and full citizenship?

The cameras flashed and microphones were shoved in our faces as we pressed our way through the crowd of news people gathered outside the Post Office building, where court was being held. Interest in the proceedings was high because the federal government had never gotten involved in state voting affairs before. If they registered us today, we would be the first people ever registered to vote by someone who was not a state official.

We went on in to join the others who had already arrived and were engaged in nervous conversation about the number of news people outside and how they were making such a big to-do over the whole thing. I looked around to see who was there and took a mental tally of who must have lost their nerve and stayed at home.

A unique group had assembled that morning for that momentous occasion. Some could barely read and write, and others had bachelor's and master's degrees. We had the old—one man was eighty-six— and we had a few younger ones. But most of us were well over fifty; the younger folks, especially the ones with young children, seemed too worried about losing jobs or they were too far in debt to speak too strongly about much of anything. We had people from many walks of life, but mostly our group was made up of people who owned their own farms, the ministers, and the people who owned their own businesses. Different as we were, though, we all had something in common that day—a common cause and a shared sense of nervous anticipation.

As it got closer and closer to court time, I started to get concerned. There were supposed to be seventy-eight people there, but I was sure I wasn't seeing nearly that many. So I started to count. I was at about forty when I was interrupted by a loud voice.

"All rise please. The United States Court, Western District, is now in session, the Honorable Judge Edwin Hunter presiding."

Judge Hunter entered and took his place in his tall leather chair high up where he could look out over his nervous subjects. Judge Hunter had been called in from Lake Charles, which is in south Louisiana. Our original judge, Ben Dawkins, was working a case over in Jacksonville, Florida, and couldn't get back in time to give us a hearing within ten days of our application, as required by the new Civil Rights laws.

Judge Hunter was obviously not pleased to have the honor of registering us. His first comments got me concerned.

"No one more than me wishes Mr. Manning had not resigned. I have never registered anybody before, and I just learned last week I had to do this."

I thought about what Judge Hunter was saying. This was no easy position for a southern white man to find himself in, since so many whites did not want us registered. But he was a federal judge, and the Justice Department was demanding that he uphold the law. I wondered if he could be fair to us and if he were fair, what would they do to a traitor to the southern cause? I figured they didn't have the nerve to lynch a federal judge, but they would surely think of something to make him pay.

Judge Hunter looked down at the papers he had in front of him and started explaining the procedure we would have to follow. He said that the state had the right to require a certain morality and intelligence from its voters, so we would have to fill out the Louisiana application blanks and demonstrate our ability to read and write by reading and writing from dictation any portion of the preamble to the constitution they selected. I looked around the room and I knew that some would not be able to pass. Reading words like "tranquillity" and "posterity" was hard enough for people who only had elementary school training, so I knew that they wouldn't all be able to spell the words correctly.

"The Louisiana law also requires that an applicant be able to understand and give a reasonable interpretation to any section of the Constitution read to him by a registrar." Judge Hunter leaned back in his chair and started to laugh. "Now if the Supreme Court Justices can disagree five to four on what the Constitution means, it would seem awfully hard for an ordinary citizen to tell what it means."

I smiled to myself as I remembered something my NAACP friend Mr. Byrd had said about the questions that they asked black people when they tried to register. "It's just like asking how many bubbles in a bar of soap or how many hairs on a hog's back. You can never come up with the right answer."

The judge had decided that he would not ask for a constitutional interpretation but would give us a citizenship test he had prepared himself. He did mention that he had prepared the test after consultation with someone from the Sovereignty Commission, the group fighting to keep segregation in Louisiana.

I glanced at my pocket watch. Judge Hunter had already been talking for about twenty minutes and the more things he said we had to do to register, the more anxious some people became. Some of them had signed up right before the deadline and had never even filled out a registration application. They would have a hard time passing.

Judge Hunter continued, "I am going to divide you into three groups. Mrs. McCarthy, my secretary, is in charge of the first group."

He went on to explain how qualified she was for getting us registered because she was a college graduate and had been an officer in the navy. He put his law clerk, Mr. Clements, over the second group and Mr. Hayes, his probation officer, over the third group.

He did a quick roll call down the listing of seventy-eight names, with those of us present responding quickly as our names were called. He dismissed twenty-five applications because the people hadn't shown up for the hearing, and proceeded to divide the remaining fifty-three of us into the three groups.

Mrs. McCarthy was assigned the room directly across the hall from the courtroom. As the judge began to call the first eighteen names in alphabetical order, each person called went up front and picked up their folders and filed across the hall. The next group was sent upstairs to the Civil Service examining room.

Then it was time. After almost twenty years of trying to register to vote, it was finally my turn. The judge rolled out the names, "Mrs. Aleazar M. Nash, Walter Henry Nash, Frank Nervis, Sr., Nancy Ruth Nervis . . ."

As their names were called, they went to pick up their folders and returned to their seats. I looked around the courtroom anxiously, giving a quick scan of the people without folders.

"Will he call the Scotts next?" I thought.

The judge continued, "John Newson, Watson Sanders, Mrs. Alease J. Scott."

I let my breath out. Finally my turn.

"John Henry Scott," the judge called.

I went up to pick up my folder, as happy as any man could possibly be. I didn't even hear the remaining names as my mind whirled with thoughts of what we had gone through to get to this place, to this moment in time.

It was 11:25 A.M. when we finally made our way up the winding stairs with Mr. Clements and entered the grand jury room to begin the process we had been denied for so long.

We started with our application cards, which many of us could complete without reading the questions. After all, we had had many years of practice. The card had the same questions that each of us had to answer in the affirmative or be disqualified—I have not been convicted of a felony. I have not been convicted of more than one misdemeanor other than traffic or game law violation within the last five years. I have not lived in "common law" marriage within the last five years. I have not acknowledged myself as the father of an illegitimate child within the last five years. These last two were the latest Louisiana "moral" rules added by the segregationists. They said these two rules, living common-law and having illegitimate children, would give registrars more ways to keep "coloreds" off the rolls.

The people who hadn't seen the cards before were struggling with some of the questions. Quite a few people in our group were around seventy years old, which meant they had been born not very long after slavery. Some had very little formal schooling. A couple of people just couldn't see too well because the print on the card was so small. Others didn't know how to figure out their age down to the number of months and days. This card was the first step and they needed to fill the entire card out correctly.

Even after thirty minutes, some of them were still sitting staring at their cards as if somehow the rest of the information would come to them through a vision. I felt bad because I knew that everyone who signed up really wanted to get the chance to register.

About that time, Judge Hunter came in to see how many had finished. He told the ones still struggling that he would give them until 12:15, forty-five minutes total, and if they couldn't complete the forms, just tell Mr. Clements and they could reapply on another day.

Those of us who had completed our forms were taken into another room where they dictated the preamble to us. Then we were given a citizenship test that consisted of twelve multiple-choice questions on the constitution and the government. We had to answer eight correctly in order to pass.

The questions were hard for some people, since they related to running a government they had never participated in and they hadn't had to use any of this kind of information since they had been in school many decades before. There were questions such as the purpose of the legislative branch or how many justices sat on the Supreme Court, and whether the president was elected by direct vote.

After we had finished everything, the judge and his assistants took our cards, our test papers, and our dictation of the preamble and they went out to grade them. We were told to reassemble in the courtroom while they determined who had passed.

By the time we got to the courtroom, all the other groups were already there. We tried to carry on normal conversations, although we were as nervous as an accused man waiting on a verdict.

After what seemed like an eternity, the judge finally came in with our results. He carried with him several stacks of papers bound together. When he was seated, he picked up the first stack.

"I have four people here that made perfect scores on the first part of the registration process—cards were filled out completely with no mistakes, all twelve questions on the citizenship test were answered correctly, and the preamble was correctly transcribed."

"The first person is Mrs. Alease Juanita Scott." My wife's name was the first one called out as qualified, and I was so proud of her. She had not only stuck by my side all these years, but had actively participated in all my causes and projects. She had taken an active role in the church as Sunday School and Baptist Training Union teacher, and she directed all our church plays. Most men in the fight couldn't say that their wives had done so much to make sure they were successful, so I was grateful to have her.

Next they called Henry O. Simmons, Eric Armstrong, and Mrs. Rosa P. Blockwood, our home extension agent. Both Mr. Simmons and Mrs. Blockwood had master's degrees from Columbia University and were the only two educators bold enough to participate. Then he called my name, saying I had pretty-near a perfect score, except for my bad handwriting, which of course was entirely true. My handwriting was pretty bad. That's why I got my wife to write up all my reports and letters. Her writing was as good as mine was bad.

After calling out the perfect scores, Judge Hunter called the names of those who failed, relieving them from the anxiety of waiting. And then he called those of us with the perfect scores to come up front to read the preamble to prove we could read. The ones with the questionable scores had to go into the judge's chambers, where he gave some of them a second chance to fill their cards out correctly if they hadn't missed more than four questions on the citizenship test. He really tried to be lenient on the oldest applicant, Mr. Baggett, who was eighty-six and couldn't see too well. He gave Mr. Baggett a second chance to fill out his card, and he still didn't get it completely right. Mr. Baggett was greatly disappointed. He had lived all his life wanting a chance to vote, and he didn't know if he'd live long enough to get another chance.

He reached out his hand and the judge asked him, "What do you want?"

"One more card, Judge, one more time," he pleaded.

Although Judge Hunter whined and complained throughout the day about the job he had to do, he turned out to be a decent kind of fellow after all. I think we weren't at all what he expected. I think he might have been a little impressed by our zeal, our unwillingness to give up after so many years of rejection. I believe he was surprised that people from this small rural town in Louisiana could be educated, aware, and articulate; that in spite of our exclusion from political and real economic power, we were indeed more capable than many of our white counterparts who had been allowed to register a long time ago. Some people in our group had businesses and farms and decent homes and cars, but many of us didn't have much. I still lived in a four-room house with a potbellied wood stove in the living room, with no running water or indoor plumbing. But yet we were capable of creating such a stir that the attorney general of the United States of America would speak for us when we were powerless to speak for ourselves. Judge Hunter probably didn't understand how a man who had found favor with God would be blessed in the midst of his enemies, by his enemies.

My wife was the first one to be certified qualified to vote—the first black to be certified in East Carroll Parish since 1922. I was second to be called. July 12, 1962 was a tremendous day for some of us and an equally disappointing day for others. Of the seventy-eight of us who applied, at the end of the day, twenty-eight had qualified.

Have you ever had a day that was so good that it made your whole life living worthwhile? That was how I felt that day. It was the culmination of over twenty years of trying to register, twenty years of obstacles placed in our way—all the injustices we had to suffer because we had no voice, no say-so on the laws that controlled our lives.

We were so excited that we forgot where we were. People were hugging and slapping one another on the back and congratulating each other. We headed back home, everybody in our car laughing and talking about who we were going to vote for and how crazy certain white people, like the sheriff, might be acting over what had happened today.

We were acting like we had won the war, when the enemy hadn't even surrendered yet and had no intentions of surrendering. Before the week was even up, our right to vote was already being challenged. Judge Voelker, Sr., on behalf of the state of Louisiana, issued some kind of restraining order, claiming it wasn't legal for the federal government to come into a state and register people, regardless of what the 1960 Civil Rights Act said. Besides, they weren't sure the act was even constitutional.

They accused Judge Hunter of overstepping his boundaries. Besides that, they claimed they could provide reasons why all twenty-eight of us should be disqualified—there was no real proof we had gone by the registration office, we hadn't lived in a precinct long enough, there was no real proof that the office was closed all hours prior to Mr. Manning's resignation, the judge helped us fill out our forms—and the list went on and on. They blocked us from getting our final registration certificates.

A hearing was called for less than two weeks later, and all of us who had qualified in Monroe had to travel to Shreveport to appear before Judge Hunter again. Court was to convene fairly late, starting at 3:30 that Monday afternoon. Actually they were to take testimony on two separate issues—whether we all met the qualifications to vote and whether we had actually been deprived of our right to vote by no one being in the registrar's office to register us. A three-judge panel had been assigned to decide the latter issue.

When we arrived at court that afternoon, quite a few people from Lake Providence were already there. Judge Hunter came out and took his place, looking aggravated before he even started the proceeding. He started court in a mood. This was a very big case being closely watched by the national media and attorneys across the South. A lot of power was at stake, and neither side wanted to be shown in a bad light.

The state was challenging Judge Hunter's actions in Monroe, and this afternoon, Judge Hunter's patience with the state attorneys was short, a fact that seemed to have no effect on the state attorney general's behavior. Mr. Gremillion's disposition had certainly not improved since our last meeting, and he took exception to almost everything Judge Hunter said. He disrespected us so much that he wouldn't stand up like an attorney was supposed to do when he questioned a witness. After a while, Judge Hunter asked him, "General, have you recovered from all your war wounds?"

Mr. Gremillion shot him a strange look.

"I know you got shot up quite a bit, so if you can't stand up too long, you can sit down, otherwise, you should stand up at the podium."

That comment finished off whatever little niceness might have existed between the two men.

Mr. Gremillion didn't want to deal with the issue of whether or not we were qualified. He argued with the judge that we hadn't even tried to register.

"That office has been open on most Wednesdays and Fridays, just like before the order, except when Mr. Manning was under the weather." He glanced in our direction. "So what could be their excuse?"

Mr. Gremillion and Judge Hunter argued back and forth for almost twenty minutes until Judge Hunter finally told Mr. Gremillion, in an annoyed voice, "I would say, General Gremillion, that the situation is that they *could* have registered had there *been* a registrar."

He leaned forward in his chair, his voice growing stern with agitation. "The court in its order previously stated that these people are intelligent people, two of them have master's degrees from Columbia University, and they should not be required to do a vain and useless thing. They know what's going on, and if they read in the paper that the registrar's office is closed, I don't think the law would require them to go to a closed office!"

So Mr. Gremillion gave up the argument as to whether we had tried to register and started arguing whether the office being closed constituted a deprivation of our right to vote. Finally the judge decided that he would just stop everything and settle the issue of what happened in June before he would even hear testimony on whether we were qualified to vote. "I'll stay here all night if we have to because we are going to resolve this once and for all."

The Justice Department called several white witnesses who had registered since June 1, some who had made special arrangements for Mr. Manning to come down and open the office so they could register. Then they called some of the black people who had attempted to see the registrar, with their principal witness being Mr. Benjamin Blockwood. It was his testimony that refuted the claims of the state and got the locals hot mad. The state had claimed that one of the reasons the office had been closed was that Mr. Manning had been laid up, flat on his back. He was supposed to be suffering from the discomfort of a crushed hip, an injury he had sustained years back in World War II when he had bailed out of a plane being shot down.

"What sort of work were you doing?" Mr. Dunbaugh, the Justice Department attorney asked Mr. Blockwood.

"I was working for Mr. Manning."

"Where were you working?"

"In the lake right behind his house. I was building a boat house for him at the time."

"Did you ever see Mr. Manning up and around his house?"

"Sure did. He was mowing his yard. Where he lives up to his store, there's a long point there with close to a quarter acre of land in there."

"What sort of mower was he using?"

"A big mower, big as they make."

When Mr. Gremillion cross-examined Mr. Blockwood, he didn't ask him one question about what Mr. Manning was doing when he was supposed to be laid up. His comments were mostly meant to discredit the witness. He shot questions at Mr. Blockwood until he got himself all worked up. At one point, he slammed his hand down on the table with anger.

"You can just stop that now," Judge Hunter warned, "because if these folks could be scared off, they would have been scared off by now."

After being chastised, Mr. Gremillion switched to asking irrelevant questions. When Mr. Dunbaugh objected, Mr. Gremillion abruptly ended his cross-examination, saying, "It was purely to show the conspiracy on the part of the Justice Department to stir up trouble in this particular community. It is the Justice Department provoking this whole thing." The low sound of approval came from the white section, like amens to a black preacher, except quieter.

Later on when Mr. Manning took the stand, the whole story changed. Now it wasn't a war injury that had kept him out of the office, but he had stepped on a round piece of brick that had "jerked him from the top of his head to the bottom of his feet, about the same as a slipped disk or something." So that turned out to be the new story.

After the first phase of the hearing ended, all the white witnesses were dismissed and told they could go home. Then almost everybody who had qualified in Monroe was made to take the stand and answer challenges to our qualifications by the state. Only Professor Simmons, Benjamin Blockwood, and my wife and me were never challenged.

Judge Hunter was almost right. We were there way into the night as the state raised every conceivable technicality they could think of to keep us from getting registered. At one point, Judge Hunter remarked, "Man, if the state of Louisiana were to be this strict in their regulations, the registration rolls would drop 80 percent."

The last person called was Mr. C. W. Baggett. He went proudly up before the judge, walking and looking a lot younger than his eighty-six years. I realized at the last hearing that Judge Hunter really wanted Old Man Baggett to get registered. Although he had left off his sex and put down "brown" as his color on his application in Monroe, Judge Hunter had still allowed him to come over to Shreveport with the rest of us. Judge Hunter said he was giving him another chance to complete his card correctly because since the last hearing, he had found out that he could verbally ask questions to a person that old and write in the answers for him. So the judge asked him the questions and ruled him qualified. Mr. Baggett's face lit up with pride.

The next day, the three-judge panel dismissed the restraining order issued by Attorney General Jack Gremillion for the state of Louisiana and made it possible for Judge Hunter to issue us final certifications. Judge Hunter certified twenty-six of us. Three people, Lehman Griffin, Sr., James Levi, and Watson Sanders, were cut from our original twenty-eight based on objections from the state and one new person, Mr. Baggett, was added.

Judge Hunter issued cards to the twenty-six of us: Eric Armstrong, Francis Joseph Atlas, C. W. Baggett, Benjamin F. Blockwood, Rose P. Blockwood, James Brown, John H. Bunn, Charles Carson, Bragg Clay, Mary E. Cole, Freddie Green, Sr., Lehman H. Griffin, Jr., James L. Hadden, Gardena Johnson, Mary E. Johnson, Percy Knighton, Adam Millikin, Jr., Walter Henry Nash, Frank Nervis, Sr., Alease J. Scott, Alfred Shoemaker, Henry O. Simmons, Laura Thompson, Fred Threats, Jr., Nathan Weaver, and me. We had gone the distance and we had won. And to top things off, the three-judge panel put the whole lot of them under an injunction not to interfere with the court's decision—the attorney general of Louisiana, Sheriff Gilbert, the East Carroll clerk of court, and the district attorneys of East Carroll *and* the four parishes nearby.

On Wednesday, we got the good news that we would be allowed to participate in the Democratic primary scheduled for Saturday, although we had just been certified. Only Mr. Baggett would not be allowed to vote because he had designated his party as "None."

It was an exciting time, but at the same time a wave of fear and anxiety swept across the black community after the ruling. People speculated over what manner of evil would befall some unlucky black person before election day. Newspaper people arrived from all over the country to cover the story, because it was the first time anyone registered by a federal judge would vote. The reporters' presence and persistent questions and picture taking only served to further agitate certain members of the white community.

When we walked down the street, we were met with glares and occasional downright sinister looks. Maids and cooks reported comments from their bosses like "We need to put these coloreds in their place" or "Those Yankee agitators are giving these coloreds some crazy ideas, got them acting like they think they're equal to us" and "That nigger-loving federal government is too powerful, dipping in our affairs." The rumors and tension had most of us anticipating some kind of trouble by election day.

Actually, it didn't take but two days for them to make up some trouble. The trouble began on Friday with the arrest of Benjamin Blockwood just one day before we were to vote in the Democratic primary. Blockwood was the witness who had disputed Mr. Manning's testimony that he had been laid up sick. The town marshal claimed that the Welfare Department had told him to pick Blockwood up for late child support payments to his first wife. On the way to the jail, the town marshal stopped to let Blockwood pick up his paycheck from his job at the light company, but when they got to the jail, the Welfare Department told him it wasn't enough. If he wanted to stay out of jail, he'd have to pay for two months, even though he didn't owe but one. So they locked him up anyway.

Most of us who had registered met that Friday night before the election to prepare for the big event. With so many news people in town and the way they were making such an event out of it, it was kind of hard not to get caught up in the celebration, even if we were a little anxious. A CBS reporter and a photographer from Dallas showed up at our meeting wanting interviews.

"And how do you feel about being the first blacks to vote in East Carroll since Reconstruction?" they asked. They told us that they had heard that one of the polling places was Mr. Manning's store. They wanted to have cameras there when the four people qualified in that ward went to vote. They said it would make a great story.

We didn't know much about voting, except what we had heard since no blacks had actually voted in East Carroll since 1878. There was hardly a black person in Lake Providence who had ever done it, maybe a few people who had lived other places, so we had to learn how to mark our ballots and such. We brought in some students who had used voting machines in college for their school elections. They drew a diagram of a machine on the black board and taught us about the black buttons and the red buttons and how to get in and out.

Although this was a truly momentous occasion for us, we decided at our meeting that we would act like nothing out of the ordinary was going on. We knew the judge had issued an injunction against the sheriff and a lot of other people, ordering them not to interfere with our voting. We had even heard that the sheriff and his deputies weren't even allowed to carry their guns around the voting places, but we still felt uneasy. So we decided we would go down to the polls, not all at one time, but maybe in twos or threes. That way, if they planned to ambush us on our way to the polls or even at the polls, they wouldn't be able to get us all at one time.

Saturday morning, the twenty-four of us went to the polls as planned, two or three at a time, starting shortly after the polls opened at 6:00 A.M. My wife and I drove uptown to the courthouse to cast our votes with some expectation of trouble, but when we got there, it was not at all what we expected. Everything was very quiet. There were no crowds of jeering, angry white people—just a few news people and the federal marshals standing around in their dark suits and dark glasses, watching all directions for trouble. We parked and walked up to the courthouse where we were escorted in by one of the federal agents.

We were taken into a room with more federal marshals and some poll workers. A poll worker asked us our names, and we showed the cards we had received from Judge Hunter saying that we were qualified to vote. Then we finally got to do what I had spent so much of my life trying to get to do. I finally got to vote. After sixty years of living, I was just now becoming a real American citizen.

Most of the news people had decided that Mr. Manning's store was the location for the best story. Later that morning, I talked to one of the people who had voted at the store and found out all the excitement had been on the other end of town.

"Rev," he said. "You should have been there. When we got to the store, Officer Bill Ragland was already there walking around with his pistol, like he was trying to scare somebody. The news people were already there too, and a good-sized crowd had gathered before the store even opened for voting. Then Mr. Manning came out yelling at everybody to get back from his store. Then he starts shoving people in the crowd, including the reporters, and they just taking his picture and writing down everything he was saying in their little notebooks.

I think they thought it was funny. I guess they got just the kind of story they were looking for."

Sometime election day morning, an FBI agent went down to the jail with Mr. Blockwood's wife to try to get him out. She paid the extra $54 for August's child support and after some going back and forth, Judge Voelker, Sr., finally signed the release papers and let Blockwood out. So he did get to vote that day. Someone must have called the press, though, because the next day the news story about our first time voting started off with a comment about Mr. Blockwood—"government red-faced because one of its court-qualified voters had to be bonded out of jail to exercise his 'federal-judge given' right to vote."

By noon all of us had cast our ballots, including Blockwood, and the day came to a close, pretty uneventfully. We thought maybe somehow the whites were starting to accept that we should have a chance for citizenship too. But we were wrong. When the sun went down and it was way into the night, when most of the federal marshals and all the newsmen had left for their respective destinations, and no one was left to record it, the night riders came. From house to house, they left the Klan calling card, a fiery cross of kerosene-soaked burlap. By morning, they had burned a cross in front of the home of every black person who had voted, whose house they could get to without being seen.

# SIXTEEN

# Creative Solutions to the Negro Problem

"What does this mean?" he demanded. "Why is the NAACP paying Negroes to move out of the South?"

The man standing on my front porch shoved this legal-sized flyer toward me. Across the top of the flyer in bold letters, I read "FREEDOM BUS TO WASHINGTON, D.C. OR ANY OTHER CITY IN THE NORTH. Free Transportation plus $5.00 for Expenses to any Negro Man or Woman, or Family (no limit to size) who desire to migrate to the Nation's Capitol, or any city in the north of their choosing." It didn't give anybody's name or the name of an organization, just a phone number to call. On the back were addresses and telephone numbers for the NAACP, the Urban League, and the welfare departments for Pittsburgh, Chicago, New York, Detroit, and Washington, D.C.

I knew exactly what this was all about. I had learned about this scam while I was visiting in New Orleans. It had started down there and had apparently now made its way up to Lake Providence. Almost every day for the last month, there had been an article about this disgusting scheme in the *Monroe Morning World*. So I was well aware of it. Blacks had already been sent to New York, San Francisco, Philadelphia, Cleveland, Los Angeles, and Sacramento and even to former Vice President Nixon's hometown of Whittier, California.

The plan, the brainchild of a New Orleans segregationist, was to relocate blacks from the South to the North by giving them free one-way tickets to any northern destination. Their plan was to embarrass the North and clear the South of the people they themselves had spent so much time creating—the uneducated and unskilled and people on welfare. People in these categories were especially encouraged to participate, although they were glad to send anybody black. I heard that anyone just getting out of jail could get a ticket easily.

The Citizens' Council, which spearheaded the program, claimed they were extending a Christian gesture by assisting "unfortunate" blacks in making new homes in the North. They claimed the local churches were helping by providing food baskets for people who accepted the offer—baskets containing possum, potatoes, onions, grits, turnips, and salt pork. A bill was even introduced by segregationists in the Louisiana House of Representatives seeking welfare help in getting needy people of any race to leave Louisiana.

I had read in the papers that several blacks had been sent to the resort town of Hyannis Port, Massachusetts, where Attorney General Robert Kennedy I believe had his summer home. This was their way of getting back at the Kennedys for filing suits against the state of Louisiana. The articles made it seem like all the blacks who went there got good jobs and a nice place to live, which caused even more people to sign up to go to Massachusetts. So it was easy for me to guess who was behind the flyer affair in Lake Providence. If desegregation and voting couldn't be stopped in the courts, they'd just fix the problem by moving us out of the state.

By the time I found out the scheme was in Lake Providence, flyers had already been distributed everywhere black folks lived. They had been distributed by a local organization, the Freedom 40 Club, which was really just an arm of the Citizens' Council. They had had a big barbecue fundraiser at the American Legion to raise money for the one-way tickets north. I guess the Freedom 40 was a play on words since the U.S. government was supposed to have given each newly freed slave forty acres after the Civil War so that they would have had a fighting chance of survival on their own. So maybe they equated shipping us to the North as giving us our new start.

Any black person who wanted to leave East Carroll Parish was eligible, and it didn't take long for them to get a person on a bus after they signed up. In fact, by the end of the first week they had already shipped out seven people to Redwood Falls, Minnesota. Redwood Falls was the hometown of Richard Parson, one of the Justice Department attorneys working on our case in Shreveport. He had remarked on one occasion that there were plenty of good jobs in his hometown. So the Freedom 40 Club decided it would be great fun, kind of like a practical joke, to start shipping blacks from Lake Providence to Mr.

Parson's hometown. They said they picked Redwood Falls because it was about the same size as Lake Providence and they wanted to send us where we'd be around some northern whites. They couldn't send us to a big city because they'd defeat their purpose. In the city, we might go months without seeing a white man.

The first people to sign up were farm workers James Reed and Eugene Cathy and twenty-one-year-old Betty Beal. To convince them to go to Redwood Falls, the Freedom 40 Club told them that jobs were plentiful and that there were lots of other blacks already living there. They were also told that when they arrived, someone would be there to help them get on their feet. So they took the one-way tickets.

Betty Beal, along with her three children, ranging in ages from eight months to six years, along with her sixteen-year-old sister, were the first ones sent to this pretty much all-white town in Minnesota. But when she arrived, all she found was a community that wasn't expecting them and there were no jobs. When the others arrived, they found similar situations. Within weeks, all of them had left Redwood Falls for other cities.

We tried to get the word out, but our main communication was through the churches. Most churches only had one worship service per month so it was slow communications at best. We explained what had happened to the people sent from New Orleans, how they arrived in California and New York with no skills and less than $5 in their pockets. They hadn't been able to find work, and some had ended up living on the streets under extreme conditions.

But in spite of our best efforts, some people still did not get informed or refused to believe it was a trick. Demand for workers was on the decline, and many farm hands were living just on the other side of slavery, so they wanted a chance to go north. It had been their dream all along. They just hadn't been able to save enough money to buy a ticket, and now they saw their chance. So more of them signed up and off to Redwood Falls they went.

Each time the Freedom 40 would put someone on the bus, they'd dash off a telegram letting the mayor of Redwood Falls know that more were coming, accompanied with some smart comment like "Business is picking up. Please continue to extend your courtesies to the new arrivals" or "What's your problem? You can't handle a few coloreds?"

Then they'd run another article in the *Monroe Morning World* detailing the next episode in their little story. The Freedom 40 members were having the time of their lives playing a joke on the North, at black folks' expense.

After only two weeks of this foolishness, I read in the paper that the governor of Minnesota was setting up a three-man fact-finding team to find the reason for the recent influx of Negroes into Redwood Falls. When the governor found out what was going on, he accused the club of having ulterior motives for sending Negroes north. He called them cruel and barbaric to deport a woman, only twenty-one years old, almost a child herself, with her children to a destination so far from home, penniless and unannounced. He appealed to Louisiana's governor, Jimmy Davis, asking him to stop the Freedom 40 Club from sending more people to Redwood Falls, but all he got was a simple reply from J. R. Dillard, spokesman for the club, "More are on the way" and a suggestion that the governor would just sing him "You Are My Sunshine," a line from Governor Davis's big hit country song.

Afterwards, I read in the paper that Jimmy Dillard had issued a six-paragraph statement about the intent of the Freedom 40 program. "We are not trying to treat the Negro people badly. Just the opposite. We have heard so much from the north about how badly the Negro is treated in the south, we want to give some of these good Negroes the chance to settle in these areas where there are no prejudices."

The statement went on to say they were "doing a favor both to the Negro people and to the people of the north" by taking money out of *their* pockets to provide transportation to "a land that promises them so much, but has actually helped them so little." He went on to chastise the people of Minnesota for not being able to retain their black population. He asked them why they couldn't handle seven Negroes, when the North expected whites in Lake Providence to deal with a "colored" population of 60% to 65%. He told the governor, whom he said appeared unduly agitated over the presence of a handful of prospective voters, that he had better save his energy for the really big test ahead and the North had better learn to practice what it preached.

It turned into a real sideshow, with all the different newspaper people coming to town to record the latest episode in what they called "the tale of two towns." CBS came down to film a documentary, thirty minutes for the southern view of the rides north and thirty minutes to the northern version. The mudslinging and name-calling was picked up by the Associated Press, getting people across the country involved in predicting the next move, either from Dillard or from Minnesota's governor. You would have thought it was a soap opera. The St. Paul paper printed a picture of the president of the Chamber of Commerce posing with his arm around James Reed, taken on the day of Reed's arrival. To this, Dillard commented, "Negroes need to be fed and put to work, not hugged."

Jimmy Dillard thought he was making a big name for himself, exposing the North's racism, when really he just showed the world the lengths segregationists would go to. And the sad part was that I don't believe it ever crossed his mind or the minds of his cohorts that there was anything wrong with shipping a young woman and her small children to someplace they never heard of where nobody expected them, with only $5 between them.

It was all a sick game to them, but it backfired on them in the end. The cost of the free tickets drained the Citizens' Council's treasury and left them begging for assistance. One of my white friends brought me a copy of a letter they had sent out to 5,000 people asking them to put a dollar in an envelope (and don't forget the stamp) to help them out because the Freedom Bus North campaign had drained their treasury. The letter ended with "or shall we close the office and forget the whole thing? Let us know." But this wasn't the best thing to come out of their campaign. Their arrogance and cruelty stirred up disgust and criticism of the South from people and organizations that had never taken any interest in the plight of the Negro. It brought national attention to the level of ignorance, sickness of mind, and meanness of spirit we dealt with on a daily basis. Finally America's eyes were opening to the truth, but many more serious things would have to happen before they would really see our lives as we lived it every day.

Television coverage of our voting in the primaries sparked interest in many of the locals, and many approached me about how they could get registered. We set up more classes to teach them what to do, but since the registration office was still closed, twenty-eight more had to apply directly to the federal courts. Judge Ben Dawkins ruled seventeen of the twenty-eight qualified in time for the September 1 election.

Almost two months had passed since Mr. Manning resigned, and the police jurors still had not hired anyone to take his place. The federal court took this to be a deliberate defiance of the May court order and proceeded to file civil and criminal contempt of court charges against Mr. Manning. While it was legal for Mr. Manning to resign his position, it was not legal, according to Louisiana law, for him to leave his office before a successor was found. So Mr. Manning found himself in trouble because no other white person would take the job.

Mr. Manning's trial was set for Wednesday, August 22, 1962. Because I had been one of the people who had gone by the registrar's office and found it closed, I was subpoenaed to testify along with only two other people—Eric Armstrong and Benjamin Blockwood. I was in St. Louis, Missouri, when the subpoena came, so I had to catch a bus back to try to get home in time for the hearing. I arrived home all tired out that Tuesday night, knowing I had to get up early in time to be in Monroe for court by 8:30 the next morning.

My wife and I lay in the bed and talked, whispering to keep the children in the next room from hearing us. "I think it was good you were out of town," she said. "The white people around here are really worked up about them talking about sending Mr. Manning to jail. You know they just about went crazy after they ran that story in the paper about "a poor gray-haired war hero being made out a villain by the government" when he was just trying to do his job. They're making him out to be some kind of big hero or something. People are even saying that they tried to run Ben Blockwood out of town. They say Judge Hester, Attorney Voelker, Jimmy Dillard, and that no-good scoundrel Captan Jack Wyly showed up at his barbecue place up there on Hudson Street and tried to pay him $500 to disappear to his brother's house up in Arkansas, at least until after the court date. When he wouldn't go, they told him he'd be sorry."

I rolled over and told her not to worry about all that talk and to go on to sleep. "Everything will be all right," I assured her. But she wasn't reassured and kept talking.

"You don't know all that's been happening while you were gone. Mrs. Blockwood got called in on her job and they told her that she had no right taking off that day we went to register and they transferred her down to Baton Rouge. And what is Mr. Blockwood going to do with his construction business if his wife is way down in Baton Rouge? That's four hours away. And you know they say his business is already falling off because the teachers are scared to go by his barbecue place, and you know that's where they all used to gather after school. I heard that the superintendent or somebody at the school board told them they'd better stay from 'round Blockwood's place if they want to keep their jobs."

"God will take care of us," I told her. "Now go on to sleep."

My wife was still uneasy the next morning. She decided that she and my three oldest daughters, Johnita, Elsie, and Sharolyn, would ride over to Monroe with me that morning. She said that would make her feel better. She warned me that I should be very careful.

"I believe they are planning something because when I was at the red light yesterday, it looked like the chief of police was writing down our license plate number."

I told her that all that wasn't necessary anyway. "This yellow and green car is easy enough to identify."

My car was a bit unusual, a sunflower yellow '55 Buick with a bright green top, like the color of a child's crayon. There weren't many cars that color around in any model. The car had also once been a police car, so there was a big ugly spot on the driver's door where someone had done a poor job trying to remove the old police insignia.

When we arrived at the federal court building, we were surprised at the number of people there. We had been told that the state had called twenty-three witnesses and that Mr. Gilfoil, representing the Lake Providence bar, was calling in a large number of witnesses, but there were white people everywhere. Some were standing around outside waving their Confederate flags; others milled about in the hall. There was almost a carnival atmosphere, with all the noise and the people.

Most every white man who had any kind of money or political power in Lake Providence must have come over for the hearing. The seats were all taken and spectators crowded into the spaces along the walls of the courtroom. As I scanned down the wall, I noticed that every attorney in town must have been in a group of people huddled near the front. I recognized attorneys Voelker (Jr. and Sr.), Ragland, Hester, Gilfoil, and my unclaimed white cousin, Captan Jack Wyly. I also noticed the federal marshals strategically positioned around the courtroom.

As we walked into that lion's den, the people turned to stare. The spectators hunched each other, looking like they could cut us in two with their eyes. We were definitely in the minority, as there were only about twelve blacks in the whole crowded place, including my family and me. As usual, I just gave everybody a smile and nodded my head in acceptance of the warm welcome I pretended I had just received. I had discovered that being nice to people when they're trying to be mean always throws them off. It makes them uneasy about how to react to you. And that's what I wanted. I knew the main reason they were there was to show that they were all united against the government and the three of us, and the last thing I planned for them to get from me was fear. They should have realized by now that I feared no one but God.

I took my place with the other witnesses and waited and waited. Channel 8 News came in to take pictures, but the lawyers for the other side stopped them and put them out. My daughters, who had sat down in the back, could see the reaction of some of the local whites to my presence. They pointed and whispered and laughed as if we were fools on display, but when Judge Dawkins came out almost an hour and a half later and announced that a compromise had been reached, they weren't smiling anymore. Manning, in spite of his seven or so lawyers there to defend him, had agreed to take his job back. He would administer registration tests under a new statewide system that had just gone into effect at the beginning of August. In return, the government would drop civil and criminal charges against him. Judge Dawkins said Manning was technically guilty, but the court didn't want to be vindictive.

Although the lawyers seemed satisfied with an amicable solution, Mr. Manning looked humiliated. And the crowd that had come over to witness a blowout by the home team had instead witnessed defeat at the hands of a hated enemy. As the judge continued to talk, you could sense anger and resentment taking life in the spectators until it became a presence you could actually feel.

# SEVENTEEN

# A Cause Worth Dying For

We hurried out the courtroom as soon as the hearing ended, past people who still appeared to be grappling with the meaning of the judge's words. Before it all sank in, I figured it would be best for me and my family to be headed out of town.

It was late afternoon by the time we got back to Lake Providence. Since it was still daylight, my wife decided to take my mother out for a ride. She was in her eighties but still traveled and had come up from Tallulah to spend a few days with us. The court had given me my bus fare back to St. Louis, which was where I was when they subpoenaed me, so I decided to stay home and try to get some things organized to head back to St. Louis.

Later, when it was time to go to Wednesday night prayer service, I decided I'd walk rather than ride to the church. I felt like the walk would do me good since I had been sitting most of the day, either in the courtroom or during the three hours of driving to and from Monroe.

I took the regular shortcut up my neighbor's long graveled drive out to Highway 65 and headed north toward town. When I got into town, I saw a group of men over at the fire station with their heads together, intently discussing something.

The fire station had gotten to be known as the meeting place for planning dirty deeds. The people who hung out around there were so offensive that black people would cross the street and walk on the other side to avoid walking directly in front of the firehouse. I was grateful that they were so engrossed in conversation that they didn't notice me passing by. I'm sure they would have had something asinine to say to me. I actually should have been wondering what foolishness they were cooking up, but at the time, I didn't give them that much thought. I figured they were up to their usual craziness.

I arrived at the church about the same time as my wife, who was just pulling up with our four youngest children. The older girls, Johnita and Elsie, had stayed home with my mother. We had an unusual prayer meeting that night. The spirit of God was present in a very powerful way. Before the service ended, two people came and gave their lives to Christ. I felt absolutely filled with the Holy Spirit, and I could feel God's closeness to me.

After the benediction, the grownups milled around the churchyard talking about what a good time we had had. It was a typical hot, muggy, August night, but Louis, Cleo, and Sharolyn had already piled into the back seat, impatiently waiting for us to stop talking and get in the car. My five-year-old, Harriet, had already claimed her spot in the middle of the front seat.

As I pulled off my suit coat and laid it across the seat, my wife, who always managed to be the last one ready to leave the church, got in on the passenger side. I left church, still feeling a strong sense of God's presence. It had been an unusual day. God had shown me his mighty power morning until evening, showing me victory both in the courtroom and in the church house. Before the night was over, he would show me still another kind of victory.

On the way home, I stopped uptown briefly to pick up a few items from Jack Yee's, one of the Chinese grocery stores, and then continued home, only vaguely aware of the children in the back digging for prizes in the Cracker Jacks boxes I had just bought and arguing over who had gotten the best prize. Harriet had already fallen asleep across my wife's lap.

I was listening to night sounds through the open windows when I noticed a rattling sound coming from one of the wheels. I didn't know what kind of problem it was, but I did know I didn't feel safe stopping on the side of the road to check it out. There were many stirred-up people around Lake Providence after court today, and I didn't believe in looking for that kind of trouble. Already that year in northeast Louisiana, one black leader had been kidnaped and beaten and several ministers had had their homes and churches bombed. Other leaders had had cats and rabbits left on their lawns with bullets in their heads and KKK notes hung around their bodies that said "Let your conscience be your guide." Of course, I didn't expect any real violence from the people in Lake Providence, but I still kept alert for trouble. I decided that if I drove slow enough, I should be able to make it home, where I could safely check out the noise.

We continued down the two-lane Highway 65 that ran south from Arkansas through Lake Providence into the rural area right past my house. We passed over First Street, Second Street, and soon we were crossing over Ninth Street and headed toward home, just outside the city limits. As I slowed down even more to ease my bad tire over the railroad tracks, I became aware of the car behind me. Actually it had been behind me for some time, but I was just now becoming consciously aware of it. It was following so close now that its headlights lit up the inside of my car. The speed limit had just gone up to 65 miles per hour, yet the car continued to creep along behind me, although I was only going about 25 because of my tire. Something didn't feel right about this. Normally the car would have passed me by now.

As we passed my neighbor's long driveway on the right, I continued to glance into my rearview mirror. Next would be the even longer dirt road that ran down behind the back of the Baptist Center building, curving around its side and ending in my yard.

The right turn to the Center was in the middle of a very steep curve where the highway suddenly changed from flat to a road where the right lane suddenly became higher than the left. The sudden incline in the highway, along with the very narrow and semi-dark entrance and deep ditches on both sides of the highway, made this a rather precarious right turn. I would have to almost come to a complete stop to make it. This seemed to be particularly annoying to drivers following me because they would just be picking up speed after leaving the city limits of Lake Providence. To keep from braking down to my low speed or hitting me in the rear, they would usually swing out wide into the left lane and pass in the curve on the other side.

Tonight when I slowed down to make my turn, the car that had been creeping along behind me all of a sudden swung into the left lane and rushed right along side me. It kept pace with my car for just a few seconds, then "Pow!" The sound rang out like the sound of a backfiring engine. Immediately pain radiated down my left arm. I looked down and even in the dim light, I could see the sleeve of my white dress shirt blown practically off. It hung off my arm in shreds. I glanced back up the highway to see if I could still see the cowards who had done this. I could still see their taillights in the distance speeding south down Highway 65.

I looked around the car and realized that no one else in the car had any idea what had just happened. "Did we get a blowout, Daddy?" Louis asked from the back seat.

My mind sped through a variety of answers as I guided the car onto the very narrow shoulder. I had just been shot, yet I could feel a strange calm coming over me, but I didn't know how to transfer that calm to my family. No great inspiration came as to how to deal with the situation, so I just said as quietly as I could, "I've been shot."

My wife shot me a look of disbelief. "How do you know you've been shot?" she asked frantically. Strange what people say in the midst of a rising panic.

I raised my left arm out for her to see. In the dim light from the Highway Maintenance Building across the highway, she could see my sleeve that was ripped from the shoulder down to the wrist, and blood was starting to form spots of red where the shredded white fabric dangled across the wound.

My wife said something. I'm not exactly sure what, because it sounded like words all caught up in her throat. One of the children started to yell and another one started to cry.

"I want you to take the car and get the children safely in the house," I said quickly as I opened the door and started to get out of the car.

"Where are you going?" my wife screamed. Panic was starting to take over.

As I closed the door, I leaned back in the open window and tried to calm her. "Please, just take the children on home," I said in a rush. I needed for her to hurry and get off the highway in case those shooters turned around and came back. I had to get her out of shock and get her moving. It could be a matter of life and death.

"I'll be okay. Don't worry. Just take them on home. I'm going to run to Dudley Green's and get him to run me to the doctor."

She looked at me with a frightened, confused look but proceeded to move Harriet over and slide into the driver's seat.

I held my arm while I ran down the steep embankment as she pulled off. The deep ditch, which was used to drain water out of the fields, was dry at the time, so I ran up the ditch a short distance, but my mind told me that probably wasn't the safest thing to do. I knew instinctively that they would come back up the highway to survey the results of their handiwork, and I planned to get me a good look at them. I thought to myself that my wife would be extremely upset with me if she had known I had gotten out of the car just to see who did the shooting.

Beside the ditch was a cotton field, and since it was almost cotton picking time, the stalks were tall and full. I figured the leafy plants would provide a better cover for me than the ditch should the car return before I could make it to the clearing by the Green's house, the closest house to me and the highway.

I looked back as I ran toward the field just in time to see headlights off in the distance. My survivor instinct switched on as I knew I'd better hurry out of sight in case that was them. I had to get myself down into the row far enough that they wouldn't be able to see me, but not so far that I couldn't see them. I had to get a look. I just had to see for myself.

The run had me out of breath, but my heart began to really pump when I saw the car begin to slow as it approached our road. What are they going to do, I thought, wondering if I had made a big mistake sending my family on without me. Surely they wouldn't have the nerve to go to the house. I tried to imagine where my wife and children would be about now. Were they already at the house, or were they maybe just coming around the back of the Baptist Center building?

My mind switched back to the people in the car. The car crept past the turnoff and then came to an almost complete stop right in front of where I was hiding. I froze as time stood still. They had the windows down, and I could tell there was a bunch of them in the vehicle. I couldn't move. Seemed like I couldn't even breathe for fear I might call attention to my hiding place.

They hesitated for what was probably just a few seconds, but for me it seemed like minutes. I guess they had looked across the long rows of cotton that lay between them and my house where, under the big light on the pole, they would have seen my car in the yard and wonder how it got there if they had done their jobs properly. As they sped away toward town, I watched their taillights disappear over the railroad tracks and out of sight. I stood there in the field for a while and contemplated my life, why I was where I was and how good God had been to me through it all. Then suddenly I remembered that I had been injured and needed to go get myself checked. I also wondered whether I should have sent the family on like that, what would be happening at the house while I was out there in the field.

I ran the rest of the way down my neighbor's tree-lined gravel driveway, as fast as my sixty-year-old legs would take me. As I got closer to the house, the porch light came on and I could see my oldest daughters, Elsie and Johnita, standing on the porch. I didn't see my mother, but I knew she knew about me because her sorrowful moaning rang out in the nighttime rural silence. "Oh, they done killed my boy! Oh, they done killed my boy!" she wailed.

As I headed up the dirt path between Dudley Green's house and mine to go show her I was still alive, the porch light went off. In the dim light shining from the single light bulb in the front room, I could see my mother through the open front door, arms flailing, my wife trying to hold her up as she looked as if she would faint away. Even when she realized it was me coming up on the porch, she continued to cry.

"You ought to be happy," I told her. "You ought to be shouting. I'm not dead and I'm not going to die." I held out my arm for her to see that I wasn't hurt too bad.

"Where have you been all that time?" my wife asked hysterically. "What took you so long? Me and the children didn't know what to do."

I looked at her and she was actually shaking. I looked at the rest of the children, and they all looked equally terrified. "Come on, let's all get in the house," I said.

After I got everyone back in the house and calmed down, I told my wife to call my brother Baker. He could stay at the house with them so that I could go to the doctor. I also had her call some of the others involved in the fight to let them know what had happened.

In probably less than ten minutes, Baker pulled into the yard in his yellow panel truck. He was pulling his rifle from behind the seat as I walked out to meet him. We talked awhile about how bad I was hurt and then we went to take a look at the car. The hole in the door was pretty big, about a couple of inches wide. They had meant business.

The older children were coming outside now to see what we were looking at and then after a while, my wife came out too. When she had driven the car home, she had apparently gotten out without looking at the door. When she saw the hole, she started to scream, "Oh God, they're going to kill us all," which of course frightened the children even more.

We got them all back into the house again and I tried to reassure her that everything would be okay, but she continued to shake. She wouldn't sit but a minute and then she would be up again, pacing around, wringing her hands and talking about all the things that could have happened. I kept repeating that it was okay and that God would take care of us, until she seemed to calm down a bit.

Baker decided to go back outside and patrol the grounds just to make sure that there were no other snipers around. With sixty acres of Baptist Association land mostly under cultivation, there were many places where someone could lurk or be parked down a turnrow, but as mad as my brother was, they would be in for trouble tonight. I had never seen Baker so angry.

We decided we'd better go ahead and report the shooting to the police, but we couldn't get through to them for a long time. When my wife finally got through and told the police I was shot, the policeman on the line asked, "How bad is he shot? Is he dead?" in a tone of voice that indicated he wished I was.

"Well, I don't know how bad," my wife said, "but I know he's shot."

"Well, we'll send somebody out there after a while, but we're really busy right now."

About the same time I was shot, a car had hit a young fellow on a bike and killed him. Now some of the policemen were busy at that accident scene, but we knew they weren't all busy because Baker, who was the first one to arrive after the shooting, had met a policeman coming off my road, before we even notified them about the shooting. But still we couldn't get a single policeman to "officially" come to the house.

Several other people arrived, and in all the excitement of telling what happened, I had forgotten about my arm until someone pointed it out to me. "Rev, don't you think you ought to let somebody take a look at that arm? It don't look too good."

I looked down at my arm. The blood had dried and caked up over the wound, and my upper arm had swollen and turned purple. I went back in the house and called the doctor, who told me to meet him at the hospital. I finally left with my neighbor Dudley Green and Rev. P. H. Henderson, who had just arrived from the other side of town.

We drove up to our little forty-five-bed hospital, where a nurse met us and took me into an examination room.

"Just sit up there on the table until the doctor comes," she said.

After a while the doctor came in. He asked me what had happened and told me that he'd need to take some x-rays to see whether any lead was in my arm. He also wanted me to take a shot for tetanus to prevent lockjaw.

"One shot in the night is enough for me," I told the doctor. "I've had more sores on me than that and nothing's happened to my jaw. Just probe on in there and see if you can feel any lead."

After the doctor had probed around a bit, he dressed my wound and told me to take an aspirin. "Now go on home and go to bed," he said. "And don't walk before any windows."

When I got home from the hospital, I was surprised to see the yard full of people. A few ladies were sitting on the front porch talking with my wife, who was emotionally retelling the events of the night. But mostly people were just kind of milling around in the yard in small groups, talking. One thing struck me almost immediately. They didn't seem afraid. I felt inspired. Some of the people there had been too afraid to stand up and participate, afraid they might lose their jobs, even when others were there to help them. And some of them knew about how Atlas had been treated and even more recently, they had heard about the cross burnings. But yet tonight, in the face of real violence, they had put their fear aside, leaving their homes at night when lately they had been afraid to be out past dark.

Later, after my wife had gotten Harriet's godmother to take Harriet and Cleo, the two youngest children, away from the confusion, I sat down among my friends and acquaintances and reflected on what could have happened that night—the plight of my family and what they could have been going through. I thought about how blessed I was and how God Almighty had chosen to protect me from a shotgun blast at very close range. Surely they had not intended for that shell to pass through the heavy steel of my door and only rip across my upper arm as I held the steering wheel with both hands. They had shot at us in the curve, right where the road slanted, like in the curve of a racetrack. Had their aim been thrown off by the sudden slant of the highway or maybe by the speed of the car?

And what about the pellets, why hadn't they spread? Why wasn't my chest ripped open? Pellets in a shotgun shell are supposed to spread the further they travel from the gun barrel. Yet tonight, somehow with my window rolled down and the way the sheet metal had caved inward, the pellets had actually channeled back together because the hole where the shell went in was larger than the hole on the inside of the door where it came out. The combination of the rolled-down windows and the metal door must have cut the force of the buckshot, because many of the pellets had battered into my lap. The rest must have exited out of the open window on my wife's side of the car. But how could that be without my wife getting struck? And why hadn't any of the pellets, glass debris, and metal fragments injured or blinded any of the children?

I was sure they had intended to rip my body apart that night. If I had gotten the full blast, it would have been a terrible bloody mess, not only for me, but also for my wife and children. Then I would have lost control of the car and surely overturned in the ditch, as steep as it was. And that could have killed anybody else who might have survived the initial blast. Or they could have come back along with their shotguns and finished us off that way. Or my baby girl could have still been sitting up between my wife and me and could have taken some of the stray buckshot. And what about Johnita, who was just about to start her first year at Southern University? Would she have been able to go on without us?

All the possibilities I thought of were bad, yet the miracle of it was that God had seen fit to see that none of them happened. I considered myself exceedingly blessed among men. As the people milled around in the yard and looked at me with sorrow and deep sympathy, it really did something to me. But mostly, it just let me know to continue to trust in the Lord because he could even bring buckshot under his control.

# EIGHTEEN

# Gross Injustice

Later in the night, two policemen finally arrived—one from the city and one from the parish. They asked a few questions and looked curiously around the yard at all the people gathered there. When they saw I wasn't hurt too badly, they went on their way.

After most of the people left, I went in my bedroom and sat on my old black trunk by the phone table, trying to figure out who I should call in Washington. I tried to get through to someone in the Justice Department, but with no results. Of course, since we were the last place in the United States to get the dial tone system, I still had to go through an operator who could let a call through at her discretion. And tonight I felt certain she was exercising discretion and listening in on all conversations.

I finally thought of a friend of mine who worked with the NAACP, a Mr. Edwards from Richmond, Virginia. I at least needed to let someone in the NAACP know about the shooting. For some reason, the operator let this call go through, so Mr. Edwards got the message to the head NAACP office.

The phone rang all through the night—people calling from in town, people calling from in the country. Everybody must have been on the phone, because the word was spreading mighty fast. For days, calls continued to come from the community and from black leaders in the movement in other places. We had to assign people to take shifts just answering the phone. I reckon practically every black person in Lake Providence must have come by or called in the days following the shooting.

The morning after the shooting, Mr. Owens, the Justice Department lawyer who had handled the case the day before, came by the house to see how things were going and there he found out, to his surprise, about the shooting. He looked as if he wanted to cry.

"Have you reported this to the Justice Department?" he asked.

"Well we've been trying off and on all night, but we couldn't get through."

"Well, don't you worry about that. I'll get somebody."

Mr. Owens left, and about five o'clock that afternoon two men from the Justice Department arrived at the house and a little later on, about three more, and the next day, some two or three more.

As the news spread, calls, telegrams, and letters went out from the NAACP, the Civil Rights commissioners I had testified before in New Orleans, and the Justice Department attorneys to the governor and to J. Edgar Hoover, FBI director, calling for a thorough investigation of my shooting. Press releases went to many newspapers. So quite a few FBI agents got assigned to the case. In fact, I believe the FBI agents would have found the men responsible had it not been for Sheriff Gilbert and his local police force that the FBI was supposed to work in cooperation with.

A few days after the shooting, I was in the house when I heard the dogs charge at something. They always barked to let us know whenever anyone came into the yard. I looked out the front room window and saw a police car. A couple of officers got out and walked over to where my car was parked under the cedar tree. I watched them carefully examine the big three-inch hole in the door, and then one of them climbed into the driver's seat. He seemed to be comparing the location of the hole in the door with the location of his chest. I listened through the open window.

"Weeelll d——!" he said in a deep southern drawl. "He must be some kinda skinny fella because that woulda blown my chest clean open."

They proceeded to take turns getting in the car and pointing their guns, trying different angles, trying to figure out why nobody in the car was dead. This was particularly interesting since I had found out from the FBI that a special ammunition load had been used that night. The lead had been replaced by steel to give it more penetrating power and make it more metal-piercing. So they really had intended to "blow my chest clean open." I shook my head as I watched and thought to myself, *Look at them trying to figure out God.*

I knew all the time that the local authorities weren't interested in identifying who shot me, but when I tried to explain this to the FBI agents, they just dismissed my comments. I gave them specific examples, yet they still acted as if all the law officers were working toward the same goal. Sheriff Gilbert had even made some comments in the *Monroe Morning World* about how he wasn't even sure a crime had been committed. He said I hadn't even been injured and called the incident an "alleged" shooting in spite of the big hole in my car door with the buckshot inside and the wound in my arm. Now I thought that should have been enlightening to the agents.

The local authorities continued to try to cover up the case. Every piece of evidence the FBI would uncover, I'd watch them cover it up again. Even some of the FBI agents made this observation to me after it had happened several times. There were witnesses who said they saw the car following me while we were still within the city limits and that five white men were in it. But when the local authorities found out the FBI was producing this evidence, they harassed the witnesses in such a way that they were sorry they had seen anything.

Local whites who were questioned by the FBI about the shooting would then call up the sheriff, wanting to know who these men were, claiming to be FBI agents, and why they were asking questions about some colored who got shot. Of course, some of them actually were ignorant of the whole affair since, as usual, the local paper was silent about the shooting.

Later FBI agent Earl Cox and a local policeman came down to the house to question Louis, my eleven-year-old. He had been sitting in the back seat on the driver's side that night, looking out the window when the car had pulled beside us that night. He had watched the car start down the highway before realizing that I was shot. He had described to the FBI a black and white vehicle with a single circular taillight on each side. He had even told them what kind of car he thought fit that description. This was very disturbing to the local authorities, because the car description from the various witnesses all matched the personal car of one of their own deputies. So they had come down to the house to gather more information.

"And how do you know what kind of car it was?" Mr. Cox asked. "Now this is real important."

"I saw the car," Louis said in his "I'm-not-scared" voice. I thought, look at that boy trying to sound and act like me.

"I could tell from the shape of the lights what kind of car it was. There's only one or two cars with lights like that."

"What makes you so sure? You some kind of car expert!" the local authority snapped. "Who made you a car expert?" He sat mumbling as Mr. Cox continued his questions and scribbled notes on his pad. "I don't know what you here asking a boy all these questions for anyway."

But Louis never changed his story, and it must have made somebody nervous because the next thing we knew, the sheriff from Tallulah, the next town down, had provided the FBI an alibi for the deputy.

Sheriff Gilbert continued to complain about the FBI's involvement in the case, and he took every opportunity to bad-mouth the agents. He told the news people who came over to interview him, "They aren't wanted, they aren't needed, and they have no authority to be here— and they need to go on back to Washington where they came from because the state is competent to handle this situation." After a while, he had other powerful politicians agreeing with him that this was a state matter and that the federal government was overstepping its bounds.

After much complaining by the right people, the FBI gave in and turned the case over to the state police. Three or four state policemen were sent up from Baton Rouge to investigate.

I didn't see how the state police were any better than the local authorities. In fact, I do not believe that the new officers even tried to find a white man because all we saw was them harassing the Negro community, asking questions, trying to find a Negro to pin the crime on. They even accused my own brother Baker of shooting me, claiming that he was on the scene mighty fast after the shooting. Baker said he started to remind them who was actually on the scene "mighty fast" since he had met the police coming off my road when he came in, but he had thought better of it. Some things were better left unsaid.

Next they tried to connect Rev. Virgil with the shooting. They claimed he was upset because he had run against me several times for the position of president of the Baptist Association and lost. Of course this wasn't true, because Rev. Virgil and I got along fine. Then they said I shot the big hole in the side of my own car as a publicity stunt to get media attention. It was awful, because local blacks passed that untruth around like they actually believed it. Now what kind of a fool would shoot a big hole in the side of his own car and include his little children in on the scheme?

They harassed my family and me and kept my wife in a constant emotional state. They'd come to the house early in the morning and say, "I want to take you up to the courthouse to get a little evidence." Then in the afternoon they'd come back for a little more evidence.

"Didn't you get shot because you were messing around with somebody's wife?" they asked me one day. All up in my face, with that foolishness.

"We know that's the reason and you know that's the reason and we're going to stay here until you admit it. Around here making all these accusations to the FBI, trying to make us look bad."

They went from one crazy thing to another, as if they could wear me down and disgust me enough to make me agree to an untruth so they would leave me alone. I began to wonder if they remembered I was the one who had been shot, the one they were supposed to be helping.

One day the local authorities showed up at the house and said they needed me to bring my daughter Sharolyn up to the courthouse to answer some questions. The children were already upset about the shooting and because they all kept up with the news, they were also somewhat fearful of policemen, considering their reputation for criminal behavior in the South. Sharolyn, the oldest child in the car at the time of the shooting, had been the most affected. She was nervous and still very afraid. She had always been the most sensitive of my children, a bit emotional like my wife, but at the time, I didn't know anything I could do to protect her as they led her away to a questioning room down the courthouse hall. I had asked them if I could go with her, but they had said, "Now what kind of sense would that make if we're trying to find out the truth about you?"

Now that didn't make me comfortable at all. I had seen strong grown men fold under police interrogation, so I could only imagine what they could do to a thirteen-year-old girl. But all my wife and me could do was helplessly wait and imagine and pray.

There was terror on her tear-stained face when she came out. She said they had taken her into a room and told her to sit at the table with four police officers. A fat, cigar-chewing policeman had sat at the head of the table asking most of the questions. Apparently they had started off easy, asking her what she had seen, trying to figure out how much she already knew. But then she said they started to tell her what she had seen and give her reasons why I had gotten shot in the first place. Then they tried to pressure her into agreeing with them.

"Looka here gal, don't you know what we do with little gals who lie? We got a place for gals like you. You ever heard of the reform school? We can have you sent away and you'll never see yo' old mama and daddy again."

As Sharolyn told us what happened, she looked like she was about to cry again. "I didn't know what to do, Daddy. You told me never to tell an untruth, but if I told them the truth, they said they would send me away and I'd never see y'all again. So I just sat there and didn't say anything."

Not long after the interrogation, they came back out to the house and picked up my car, saying they needed to keep it at Rentz's Garage while they did their investigation. So we had to walk most everywhere we needed to go. I came by Rentz a couple of days later and the door and the front seat were missing. They said they had to take the door off to collect the buckshot that had been trapped inside the door during the blast. They were going to send the pellets, along with the door and my shredded shirt, off to the state police headquarters in Baton Rouge to determine something about where the shot came from.

Not long after that, the state police called me down to the courthouse again. They asked me whether I would take a lie detector test.

"Would I be willing!?" I was getting mad. "No, I wouldn't belittle myself with such a thing. I've told you the truth and actually I didn't send for you. You're here and seem like you're trying me. I'm the one shot. Now you're trying to try me."

I was about fed up with the whole affair and I didn't care what they did at this point. Ever since slavery, the victims of racial crimes had been made to hold their heads down while the perpetrators and beneficiaries of the crimes walked around with their heads up high. But it was not going to be that way today.

I rose to leave because I didn't want to hear anymore. "This case rests on the bedrock of eternal justice and God himself will vindicate it," I said. "I'm not worried about the man who did the shooting, because God will handle him. However," I hesitated as I thought about what I was about to say next, "if he would be willing to come and beg pardon for what he's done, I'd be willing to forgive him and not even mention his name."

Without turning my head, I shifted my eyes toward the deputy standing by the door. His eyes caught mine and locked for an instance, just long enough for him to realize that I knew. Then he turned his eyes and looked down at the floor. He couldn't look at me. I'm sure it wasn't because he was ashamed of what he had done, but because someone who has done a great evil feels great discomfort when faced with genuine, unmerited forgiveness. "Besides," I continued, "the people who did this were cowards. I pastor a church over across town and I walk that road day and night. They didn't have to try to steal my life in the dark of the night. They could have gotten it in the daytime."

They stopped calling me in after that.

A month passed and we were still walking or catching a ride everywhere we needed to go. Since there were so many of us, I would often let the five children still at home get the ride and my wife and I would walk. One particular day, my wife and I had walked up Highway 65 into town when we noticed a white fellow leaning against a pickup truck. He was standing there glaring down the sidewalk toward us. He looked like he was about to boil over, just watching me walk up the road.

Whenever I would go up town and walk down the street, most white men I saw would grit their teeth and roll their eyes. I would see them whispering and poking each other and pointing, saying, "That's him right there. That's the one." Quite a few whites didn't know me at that time, and they would stretch their necks to see what I looked like when I passed by.

The police department seemed to have no plan to return my car, so I went to see the sheriff about it. Leaning back with his feet up on the desk, I could see him just running over with concern for my situation. He said flatly, "Well, as soon as the state police get through with the door, why they'll send it."

After the shooting, I hardly knew what to do. It was like a war going on within. Most times I felt peace and rest in the knowledge of God's protection. But other times, I felt plagued with a vague sense of uneasiness—uneasiness not because I was afraid but because of the uneasiness of waiting for the next attack to come. For the first weeks after the shooting, men from the community—Curtis Klienpeter, Joe Shoemaker, W. J. Matthews, Jack Matthews, Percy Morehouse, and a few others—formed a security force to keep watch over the house and property. There were generally three armed men (other than me) on the property at any time—one in the house, one on post on the porch, and one somewhere hidden on the grounds. During the night, they worked shifts, with the one inside catching a nap on the front-room couch, then relieving one of the young men on the outside. They generally left about daybreak before the children got up.

I had hoped that their presence would help my wife relax some, but nothing seemed to help. The whole affair had her jumpy. She barely slept at night, and every little sound seemed to startle her awake. She'd jump up, shaking me. "Did you hear that? Did you hear that? Sound like somebody's out there."

Sometimes I would hear her on the phone retelling what happened that night to each new person and speaking about all the "what ifs" if I had died or been seriously injured that night. And every time she retold the story, she got all shaky and nervous, as if she had just relived the experience.

I had two dogs at the time that I used to guard the house. Joe, the one with hair the color of a fox, was quite ferocious-looking. He would bare his teeth at unfamiliar guests in our yard, and his hair actually bristled on his back when he got angry. But it was more for show than anything. He wouldn't bite anyone, but most visitors didn't take the chance. They'd sit in their cars until someone came out to walk them to the house. Our other dog, Black Eyes, was more the children's pet. He liked performing tricks and was very gentle, except when he thought someone in the family was in danger. Then he could be almost as protective as Joe.

After the shooting, we'd often be startled awake by the dogs' persistent barking. I'd lay there for a while listening so that I could decide what to do. They had a certain bark if it was a human intruder and another if they just happened to be barking at some animal. I could even tell what kind of animal they were after in most cases.

Sometimes I would hear that alarming bark, the one that indicated that the family might be in danger. I'd ease out of bed, in case the children were still asleep, ever mindful of the racket my weight made on the squawky springs of my iron bed. I'd find my gun in the darkness and move noiselessly, crouching down under the open double front windows, straining to hear what had made the dogs start. Sometimes I would hear the crunching of tires passing over the gravel-filled ruts as someone made their way, headlights out, down the dirt road that ran behind the Baptist Center. I would listen for evidence of movement toward the house, but when the dogs made no more sounds, I'd know the trespassers were just sitting, making no move to get out their vehicle. So I would sit listening and waiting, every nerve aroused, until I'd hear the sound of an engine restarting and the occasional crunch of gravel as the car made its way back out to the highway.

Sometimes the dogs would start at something and then stop suddenly. In the quietness, I'd strain to hear human sounds above the croaking frogs and humming mosquitoes. I'd also listen for the silence. The crickets' silence meant someone had come around. Occasionally I'd hear the restless tossing of the children. I worried that they might be awake too, lying there, straining to hear in the darkness, waiting in fear for the danger that might seem so imminent. Sometimes the waiting would become unbearable, and I would take my shotgun and go outside and walk around the grounds. On some occasions, it was only some young couple who had taken the dark road behind the Center as a lovers' lane. Sometimes I never figured out what had made the dogs start so I'd just come back in and go to bed.

After several weeks of not enough sleep, my wife had become extremely edgy. "We cannot live here under these conditions," she told me one night. "We have to think about the children."

I was in sympathy with her, because it was a dangerous time to be a black leader. The Klan was reorganizing in north Louisiana and rebel-flag-flying, cross-burning rallies were being held all over our part of the state. We could only guess that times would get more dangerous as their movement grew.

Sometimes it seemed just like how Papa Charley had described the times after Reconstruction. Any kind of criminal behavior seemed to have become lawful and acceptable to ordinary people. It seemed from the stories I read in the papers that white people were even turning on their own in north Louisiana. Whites who sympathized with the Negro plight had been beaten in some cases, and some of them had their homes burned. Any politician who had the courage to be openly sympathetic to treating black folks as equals was blackballed and promptly run out of office.

I was seriously considering moving, but when I discussed it with the children, one of my daughters said, "That's what they want us to do. Can't you see they're trying to run us away? If you go, you'll be playing into their hands. Daddy, I think we really ought to stay. If you run now, anybody else that tried to do anything, they'd work the same trick on them."

I agonized over what to do, not because of me, but because of my wife and the children. I would have never considered leaving for my own account. The children seemed ready to stay, but when I'd walk around and listen to people talk, I'd get mentally tossed about between two opinions. My shooting and the recent killings over in Mississippi had some people pretty shook up. Some were even scared to stop and hold a conversation with me, afraid of punishment just because of association with me. In some ways it made me feel ostracized. Even some of my out-of-town friends stopped calling because, as they told me later, someone might be listening, and they didn't want to say anything that might make them come down harder on me.

Eventually I had to realize that I shouldn't have been concerning myself with what the people said anyway. I was not alone and never would be. God had always been there, especially when I felt discouraged, and this time was no different. In the midst of my discouragement, God sent me encouragement. Almost one month from the day of the shooting, the community came together and put on a two-night testimonial program for me. As the people came forward to tell their stories, I realized that my living was not in vain—there were stories from the sick and the elderly people I had visited and prayed for, stories of rides to the doctor and letters and visits to the jails and prisons. There were tears over children saved from prison or defended before a partial school board. Appreciation for counseling to save a marriage. Stories of legal issues settled without having to hire a lawyer. Young people who had learned their history and were interested in current events and understood their impact. Young people determined to go to college. Young people who stood tall and strong against the competition. I felt humbled that God should have given me such an opportunity to serve. Even the ones who didn't support me seemed to have decided that I did serve some useful purpose.

They raised about $700 at the program that helped me take care of my bills and some of Johnita's first-year college expenses at Southern University. I learned I was not in this thing by myself. There were people who appreciated the sacrifices I had made, even the ones who acted scared. One man told me one day, "We need you to stay alive. You're the only one they can't scare." Sometimes people would meet me on the street and slide a dollar or so in my hand. "Just to help you out," they'd say. "I can't participate myself, but I want you to have this." So I was able to go on a little further, although every day was still a struggle.

Another two months passed. A little nip was now in the air, and I was still walking the mile or so to town and to church and to meetings. I had to go down to Baton Rouge for an NAACP planning session so I decided that while I was there, I'd just call the state police headquarters and ask them about my door. After all, they had had the door down in Baton Rouge right at three months by then. It was too cold for my children and me to be walking.

When the person handling my case came on the line, they said, "Well, we've been through with that investigation a long time. We've been just waiting for your sheriff to send for it." He told me they would get in touch with the sheriff to see about sending the door back to Lake Providence.

They must have gotten in touch with the sheriff because not long afterwards, the door was sent back to Mr. Rentz's garage. They put the door back on and told me to come and pick up the car and the clothes I had on when I was shot but when I got in the car, the seat slid and tilted backwards. They hadn't bothered to rebolt the front seat.

I never got the hole in the door repaired, and for a while I didn't even fix the hole in the window. When the window was up, the big gaping hole so close to my head was a constant reminder of the nearness of God and also the nearness of eternity. It let me know that the hand of God holds the destiny of man. Also, I let the hole stay there because it seemed to do something to certain members of the white community. Whenever they looked at the jagged-edged hole, big enough for a ping-pong ball to pass through, it seemed to work on whatever little conscience they had, especially those I knew were connected with the crime. So I let it stay there as a symbol and a reminder.

Unfortunately, later I found out it was also working on my family's mind too, causing anxiety for my wife and embarrassment for the children. So I went out in search of a new vehicle. I replaced my bright yellow '55 Buick Special with a much later model Buick Le Sabre. The whole family acted so happy the day I brought the new car home that I guess they hated that yellow car a whole lot more than I realized.

From time to time, my out-of-town friends would write and send word to me about our situation. One of my friends from New Orleans told me, "I got a house here. Bring your children and your wife and y'all come on down here and stay at my house. We can stay together."

When I went out to California a little while later, some of my friends out there said, "You ought to leave Lake Providence. We will raise a hundred dollars here and a hundred dollars there to help you until you can get settled in. And you know how everyone out here loves to hear you preach. It wouldn't take you long to get a church to pastor."

But I made up my mind to stay. I told my friends, "I've got to die sometime, and it's just as close to heaven from Lake Providence as it is from California."

The movement had fallen by the wayside in many towns when the leaders bowed under pressure of violence and threats. So I had to stay. It was as if it was my destiny to stay in East Carroll Parish. My wife and family agreed we should stick it out, but in the meantime, I decided we needed to get more prepared. I had kept most of my guns together in one room, but I now placed my rifles and shotguns throughout the house, all within easy reach, if the need should arise. My two oldest sons, Leon and Leotis, were out of school and living elsewhere, so I gave my older daughters Johnita, Elsie, and Sharolyn and my youngest son, Louis, some target practice, so if we ever got into a tight corner, together we might be able to get out.

# NINETEEN

# Trouble on Every Hand

My commitment to stay cost me, and I often wondered whether I could endure. It was like living under a continuous test of how much the human mind could take, four or five years of feeling like I was being hunted, ducking and dodging for my life, like a buck during open hunting session.

One thing after another happened. After their botched attempt to murder me, they started doing things to play with my mind. One day when I picked up the mail, I found an empty envelope in my box. It had my address on it and a stamp, but there was nothing inside, just three teardrops drawn on the outside. I didn't know what those tears meant. Tears could mean so many things, maybe that someone would be crying soon.

I figured the Klan was probably behind a lot of the racial things going on around town, so I checked with the judge to see whether Lake Providence had an active Klan. He told me that the local group wasn't active at the time, but later I found out that the Lake Providence Klan was very much active.

Not long after I received the envelope, the Lake Providence telephone directory came in the mail. Walking from the highway back to the house from the mailbox, I happened to flip through the directory back to the S's. There it was—a big black blot of ink. They had blotted out my name. I assumed it was yet another warning that they still planned to blot out my life. It also showed me the free access they had to my mail and how easily they could tamper with it. I wondered how much of my mail was being taken. Somebody who worked at the post office had already warned me that they were checking all my mail from the NAACP, but here I had sure proof that they were messing with other mail too.

I had to make up my mind that I would just ignore all the things that were happening. I would hear comforting scriptures in my head:

"God hath not given us the spirit of fear" and "I can do all things through Christ which strengtheneth me" and "No weapon that is formed against thee shall prosper." That was how I kept going on.

I didn't share with other people the things that happened to me, because I figured if I talked about them, the people who were playing these mind games might think they were getting to me, and they might try more. So I went on following my daily pursuits. I did have to be careful, though, because one of the cooks told me that someone told him that the guy who shot me had a $1,000-dollar shot. That was real money back then, about a third of the cost of a new car, and I didn't know how many more thousands were up for my head. Or maybe the same thousand was still available since the first shooter hadn't done the job properly. So I always tried to keep my eyes open, but I couldn't let them stop me from living. When I wanted to go fishing, I fished; when I wanted to go hunting, I hunted. The woods were still my place of peace and communication with God. Still, I was always on the lookout for another attempt on my life.

One day I decided to go over the levee and spend a little time at one of my favorite fishing spots. The levee was only about a mile from my house, just on the other side of Highway 65, running parallel with the highway. Over the years since I was a child, the Mississippi River had periodically changed courses, moving further and further back from the levee. It now ran about a mile back, leaving behind in the woods an abundance of good fishing holes.

I parked my Buick on top of the levee and dragged my two cane poles out through the back rolled-down window. Carrying my can of worms and my big bucket for all the fish I knew I would catch, I made my way down the short narrow path that led through the woods to the fishing hole. I used my extensive knowledge of fish behavior to determine where my dinner would most likely bite, baited my hooks, and dropped my lines in the water to wait. It was a clear, sunny day with an occasional cool breeze, a good day to be outside. I settled in, feeling relaxed and almost back to normal again, enjoying the color of the leaves that covered the ground and the sounds of the outdoors—birds flittering from tree to tree, the periodic rattle in the bushes as some small animal scampered past.

That was where I was, all alone, out next to the woods, thinking good, peaceful thoughts, when I saw several white fellows approaching in a boat. They hadn't noticed me because they were busy doing something—I couldn't exactly tell what, at that distance.

As they got closer, I could see that one of the fellows had a .22 pistol that he seemed to be using to shoot some garfish or something on a line. Then I saw the other one look over toward me. He said something to the fellow with the .22, pointed at me, and then headed the boat straight in my direction.

My heart started to race, beating faster, faster, faster as the motorboat skimmed across the water straight toward me. I was too far away from the car and I didn't have a weapon with me. There was no one out there to help me, no one to hear my shouts or even serve as a witness. I wondered if I should run for the woods.

They pulled their boat up close to me and yelled out over the drone of their motor. "Do you like gars?"

I said, "Sure do."

"Well, we got some here we don't want and you can have them if you want them." They threw the gars out of the boat to me.

So I thought to myself, as my heart settled back into my chest, *Well, what I thought was meant for harm was meant for my good.*

This incident, however, turned out to be the exception. Mostly, they did mean harm. It was a very hard time for me but I took my burdens to the Lord and tried to leave them with him. The Lord and I spent a lot of time together those years, because every time I'd give him one burden, old Satan would make sure another one came my way.

One day as I was walking from town, a vehicle coming up the highway caught my attention. I had been on the lookout for trouble ever since the shooting and had tried to keep my eyes open, especially when I was out walking. The car seemed to be the same make and model as a car that one of the town troublemakers drove. Even in the distance, I could make out a carload of young white men. As it got closer, I noticed that the car was slowing down, and it looked like they were all looking at me.

My mind told me to start moving from the edge of the road in case they tried some foolishness. If I walked close to the edge of the ditch, I might have a chance to put some distance between them and me if I needed to.

In the few seconds it took me to think about this, the vehicle was already starting to cross the center line and move in my direction. I ran for the ditch and scrambled down its side just as their tires left the pavement and the vehicle sped in my direction. They were laughing as one fellow yelled out the window, "Dead nigger today!"

I was over sixty and practically bald by now, but I was still skinny and quick and could probably outrun a lot of young people. Through the grace of God, I was able to move just in time, and they had to swerve back onto the highway to keep from crashing down into the steep ditch.

I walked the rest of the way home by way of the cotton field, adrenaline turning into just plain anger. The voice in my head kept asking, "Why does a man have to live this way? Will it ever stop—other than when I am dead?" I remembered the laughing and wondered about a society that could create the kinds of animals that found pleasure from crushing a human body under the wheels of a car.

I had seen their faces and knew who the men were. I had already been watching one of this gang in particular, because he seemed to be under close surveillance by the sheriff after I was shot. I would always see him riding around in various police cars, talking to the sheriff or the deputies. It was only later that I found out he was the Ku Klux Klan leader of the parish, and the meetings weren't about surveillance after all.

I had no one to turn to for help. The FBI had gone back to wherever they came from, after turning the investigation over to the state police. That was like giving the fox the job of watching the henhouse. And I didn't want to tell other people because it might make them too afraid to participate. They would have given up the fight. So all the things that happened in the years following the shooting, through all the violence that was heaped up on me, I tried to keep it from the people.

I wouldn't even tell my wife. If she didn't witness it, I didn't tell her because I wanted her to sleep at night. And I especially didn't want anything to get back to the children to worry their minds.

When the FBI agents finally came back to Lake Providence to check on me, I related the various incidents to them. They went to ask my wife about them, but of course she didn't know anything, and because she didn't know anything about the incidents, they acted as if I wasn't telling the truth. And of course my wife was very upset with me for keeping things from her.

After her discussion with the FBI agents, my wife called a meeting with Elsie, Sharolyn, and Louis—the oldest children at home at the time—to talk about our situation and to prepare them for what might come. She told them that even if they ended up with no parents, she expected them to all become good productive adults. They had already been trained in what to do, so there should be no excuse. She told them not to let anyone separate the family. If someone wanted to raise just some of them, then none should go. It was to be all or none. She reminded them of how she had already assigned the younger children to an older sibling, so the older ones were to maintain that responsibility, no matter what.

She told them that we would always try to get back home by sunset, but if we weren't back by dark, they were to go in the house and lock the door and not let anyone in that they didn't know. Then she started talking about school and their friends.

"Now I don't want you talking at school," she said, "about any of this that is going on at home. Don't mention the cross burnings or the telephone calls or anything else. You don't know who we can trust or who might be against what your father is doing. And you don't want the other children scared to be around you. And be careful what you say on the phone. It's probably bugged, so you should assume at all times that someone is listening."

I suppose this was a conversation that needed to be held, but it wasn't one that I probably would have brought up. With the children, I tried to keep things light and humorous, and I always showed them an unwavering determination and a total lack of fear. Sometimes, the children got so caught up in what I was doing and saying that they would take lightly or act too boldly in some fairly serious situations. They tried to act as invincible as I talked. But that was the way they adjusted themselves to the craziness of the times. Everybody had to deal with the situation the best they knew how. They had their way and I had mine.

When I was growing up, boys were taught to conceal their emotions. I perfected this skill through a schoolyard game we played called rap-jack. In rap-jack, we used a switch called a rattan, the same kind the teachers used to whip us with when we misbehaved. We would join hands and whip each other with the rattan until the first person hollered out in pain. I learned in the game of rap-jack that the best way to outdo the others was to act like it wasn't hurting you. Even though they might be killing you, if you kept smiling, pretty soon they would say you didn't have good sense or you couldn't be hurt and they would leave you alone. They wouldn't even pick you to whip on the next time. But if the other person sensed he could get the best of you, why he would whip you even harder.

So the lesson I learned from childhood showed me how to carry on the struggle for civil rights. No matter what they did or said, I could mostly ignore it. When they confronted me face to face, I would choose either to ignore them or challenge them back. I had been doing this since my days as a tenant farmer, and I had earned the reputation of being crazy because no one could scare me into backing down when I put my mind to something.

So I continued to come and go as I saw fit, although every pickup truck outfitted with a gun rack with one or two loaded shotguns could have contained a killer. I refused to give up or give in, even when they tried to run me down a second and a third time. The third time I was walking down the highway again when a fellow drove all the way off his side of the highway, across the other lane and onto the shoulder of the road to try to hit me. I recognized him. He had been in the automobile that tried to run me over the first time.

I tried to control my feelings, but this attack aroused my deepest emotions. I couldn't keep it to myself any longer. Something insane triggered inside my head. I felt sort of like a dog when his tail has been pulled for a long time—he gets to the place where he's going to bite or fight. I wanted to get my guns and kill these people.

But it's times like these that God has to make his presence known, even when we don't ask for it. He reached through my anger to give me the comfort and peace I needed. He opened my eyes to see that out of all the bad, good had come out of it, and that he was the same God who had been the leader and the protector all the way through the fight. He made me see that I was about to lose the war in an attempt to win one battle. My enemies would have had me just where they wanted me, in a position where they could "justifiably" lynch me.

So as the months passed, I had to learn what it meant to totally lean on the Lord. He had to show me that he was all I needed and that he was in control of life and death. He protected me and warned me in the time of trouble, sparing my life over and over again. He gave me the courage to go on.

Since the children had had their talk with their mother about our situation, they had gotten serious about protecting themselves. If my wife and I got home after dark, which we tried to avoid doing, I would find them all inside with the doors locked tight. They told me that they would go in and pray until we got home.

One night my wife and I were uptown when a young man came up to me and introduced himself as Ronnie Moore from the Congress of Racial Equality (CORE). He said, "You know I almost got myself shot at your house tonight."

"What do you mean?" I asked, feeling a little worried.

"Well, I came up on your porch and knocked on the door and your daughter answered the door with a gun barrel in my face. I had to do myself some fast talking to assure her I wasn't an enemy. You've got them trained well."

When I got home, I found out that the story was indeed true. The young man had come in the yard in a small sports car, which the children hadn't been able to see when they looked out after the knock on the door. Johnita had answered the door with the shotgun. They had taken things a little further than I had expected them to.

The family survived the summer and most of the fall, and winter was now fast approaching. It had started to turn cold, and my son Louis and I were out working in the woodpile cutting up some logs one of my friends had brought. We finished about first dark and were headed around to the front of the house when I heard the report of a rifle. Out of the corner of my eye, I glimpsed a flash of light as a branch fell from the peach tree I was just walking past. My mind immediately began to tell me that I hadn't really seen or heard what I had just seen and heard. So I kept walking as if nothing had happened. I didn't even look at Louis for fear that the expression on his face might make me acknowledge the truth. So I pretended for his sake and mine that nothing had happened and went on in the house, but not before I looked toward the levee and saw someone hurriedly getting in a vehicle.

Thanksgiving 1962 came and went, and not long after the holidays, my wife received a letter from a Miss Arnetta Pierce, counselor for the Young Adult Branch of the NAACP over in Monroe. In her letter, she talked about how her newly formed young adult group had registered more people to vote in three months than the adult group had registered in six years. She wrote that it was me and my wife's courage that had inspired them to continue working, even when one of them had been thrown in jail. They had met and decided they wanted to show their appreciation by doing something for my children for Christmas. We were surprised that we had inspired these young people and that they wanted to do something so nice.

Miss Pierce and her group came over right before Christmas and gave the children a surprise Christmas party. They bought each child the toys and new clothes they had wanted and presented us a family gift of a record player. They bought the kinds of things I couldn't afford to buy from the $100 or so the church paid me each month. We all had lots of fun that day, and when I looked at these young people, all under the age of thirty and so eager for the fight, I had all the encouragement I needed to carry on.

So I stopped thinking so much about just staying alive and started concentrating on the things I could accomplish in whatever time God afforded me. Maybe the middle-aged people were scared, but I had another generation coming along who were not afraid, which gave me hope. I set about the business of making sure that as many people as possible got to take advantage of the opportunity to vote. We began a serious campaign to get the people registered.

We started meeting regularly at the Baptist Center across from my house. The entire parish was organized by ward and precinct, and coordinators were assigned to each area. Eric Armstrong, Rev. Atlas, Mary Liza Cole, and a few other ladies headed up the registration effort inside the city limits. We also assigned Mrs. Annie Wiggins, a lady who had a lot of influence with the older women. South of town, in the first ward, we had Watson Sanders and James Levi and another group who lived on the Henderson Project settlement we had won from the Farm Security Administration back in the 1930s. West of town, out in the Pilgrim Rest area, the sixth ward, we had Lehman Griffin, Sr., and Lehman Griffin, Jr., and the pastor of the church in that area, Rev. Freddie Green. In the fifth ward, north of town, we had Clyde Robinson, Walter Nash, and Frank Nervis. In every area, we had someone to carry on, except in the seventh ward, which was a long ways out and practically dominated by the poor whites.

We canvassed door to door and tried to talk to every black person old enough to vote. Every day we got a new story or a new excuse. "Rev, y'all need to leave this thing alone. Didn't you see how they burned those crosses? I saw two on the way to work this morning. That's message enough for me. They don't have to come tell me to my face." Or, "You going to have it so none of us will be eating."

I couldn't really fault them for how they felt, because they had to have heard stories from the people already actively involved, how some of them couldn't even buy their own groceries because no one except Wyly Jong, one of the Chinese grocers, would sell to them. Or how in other stores, the clerks would reach around them and serve the next person in line, just like they were invisible. And all of them seemed to have heard about J. J. Ellis's furniture store, the one with easy credit and even easier repossessions, where they would ask, "Are you involved in this voting thing?" and if someone answered yes, they would say, "We can't sell to you." So voting required a level of courage, because people had to put something on the line, sometimes even their jobs, to register.

Benjamin Blockwood, one of the witnesses at the last two hearings against Manning, had already been forced out of town by now. He had tried to carry on his business for a while after his wife was transferred to Baton Rouge, but they fixed it so he couldn't make a living. After the school officials told the teachers that they would lose their jobs if they went to his barbecue place, everybody stopped coming except for a couple of teachers who still had the nerve to defy the order. Then they went after his construction business. He said that the owners of Madden Lumber Yard and the East Carroll Lumber Yard both told him to get out their places and never set foot in them again. He had the same problem at Schneider's hardware store, so he couldn't get any supplies. Eventually, after more than fifteen years in the construction business, he had to close his business down and move to Baton Rouge, where his wife had been transferred.

The registrar, Manning, was back at work but obviously not happy to be there. When people went to register, he would make them wait a long time in the hallway outside his office before he would serve them. And when he let them in, he was unpleasant, and nobody seemed to be able to answer the questions to his satisfaction. So he found a way to turn away a good many of them.

The sheriff, whose office was near the registrar's office, kept a watchful eye on our activities. The whole affair seemed to make his blood boil. One day he walked in the courthouse and saw a group of blacks along with a few whites waiting in line outside the registration office. He walked over and pushed the white people up to the front of the line, in front of the blacks already there. "I don't see what these d—— niggers are here for anyway," he mumbled as he walked away.

So there were many reasons why people might not try to register, but that didn't discourage us. Those who we could convince were told to come down to the Center, where we taught them how to fill out the registration cards. If they made it through this procedure, they were assigned to a voter registration teacher who would teach them the answers to all ten versions of the constitution and government test. Each version had six questions, and they had to be able to pass any version randomly selected for them to take when they went to register. We had volunteers assigned to teach at five locations—the Baptist Center, my house, where my wife taught, Mr. Eric Armstrong's house, Mr. Weaver's house, and Progressive Chapel Baptist Church. My children and some of the other young people around town assisted the teachers in preparing the candidates for their tests.

Most of the people who registered finished one of our classes. People sometimes came by the house after working late in the evening, and my wife and I would stay up way into the night carrying them over the test questions. Alease wouldn't give up on anybody. She actually taught one lady how to write and fill out everything. She couldn't make her letters right, but she wanted to register so badly my wife taught her how to make the letters. It took her five or six trips to the registrar's office before she finally passed, only to be told by the registrar that he couldn't certify her anyway because she owed some rent on her house.

Soon after we started our registration drive, people attending the meetings at the Baptist Center started complaining about getting flats or finding nails in their tires. I was working in the yard one day when an old man carrying a tin can walked up in the yard.

"I needed some nails and tacks," he said, "and I saw a bunch of them at the end of your road. I picked up nearly a can full. They were just what I needed."

I got my children and he and I went back and picked up all the nails and tacks we could find. We found out that at night while we met, someone was scattering nails and tacks up and down the road where the people had to come out. From then on, we kept a close check on the road to keep it clear.

Election time rolled around again. Some of us had voted before, but for most people, this would be their first time. Certain members of the community who liked wearing sheets thought this would be a most opportune time to play on the fears of the people who had just registered. They must have opened a cross-making factory, because the night before election day, there were crosses burning all over the parish.

All into the night, the phone rang with reports of cross burnings. One frightened lady called me and said, "They're burning a cross in front of my house." She sounded hurt. "I don't bother anybody. I don't see why they have to be picking on me."

I told her, "Well, that's only a reminder that tomorrow is the day for you to go out and vote. They just didn't want you to forget. Don't disturb yourself about the cross burnings. Some people use the cross all kinds of ways. Some wear the cross and some burn the cross. Some of us choose to bear the cross."

That night, I decided that I was going to take my gun and go hide out and wait for them to come down our way. I told the children, "I think I'll go hide in the bushes and when one of those Ku Kluckers gets out the car, then I'll shoot him, maybe in the kneecaps. That way whoever we see limping tomorrow, we'll know who was under that sheet."

The children started to laugh and urge me on. "Yeah, Daddy, go do it, Daddy!"

I looked over at my wife, who was rolling her eyes at me, giving me her "this is not funny and don't play about this" look. I went and got my guns and started to load them.

"You can't be serious," she said. "You go out there and you could be the one getting killed."

We sat around a long time joking about the whole thing as the children created funnier and funnier scenarios. Of course my wife wasn't included in that "we." I really was halfway waiting around for them to come, but they were so long getting down my way until I decided to go on to bed. Later on, my daughter, who was still up, heard a truck pull off. She looked out and said, "Oh, they're burning our cross now."

In the morning, I walked out to the end of the road and pulled up the charred remains of what had been wood wrapped in gas-soaked burlap rags. This would be one of many trips to the end of the road to remove this symbol of the Klan. One time they ventured onto the property to burn a cross down near the Center, but all the other times, they burned them way at the end of the road, out at the highway.

Most of the crosses were burned out in the rural area, where it was easier to get in and out without being seen. But after a while, the cross burnings got to be so commonplace that people began to take it as a symbol of fun, though as far as I was concerned, they were still trying to work on me.

Most people in Lake Providence hadn't experienced real deep-seated racial violence up close and personal, but many of them read the black papers enough to know that in towns not very far away, leaders were getting their homes firebombed, churches were being burned, and people were occasionally being lynched. So there was always an undercurrent of fear in the community that paralyzed people into inaction when it came to taking an open stand on civil rights.

In February 1963, some of the NAACP branches in northeast Louisiana got together to discuss how to deal with the growing fear in the community. As a few of us sat around waiting for time for the meeting to start, the conversation turned to the recent violence.

Two men sat behind me talking. "You know things have really gotten crazy since that Meridith boy integrated Ole Miss," one of them said. "Did you see how they carried on about a boy trying to get a college education? College students screaming "kill him" and throwing bottles full of acid."

"Well at least he had the protection of the federal marshals," the other one interjected. "What about Clarence Shaw who they grabbed because they were so mad about their school being messed up with colored people? They beat his head in, and if that wasn't evil enough, they threw him on the railroad tracks to be run over by the train. That train cut off both his legs and about cut off his arms too."

"Well, don't forget that back in December, they shot up the house of the Meridith boy's parents too," the first man countered.

A young man who looked to be in his twenties had been leaning against the wall listening to the exchange and decided to add his two cents' worth. "Have you all heard the latest? Not only are they shooting at folks, but now they've got a whole new game. Like what happened to the SCLC director from Shreveport when he was over in Georgia. He was outside in back of this church trying to provide some security where Dr. King was speaking, when the police came up and arrested him. Guess what they charged him with? Lunacy! Can you believe that?! The sheriff actually had him committed. I was told they tested his sanity by asking him stupid questions like 'Do you believe in integration?' and 'If you had to choose to defend the state of Georgia, which would you choose?' Now you tell me who's the lunatic!"

With that, he strode off and took a seat on the other side of the room with some of the other young adults.

I looked back, and the two men were looking over at the young man with that look that said, "You don't know enough to be dipping in old people's conversation."

I turned back around as one of them said, "These young people just don't know. In Louisiana, they've been committing people all last year. People who try to stand up to them, they been sending them to the insane asylum in Jackson and not a thing wrong with them."

The other man nodded his head in agreement. "And you know they don't want anybody to know what's going on down here either. You saw how they shot that reporter from London in the back and killed him while he was trying to cover that Meridith story. And what about that television show on voting in Mississippi that aired on CBS back in October? You see how they blacked it out completely in Mississippi and in part of Louisiana, and I heard Tennessee too, so that colored people wouldn't know that a change was a-coming, whether they want it or not."

By now, it was time for the meeting to start. After much discussion about recent bombings, fires, and threats, we had to agree that the danger was real. So how did we convince people not to be afraid when there was definitely something to be afraid of?

In the end, we decided we needed to generate a propaganda war just like our opponents. All the way home, I tried to think of something to say that would move the people to go get registered. I was still the president of the Baptist Association and because of my office, I was a sort of missionary. Most churches back then only had one service a month. At my church, North Star, we had preaching and communion service on the fourth Sunday, so the remaining three Sundays, I would visit other churches. Whether they let me preach or just make remarks at the end of the service, I would always find a way to make my pitch for voting and for standing up to be counted. Certain churches, I didn't even try to visit because I knew that the members and sometimes the pastor were too afraid to even have me in the building.

By the time I got home, I had come up with a plan. My theme became "Get Your Name on the Books." First I would talk about the Fair Lamb's Book of Life. I'd say, "Don't forget to get your name in it. Is your name written there? You won't be known, your name won't be called in heaven, unless you get your name on the book." Then when I'd finish talking about that book that's so precious in heaven, I'd talk about the earthly book down at the registration office. "If you don't get your name on there, you won't be counted. Your needs won't be recognized. For goodness sake, get out there and go get your name on the book."

I'd tell the people a story about how I overcame fear when I first started going out to see girls. I was afraid to go out at night in the country by myself, so I would always take a friend along with me. One girl I was visiting really got my heart. I was in love with the girl so deeply that it worried me to stay at home, but yet I didn't have anybody to go over to her house with me. So I decided I had to venture out alone. Nothing got me that night, so I ventured out again, and I began to overcome my fear. I told them that if I had not ventured out, in spite of my fear, I would have missed out on something I really wanted.

I would also tell another story about a soldier who was about to be shipped out. He was standing there shaking, with his teeth knocking. His officer walked up to him and said, "Fear is a healthy sign in a soldier."

"Yes sir, Captain, this is one of the healthiest soldiers you got," the soldier replied.

I would say, "Now the soldiers, they don't stop because of fear. They feel like there's a job to be done and they've got to do it. That's how we've got to face this situation. There's a job to be done and we've got to do it. I don't care if our teeth are knocking and our legs feel weak, let's march on together and do it." Of course that created some interest.

I tried to take advantage of every bad incident to kindle the fire. I'd tell the people, "Now if you were a voter, they wouldn't disrespect you like that. You would be able to do something about that problem. You would have a voice in it."

Sometimes I felt like telling them that if they didn't want to help themselves by registering, then don't come calling me when they got in trouble, but I didn't have the heart to turn people away when they were in trouble. It was downright discouraging, how the people couldn't see the amount of power they actually had. When we started voting, the politicians started changing. I would tell the people, "You see what has happened since just a few of us started? What would it mean if we all got involved in this thing?" Still, most acted as if they still didn't get the point.

# TWENTY

# One Hundred Years

We continued to work through the spring of 1963, but as hard as we worked, we still had minimal success. From my reading and conversations with other civil rights leaders across the south, it was clear to me as early as April that 1963 was going to be a year of confrontation. Leaders of the struggle and people who opposed us were both digging in their heels. Both sides were refusing to give an inch. I believed we were headed for a crisis of some sort, but I just didn't know what kind. Back in February, there had been a big confrontation over in Greenwood, Mississippi, over people protesting the attempted murder of a civil rights leader. The police had beaten the peaceful demonstrators with billy clubs and then turned the dogs on the people. Some were already injured and couldn't get away, so they were bitten by the German shepherds too. Then in April, Dr. Martin Luther King had arrived in Birmingham and declared that he would lead demonstrations until "Pharaoh let the people go."

The year 1963 marked one hundred years since the Emancipation Proclamation, and a national centennial celebration was declared. President Kennedy went before Congress and made a speech about the many injustices against the Negro and what needed to be done to correct them.

Although we were happy not to be in slavery, somehow the celebration seemed empty when we were still denied so many basic rights. Viewing things from a hundred years back made a lot of people see the injustices for what they were, and it made some people mad. A hundred years was a long time for so little to have changed. Yet there were white people who were still saying that we needed to take it slow. If we moved any slower, I thought, we wouldn't be moving at all.

I spent a lot of time thinking in those early months. Often at night in the quiet, with the croaking frogs and the chirping crickets in the distance, I would walk around outside and think. In the quiet, I would watch the stars and the clouds and maybe an occasional lightning flash off in the distance, and contemplate where we were. Is this what being patient and never speaking out and complaining had bought us? Why did we smile and go along as if everything was okay, when we were so filled with hurt and anger over being separated and being treated different from every other American, or immigrant too, for that matter? If we had forced our history to be told honestly like the Jews were doing, would the Negro now have some respect? Had we made it easy for whites to pretend that they were all good Christian people?

And why were people talking about us, why did they expect us to have accomplished so much in a hundred years when we started off with nothing and when what we had worked for had made others rich? Hadn't we tried to make our way after slavery only to be constantly robbed of our goods, our labor, our livelihood, our dignity, and our rights? Weren't black leaders being killed off in record numbers all across the South? We still didn't have basic human rights, not legally or otherwise given. Good-paying jobs weren't available to us. And why would anyone compare us to immigrants? No other race had their separation and poverty mandated by law and affirmed all the way to the Supreme Court.

Hadn't we just gotten rid of the split school term a few years back? Weren't our children still in segregated and substantially underfunded schools, and weren't we still getting desks and books after the white children finished with them? Didn't we still have colored entrances to some businesses? I wondered what most white people *really* thought about racism, or whether they bothered to think about it at all. Could they really be *that* blind to discrimination, or were they blind because we allowed them to be? Or could it be that they really lived under such a thick cloud of historical lies, some kind of fantasy South that their minds couldn't even accept that so much was being done to us every day? Because surely if they saw, wouldn't decent people be moved to action? Or was it because the politicians had made the rules by which everyone played, that the players could no longer be held account-able? Was no one accountable for the situation we were in?

I continued to dwell on these questions as the number of racial confrontations continued to increase. By May of 1963, the Klan, which was reorganizing extremely fast, had created hit lists of people targeted for vigilante acts of violence. One of my white friends told me about some of the meetings they were holding locally and told me to be careful. "You know they still mad about how many times they have missed," he said. In some cases, the NAACP managed to get copies of the lists, which included the names of some people I knew and had worked with through the years. It seemed our enemies would stop at nothing to reach their goal.

One day I had walked to town because of a problem with the car. I had gotten to talking and had let night about catch me before I hurried home. As I came up on the edge of Dudley Green's property, something moving in the leafy branches of the pecan tree caught my eye. When I looked up, I discovered a man up the tree with a rifle turned toward me. My friend had told me to be really careful, and now here I was staring at a man with his finger on the trigger and one eye closed as he set his aim on me. I stopped dead in my tracks.

I turned toward him and said, "Take your best shot, and if God is ready for me, then I'll go. If he isn't ready for me, there's nothing you can do." I stood still in front of the tree, looked him straight in the eye, and waited for him to pull the trigger. He hadn't expected anyone staring at death to behave that way, and he slowly lowered his weapon and just looked at me in a dumbfounded way. I turned and proceeded to walk the short distance to Dudley Green's drive. I turned down his road and walked on home, never looking back.

In other parts of the country, the same craziness was going on—a bombing here, a lynching there. Then they dynamited a black hotel and Dr. Martin Luther King's brother's house all in the same day in Birmingham, and all the pent-up anger must have just come out all at once because the people in Birmingham took to the streets. They attacked the policemen, and when it was all done, a big section of the city had been burned down. After that, race riots broke out all over the South, and all the white hatred and all the bitterness that black people spent so much energy trying to hide flowed out into the open.

I had complained about my sister Annie B. giving my wife a television, but now I could catch the television news, which was a lot different from listening to the radio. On the screen, I could see the large numbers of people following Dr. King and other leaders in their nonviolent demonstrations and sit-ins, but I could also see what the police were doing to the protesters. And if I could see, that meant that America and all the foreign countries had to see too. They would see the water from the fire hoses so strong that it pushed the people down the street and tore off their skin. They would see the pictures of college students trying to get served at soda fountains, being beaten across the head by the police until their faces couldn't be seen for the blood.

It wasn't long before the foreign press began to ask the questions Americans had never been forced to answer before—How can you protect the rest of the world from loss of freedom if you deny freedom to your own citizens? As they plastered the pictures and inadequate answers in their newspapers across the world, I began to feel that a little change was right around the corner, because America did not like to be embarrassed.

As pressure mounted from within and without, in June 1963 President Kennedy decided to address the country about race. We gathered around the radio, straining to hear his every word over the crackles and static. In his strange Massachusetts accent, I heard him say, "We preach freedom around the world, and we mean it. And we cherish our freedom here at home. But are we to say to the world—and much more importantly to each other—that this is the land of the free, except for the Negroes; that we have no second-class citizens, except for Negroes; that we have no class or caste system, no ghettos, no master race, except with respect to Negroes?"

It was a significant speech, because it was the first time we had heard a governmental leader actually admit that something very wrong was being done to us. He had said, "We owe them, and we owe ourselves a better country." But the response to the call for improved race relations I heard from my part of the country was quite the opposite. Right after President Kennedy's speech, some coward had hidden in the flower bushes at the home of Medgar Evers, an acquaintance of mine and NAACP field secretary for Mississippi, and had blown him away with a high-powered rifle.

In some respects, the president's message gave black people courage to defy discriminatory practices and it caused us to start expecting real change, but on the other hand, the violent response from the South made many more people afraid. Certain people felt the president's speech meant the end of their power and control, and we knew they would not go down without a fight. So there was a new fear when people left their houses unattended or when they rode down a lonely stretch of highway or when they left their children at home alone.

Although violence was prevalent throughout the South, things had actually been kind of quiet in Lake Providence for the last month, except for some cross burnings and a few white teenagers in cars meddling with black people who walked along the highway. But that didn't mean we didn't expect something big to happen every day. Violence seemed to be creeping closer. One recent morning as I was getting ready to go out before day break, a man had come knocking on the door. He was shaking scared, saying that he was from Mississippi and that a white man had come to kill him in his own house after he had stood up for the right, but he had killed the white man instead and was now running for his life. Another civil rights leader in Mississippi had told him that when he got to Louisiana he should look me up and I would tell him what to do. I gave him bus fare and told him to head for Chicago.

Trouble did come soon, and it started with a campaign to cut as many black mothers off welfare as possible. The cuts were so severe and the politicians were starving so many children in Louisiana that relief agencies from foreign countries offered aid to the children. Soon after the campaign to starve the children started, two churches where we were holding registration meetings, Pilgrim Rest Baptist and Cain Ridge Baptist, were gassed and torched in the middle of the night. They burned to the ground. We tried to carry on at the Baptist Center across from my house, but only the very brave continued to come.

One Friday night, not long after Medgar Evers had been murdered, my wife and I were attending one of our registration meetings at the Center when devilment got into somebody's head and told them to call my house.

The children were at home, and my teenage daughter, Elsie, answered the phone.

"May I speak to Rev. Mr. Black?" the voice on the other end had asked.

She told him that he must have the wrong number.

"Oh yes, we have the right number," the voice said. "You tell your Daddy that we're going to come down there and kill him." Then the man had hung up.

*Rev. Mr. Black* was a top-ten country song about a preacher under attack. It said something about the preacher having to walk a lonesome valley and having to walk it all by himself.

A little later the phone rang again, and Elsie again answered the phone.

"May I speak to Rev. Mr. Black?" It was the same man calling again.

"No Rev. Mr. Black lives here!" Elsie angrily told the man.

The man laughed a sinister laugh. "Oh you know who I'm talking about. I want you to deliver a message to your old daddy. Tell him that if he's not out of Lake Providence by tomorrow, we're coming to get him and he won't live to see the next day."

Elsie, who was the quietest of my children, told the man, "You'd better come prepared then, because my Daddy will be ready for you!"

"Who you talking to? How old are you?" the voice on the phone wanted to know. "Little gal, don't you know that I'll kill your Daddy and when I'm done with him, I'll rape your Mama too?"

I was up front presiding when I saw Elsie come into the Center. She went over and whispered something to my wife, and they both left out. When they got back to the house, the phone was ringing again. My wife answered this time, and the man on the phone described to her what they were going to do to me. The man spewed out all his racial venom, calling her a b——, telling her how much he hated her just because she was a nigra and how he hated me because I was an "old NAACP man." He proceeded to tell her how after they killed me, how they were going to rape her.

I could see the distressed look on my wife's face when she came back in the Center to get me. It reminded me of the look I often caught on her face during the days immediately following the shooting in 1962.

My wife recounted what they had said as we walked back to the house. She was very frightened, more than I had ever seen before. I was so mad I could hardly stand it. I had always worked to see that my wife was respected. In fact, she was one of a very few black women white people did not address by a first name. They addressed her as

Mrs. Scott or Mrs. A. J. Scott or Mrs. John Henry Scott, so they certainly couldn't disrespect her by calling her out of her name. And nobody had a right to be threatening my wife with rape or to call and frighten my children that way. This time they had crossed the line.

I asked her what the man sounded like. She said, "He didn't sound like those others you've been talking about. This man actually sounded well-educated, but he said to tell you that he was speaking for the Klan. What are you going to do?"

When I got to the house, the phone was ringing again. I told my daughter to let me answer it. I had planned to give them an earful, but as soon as they heard my voice, they hung up. They kept calling every couple of minutes, but they never said anything.

After a while, I decided to go back over to the Center since I had left so abruptly and because the caller obviously didn't want to talk to me. After I got the meeting closed out and locked up the Center, I came back home and started getting my guns together.

"What are you getting ready to do?" my wife asked as she followed me around the house.

"I'm just getting prepared. You go ahead and get the children in the bed."

My wife got the younger girls put to bed in the front room while I loaded my guns. I told the older ones, "I'm going to get prepared. That call probably was a trick to get us all out on the highway so they can ambush us and kill us all. But we're not going to fall for that. I've got a much better chance defending us if we stay right here at the house." I looked at my wife, who was looking undecided about the whole matter. To give her some assurances, I told her, "I don't really believe they will come if they call and say they are coming. If they were actually coming, they would have never called. But I want you to take the .410 and Johnita, you take the .22, and Louis and I will watch outside in case they've changed their ways. You know a man's got a legal right to defend his own home. I might die here tonight, but I guarantee you this, I will take someone else with me."

The older children were starting to look frightened too, probably because they had never seen me like this, never seen me this angry. I picked up my 12-gauge double-barrel shotgun and my .38 revolver and put extra ammunition in my pocket, and Louis and I went outside.

Glancing around the yard, I decided that the best place to hide was behind a clump of four-o'clock flower bushes growing off to the front right of the house. From our dark hiding place, with the light shining from the light pole between the house and the Baptist Center, I could see across the yard toward where the road came in from the highway. If they came up in the yard, I should be able to pick them off before they could harm anybody.

We waited a while, and then I sent Louis back in the house. I continued to wait until way over into the night. Then it finally occurred to me that I should pray. After I prayed, I thought to myself, *Why am I saying I'm going to trust in the Lord and I'm afraid to go to bed?* So I got my guns together and went back in and got in my bed and went to sleep.

The next evening after the phone calls, I went to town. I had stopped across the street from the Fireman's Hall to talk to a fellow when I happened to look up and see a group of whites gathered outside the Hall. One of them looked and saw me, and they started poking one another until they were all looking at me.

The man I was talking to said, "What they looking at you for?"

"Well, maybe that's some of the group that told me to be out of town by today and I'm still here. I guess that's what they're looking at."

After that incident, I put Elsie in charge of manning the phones, but they never called back after that. Those phone calls had come in on a Friday night, and almost all the other dirty deeds were done on Friday nights. We decided that Fridays must be Ku Klux meeting night because most everything that happened bad, happened on a Friday night.

The policemen had always had a pattern of arresting black men for any old thing, even if they had to make up something, but after we began to vote, they seemed to press this pattern much harder. They would pick up black boys and claim they had stolen something. Once they had them in custody, they'd beat them to make them confess to things they hadn't done. Sometimes they would just stop them for personal entertainment and make them lie in ditches of foul dirty water or they'd do other kinds of humiliating things to the boys and then let them go. The parents kept worrying me about what the policemen were doing to their children, and I really didn't know what to do to solve the problem. Finally I told them to just write out their complaints and sign them and I'd see what I could do.

In June 1964, I caught the bus up to New Jersey to attend the Baptist Jubilee Advance in Atlantic City. I even took a little time for some fun, going over to the World's Fair in New York. On the way back down, I stopped in Washington, D.C., to visit my friend Rev. Stovall. I decided that since I was in Washington, I'd call over to the Justice Department and talk with some of the people I had worked with through the years. They invited me over for lunch the next day, and during the luncheon, I happened to mention the complaints I had about the boys. They told me if I gave them copies of the complaints, they would investigate.

In a few weeks, the FBI started their investigations, and in about six months they had the case brought before a federal grand jury down in Lafayette, Louisiana. I had been under so much pressure, I really didn't want to be directly involved in this case. But when the day came for the boys who had been beaten to go to Lafayette, the man who was supposed to take them backed out and wouldn't go. So I had to take them down to Lafayette myself.

The grand jury indicted three police officers, Junior Thornton, Johnny Warner, and Kenneth Parks, for assaulting, beating and kicking three teenagers to secure a confession during the spring of 1964. Thornton and another police officer, Wilson Boudreaux, were indicted for depriving three other teenagers of their rights by beating them in the summer of 1963. The police officers were not present at the hearing, and the decision was kept secret until the federal marshals came to arrest them. This case played a great part in helping to straighten out policemen in the area. Before the indictment, they had thought they could do anything and get away with it—including shooting me.

During the summer of 1964, we decided to put on a big pageant called "Youth at the Crossroads" for our annual Baptist Association meeting. The parts to the play were given out to youth representing all the different Baptist churches in the parish. In the evenings, when the young people would come down to the Center for rehearsals, large groups of teens would be milling about in the yard waiting for their turn to perform.

The Baptist Center, being off the highway, was somewhat remote, and the police really had no business being on the property unless they were coming for official business. But during the rehearsals, policemen would turn off the highway and drive slowly up and down the road, looking at the crowd. I don't know what they thought we were doing—maybe planning a demonstration or a boycott or something. But whatever they thought, it was clear they were concerned about what we were doing.

The new Civil Rights Bill was coming up before Congress, so I decided to go up to Washington. I figured I would have plenty of time to get back before the start of the week-long annual Baptist Association meeting. I secured a pass ticket from Senator Long's secretary that permitted me to sit in the gallery during the debate. Senator Humphrey was making every effort to get the bill through, but there was a filibuster by the southern senators. I sat in the gallery and listened to them hold up the debate, making speeches on all sorts of irrelevant subjects. The filibuster went on and on and on. I started praying. I asked God to give Mr. Humphrey courage and strength to hold up and to carry the fight on through.

Our annual association meeting was to be held the first week in July, so I had to leave Washington before the filibuster ended. I had some things I needed to get done before the association started, and I needed to get with my wife to get my annual address written. I had discovered early in our marriage that speechwriting was one of her very strong talents. I was good with sermons; she was good with speeches. I could give her an outline on any topic and she could write a speech about it, which she also routinely did for many other members of the community too. So I started outlining my annual address on the way back home.

After the long bus ride back, I was surprised to find out that the filibuster was still in full swing. I listened to the radio the next day and the next, wondering how long a filibuster could last. The third day after my return, I heard that the senators had put a stop to the filibuster, 71–29, and the civil rights bill was going to pass.

Our association turned out first-rate, and the young people put on one of our best programs ever. I gave my annual president's message, making reference to the great turn of events in the last twelve months—the big March on Washington last August when more than 250,000 people of different races and denominations united for civil rights, the fear that gripped the country when everywhere black people, North and South, poor and middle class, all began to speak publicly for the first time of their collective pains and humiliations, the anger in September, less than three weeks after the March on Washington, over the four little girls blown up by a bomb planted outside their Sunday School class in Birmingham, and the disappointment and fear associated with the assassination of President Kennedy two months later, in November. And I talked about how after all the sadness and hatred of 1963, how the new president, a southerner no less, had pushed the Congress to pass President Kennedy's civil rights bill in the past president's memory, how the Senate had finally taken a stand for the right and put a stop to the southern filibuster on the civil rights bill, and how just this very week, on July 2, 1964, President Johnson had signed the bill into law. I told them it was like watching a great drama going on. Before you could get used to one thing, something else was happening. God had not let our work and dying be in vain.

My oldest daughter, Johnita, was home that summer after her sophomore year at Southern University in Baton Rouge, and Elsie was getting ready to start there in the fall. Johnita had found a little job at White's Motel, up on the lake, working the evening shift to earn money for expenses not covered by her scholarship. She generally got in around one in the morning when Mr. Slim, a man who worked at White's, would drop her off at the house. I thought that her late arrival would offer some protection from intruders coming on the property.

One Friday night, sometime before Johnita got home from work, I was startled awake when the dogs broke at something and then suddenly quit barking. This should have caught my attention enough for me to go out and check, but it didn't. I dozed off again only to be awakened an hour or so later by the dogs barking at Mr. Slim's car. I got up to let Johnita in, and we talked a short while. She said she was going to stay up a while and read. I went back to my room and lay down and after a while, I saw the lights go out and heard Johnita turn in for the night. I fell back to sleep soon afterwards.

I pulled to get away from something that was grabbing for me in my sleep, but it pulled at me again.

"Wake up! Wake up!" a voice was calling.

At first, I had thought I was in a crazy dream, but I now realized that it was my wife's voice and her pulling at me and screaming and scrambling out of the bed, all at the same time.

"Get up! Get up!" she yelled. "The car's on fire!"

I looked through the open bedroom door toward the two front windows in the living room. A reddish glow filtered around the edges of the window shades. Leaping out of the bed, I calculated how much time it would take the flames to leap the four feet between the house and the makeshift wood-and-tin carport I had built. We might have minutes, even seconds, to get the children out, and all six of them were sleep on the carport side of the house. I pulled the string to turn on the light bulb that hung from the center of the room. No lights. We had no lights! They had cut off our electricity.

"Get up! Get up! There's a fire!" my wife screamed, as she ran through the front room into the back room calling the three children back there. "Get up and grab your banks and let's try to make it to the Greens'!"

I was grabbing for the two children sleeping on the cot and the one on the sofa when I was struck with another realization. Something else was wrong. The dogs hadn't barked. Why? Maybe they had been poisoned. I stopped to peep out the window and that's when I realized that it wasn't the car on fire after all, but the Baptist Center building all in flames. The flames were sweeping through the place like wildfire.

All the children were now huddled at the front door, wide-eyed in their sleeping clothes, waiting for me. I told them that it was the Center on fire and that I needed to call the fire department.

"Number, please," whined the operator. She sure did take her time coming on the line, I thought to myself. She must have been sleeping. I grabbed my flashlight and shined it on the wind up clock on the dresser. It read 2:45 A.M.

"We need a fire truck sent to the Baptist Center building just as soon as possible!"

"Sorry," came the nasal answer at the other end of the line. "All the fire trucks are at another fire." Click.

On a reality level, I should have known they wouldn't come to put out a fire that might have been planned at the firehouse in the first place. But I always tried to live in expectation. I really hoped that these people would just wake up one day and say to themselves, "Does this make any sense what I'm doing? Isn't there something just a little insane about hating a group of people and destroying their property just because of the color of their skin?" But tonight was apparently not a night of revelation, so in the wee hours of the morning, I ran over to the Center only to discover that it was already almost totally engulfed in flames. Flames were starting to leap out of the top of the Center building, and I could see fire through all the windows.

I had put some records near the front door, figuring that I would have a chance to get them out in case of a fire, but the fire was so intense, I couldn't get anything out. The wood-frame building looked to have been oiled down so well that no fireman would have been able to slow the fire down anyway.

My wife had taken the younger children over to the Greens' house, and Mr. Green had come back over with her. We stood there together along with the older children, watching the fire spread. Without the light on the pole, since the electricity had been cut, the only illumination was the flickering flames that danced in the wind. Fortunately for us, the wind was blowing away from our house, or the house would have burned down too. The flames cast ominous shadows over the surrounding trees, making everything look as gloomy as I felt. We stood watching the flames as they licked through the roof and the sides of the Center finally came crashing inward.

When the Center was almost burned to the ground, the firemen finally arrived. They had been up on the opposite end of town fighting a huge fire at an old abandoned barn. We always suspected it had been set deliberately to divert all the fire wagons up there so that none would be available to come to the Center. They parked the fire truck on the dirt road that ran in back of the Center. Then they got out and had them a little party, laughing and drinking as they watched the Center burn itself to the ground. I turned my head to God and prayed for their deliverance from such a sickness of mind.

It was almost daybreak when we settled back into bed. I wanted to get just a little sleep before the long day ahead but soon discovered that sleep eluded me, and the rest of the family too. The children tossed and turned and my wife was as jittery as I had ever seen her. After lying there awhile, I finally heard the rooster crow, and I knew daybreak was upon us and I could go out and survey the damage.

I made a few calls to association officers and went out to look around. As soon as I came out of the house, I discovered we still had a problem. A tall, narrow flame was shooting out the top of the butane gas tank that had once supplied gas to the heaters and stoves in the Center. I feared that the tank would explode, and I didn't know what that much butane might do. Would it create a fireball and hurt the children, or set the house or the car on fire? I went back to the house and called the fire department again, and the butane gas supplier. I waited a long time for someone to come out and cut the gas off, but no one ever came.

Rev. Atlas arrived, and we talked about what to do. It seemed that no one was going to come, so we decided that we'd just have to do it ourselves. Although we feared that the tank might explode at any time, we made up our minds that we had no choice. With hearts beating fast, we went over to the tank and, by the grace of God, we were able to shut off the valve supplying the gas and prevent an explosion.

After the tank problem was resolved, I was finally able to turn my attention to what was left of the Center, and my heart sank to a new low. Everything was gone. The building that belonged to all the Baptists was gone. All our historical records from the early 1900s, the voter registration materials, the tape recording and public address systems, the school books, the song books, the fully equipped kitchen, and the piano—all the things we had toiled so hard in the cotton fields to make the money to buy—all of it was gone, burned to the ground, not even a scrap of charred wood remaining. There was hardly evidence of what had been, the fire had been so hot. The concrete blocks that had once held up the building now crumbled when touched with the toe of my shoe. The metal tracks that had once held the large sliding wooden doors between the main building and the dining hall now resembled twisted spaghetti.

All that remained of what had once been the kitchen area was a burned-up stove and the gas heaters and lumps of melted glass sticking out of smoldering ashes. The crape myrtle trees, with their pretty red flowers, were now just skeletons of charred sticks jutting out of the ground. No life would ever spring from them again. There was no sign of my prized rosebush, which had produced giant perfect red roses that had made many a beautiful bouquet. The only things that remained intact were the cement front steps and the side porch.

My dog Joe came up beside me and just kind of stood there looking toward the Center, as if he too could recognize just how much we had lost. Hadn't I just stood there in the Center the month before, talking to the people about the great turn of events? I bowed my head to send my petition before the throne of God, "How long Lord, must the Negro suffer so?"

Many churches would be burned before our registration campaign reaped its full harvest. Rev. Green's church had already been burned once because his members were heavily involved in the movement. The plantation boss who owned the land on which the church had set told them they couldn't rebuild it there, so they bought some land and rebuilt their church at another location. The new church was burned too. On the same night of the second burning, crosses were burned in front of Rev. Green's house, and a little Methodist church further around the bayou from Rev. Green's house was torched. Vandals broke into another church and desecrated the Lord's Supper table by moving their bowels on it. They later burned this church too.

Practically all these churches were in the rural area, and many were on land owned by white men. The churches had no insurance for arson. Later on, we asked the Masons about using the Masonic Hall as a place to hold our activities. Then one night someone looked out and saw it engulfed in flames, too. Arsonists had fire-bombed the Masonic Hall.

It seemed that even though the civil rights bill had passed, locally the political structure and nearly everybody tied into the political structure were united in keeping the Negro from his right to vote. First it had been the Citizen's Council, made up of the more well-to-do whites. They exerted economic pressure on the Negroes who attempted to go forward. Then the parish officials got together and decided they could punish us by refusing to apply for federal education and anti-poverty funds to help the people. Then came the Ku Klux Klan that was made up of mostly poor whites, the ones that I believe did the church burnings and the ones I knew did the shooting and tried to kill me on the road. But it didn't make much difference who the people were or what method they chose to use. They were all bound and determined that the Negro would never be treated equally, that he would always be poor and fearful, and that he would always be made to feel less than the rest of society.

# TWENTY-ONE

# Deliverance

Black voters in East Carroll Parish operated under the guidelines of our 1962 lawsuit until 1965. The suit required people to register under the Louisiana voting restrictions, which were many. We had only registered about two hundred people in that entire three years because of all the people had to go through—the constitutional interpretation test, the citizenship test, the literacy test, and the registrar who just didn't want Negroes to pass. And on top of that, potential voters might also have to go through the cross-burning test, suffer a few economic reprisals, and maybe even have their church burned down. So we looked forward to and hoped for something better to come.

I sometimes wondered whether anything could happen that would be awful enough to wake up the masses. I wondered what would it take to make regular, ordinary people acknowledge that America was wrong in how it treated the Negro and make them want to change what America had become. Yet person after person was brutally murdered, like the CORE members James Chaney, Andy Goodman, and Michael Schwerner, whose bodies were found buried in an earthen dam in Mississippi. Even women and children were being killed, and still the politicians didn't change their racist positions and the regular white citizens seemed untroubled by crimes against black people. Then the Selma, Alabama, incident happened.

Dr. Martin Luther King had recently returned to the United States from receiving his Nobel Peace Prize in Norway. Some of his aides were leading about five hundred demonstrators from Selma to Montgomery when two hundred state troopers and sheriff's deputies ambushed them as they came over the Edmund Pettus Bridge. The policemen blinded the demonstrators with tear gas, and when they couldn't see, they beat them with billy clubs and whips. But this time it was on television, and millions of people saw it in the United States and in other parts of the world.

For a long time the bad things done to black people had been kept out the newspapers. But now it was getting hard for ordinary white people to pretend that nothing was happening, when they could see for themselves how peaceable people were being clubbed and killed. Maybe they were moved by seeing on the evening news how the policemen beat those white ministers bloody for trying to stand up for the right, how they had killed one of them. Maybe it was the contrast of the peaceful demeanor of the demonstrators against the wild animal behavior of the police. But whatever the reason, three weeks later, when a second march from Selma led by Dr. King ended in Montgomery, 50,000 people, both black and white, stood before the Alabama capital.

Not long after the Selma incident, President Johnson went before Congress about voting rights, and by September 1965, we had a Voting Rights Act that changed everything in Lake Providence.

The new law threw out the citizenship and literacy tests (writing and reading the preamble). Federal registrars were assigned to counties and parishes where less than 50% of the voting age population was allowed to vote. Probably because East Carroll's record ranked right up there with the worst in the country, we were one of the first places to receive federal registrars under the new legislation. Four other parishes in Louisiana also received federal registrars.

We found out the registrars were coming about two or three days before they were scheduled to arrive. So on the Monday night before their arrival, we held a big mass meeting to tell the people to get out and register. In the meantime, President Johnson had made a speech broadcast over the radio when he signed the bill. "It's up to you now. You've got to get out there and register," he said. Quite a few people thought that he meant they *had* to do it—so we didn't have much trouble getting them out.

The first day the federal men came and opened their office at the post office, the people were lined up early, long before the 8:30 time for the office to open. Some of us went up there and walked the lines to make sure that everyone knew their wards and precincts before they got up to the registrars. I walked around practically all day and got another man, Mr. Clyde Robinson, to walk the lines when I had to leave.

We had a long line all day long. By the end of the day, we had 125 new registrants, compared to only one that had registered under Manning the month before. The politicians and policemen rode by, looking, but they could not dictate or say anything. We were on U.S. government property.

For several days, prospective voters continued to line up. They came from town and off the plantations. When one would go, he would tell another one "the president said we need to go register." Actually, some of them didn't know they were registering to vote. They just knew that they were signing up.

During the main registration period, we had three federal registrars most days, and I think as high as five registrars here at one time. They stayed until nobody was coming anymore. The federal registrar told me they had registered 88% of the eligible voters.

After that first registration period, they sent a man back to Lake Providence once a month, on the first Saturday, and sometimes on the second Saturday of each month. When we were having elections, they sent federal registrars back to help the people who might have trouble with their forms at the polling places and to prevent the local officials from interfering with the voting.

After a lot of us got registered, the whole political structure changed. The white people began to shake hands with us. One white man worked out a clandestine operation of sorts, where he secretly passed on information to me on Klan activities and other secret meetings. He said he did it because they were wrong and he could do something to stop them.

When the chief of police who seemed to hate me so badly and would barely speak, looking away whenever he met me, ran for election, he came out to the house to talk. And I wasn't even a voter in the city elections. We talked about some of the bad things he had done, and he actually begged me pardon for doing them. He acknowledged that he had done wrong in many instances, some things he did totally on his own and other things he did because Sheriff Gilbert wanted him to. And the other police officers, even those I helped to get indicted, they all started to speak. The officers asked me, "Do you need any help? If I can be any assistance to you, I'll be glad to do so." So the pattern changed and everybody could sense it. The vote brought us respect.

By this time, we had rebuilt the Baptist Center, but the dirt road to the building was as rutty as ever. I used to fight the parish to get them to come down and occasionally scrape the road with a grader to fill in some of the ruts. After we started voting, they came and blacktopped the road. They hated to see the Center rebuilt, but yet they fixed the road. This was done though our representative, Mr. Vail Deloney, the sixty-four-year-old House Speaker in the state legislature at that time. He was the same one who had once said, "I won't stoop to entice these niggers. They either vote for me or they don't." Later he wrote me saying, "Whatever I can do to be of service, just let me know." That was the power of the vote. The vote gave poor people power that could sometimes be as strong as money power, if exercised properly. I was beginning to understand why they fought so hard to keep it from us.

We formed an organization called the Grassroots Democrat Club. We held citizenship classes that taught the people the rights and privileges that came with true citizenship, the right to have a voice in the governing of their country. We taught everybody willing to come, but many of the new voters did not realize that it took intensive study to start making up for three hundred years of not having rights. The people learned how the government was made up and how it worked, and practically everybody who ran for office came before our organization—the candidates for mayor, chief of police, and the board of alderman.

After the chief of police had come by the house and asked me for forgiveness, I asked him to come before our organization and make himself clear. He did, and he told the organization that he had done many things wrong, some on his own and some he did because somebody else wanted him to do it, but if he was elected, he would be fair to everybody.

"That's what we want, is for you to be fair," I told him. "We don't want to be treated different from the rest of the people. We don't expect special favors. We just want you to carry out your responsibilities as the chief of police. We expect you to treat our children just like you treat the white children. If you carry the white children to their parents rather than to jail, that's what we expect you to do for us."

The chief said he liked his job. "I don't have any other job, and I certainly would appreciate you letting me stay in this one."

Whether or not he meant all he said about being sorry and all, he made a big impression and a lot of people believed him. Our organization endorsed him for the chief and of course, when the elections came up in April 1966, he was elected. The person we endorsed as mayor was also elected. One of the candidates for board of aldermen had a liberal view, and the white power structure disliked him so much that they used threats and cash bribes to Negroes to try to keep him from being elected. So we put him in office too.

Our organization only nominated one Negro. In the first primary, he was the high man, but when it came down to the runoff, it was a different story. It took a bit of study, but we figured it out. Everybody had to vote for five aldermen in order for their vote to even count. Most of the white people were not going to vote for a Negro, but every Negro had to vote for at least four whites to make their vote count. If all the Negroes voted for some whites, then the white candidates were all bound to be ahead of the Negro candidate, who would receive only Negro votes. Then some Negroes didn't know anything about the voting machine, and they spoiled their ballots. They would come out from under the curtain without pushing the lever, and their vote wouldn't count. So it was not understanding politics and not knowing voting machines that helped defeat our candidate.

We would have nominated more Negro candidates, but after being out of the political business for seventy-five or eighty years, maybe we just didn't have anyone who wanted to run—no one with political aspirations. The Bible says to train up a child in the way he should go, and when he is old, he will not depart from it. I think that's why Negroes have been trained away from politics—trained to think that their votes don't count or that they can't win if they run, trained to believe in their own powerlessness. It never seemed to occur to the Negro that certain people wouldn't invest that much money, alcohol, drugs, violence, and political control on a people who did not have the potential for greatness, if unbound.

So it was hard to awaken the Negro and let him know that he was a part of this thing. Black people were never that interested in politics anyway. They just wanted to make a better living and to be treated with respect. They were just looking for any way out of a bad economic situation, looking for any way they could find to relieve themselves of economic oppression. That's why the blacks with the most money generally participated the least. The problem was that most people didn't understand that economics and politics were connected. Failure to exercise political power *always* led to economic loss and disrespect, because politicians controlled almost everything. They determined what communities got the good schools and good jobs. They determined when a community got electricity and water service. Indirectly they decided what we read and what we thought, and how much we paid for things. And the worst thing about politics was that if a bad law was passed, politicians rarely admitted it, even when it was clear that the law was harmful, so the people were always stuck with bad laws for a very long time.

Politicians had made the laws that put black people in slavery in the first place. Then politicians made the laws that created the doctrine of separate but equal that put us in a new type slavery for another hundred years after the Emancipation Proclamation. Politicians appointed the Supreme Court justices that made separate and very unequal the law of the land and, years later, politicians appointed the justices that threw the discriminatory law out again. But the people hadn't been trained to understand that the vote was the great equalizer, and that was why people would kill for it or find other indirect ways to make our vote not count.

So we continued to work with the people, to teach and educate, and we began to see a difference. When the Ku Klux Klan leaders went before the new mayor to get a permit to hold a rally in town, he refused them a permit. So they picked another spot down the highway in the country. When the sheriff heard about it, he came out in opposition to it and put out handbills asking them not to hold the rally and asking the people not to come. The Klan leader worked for the city of Lake Providence and had been treating black citizens disrespectfully for a long time, but it wasn't long before he no longer had a job with the city.

In the next election, which was for the school board, we were successful in getting two black people to run, and at the end of the day, we had elected our first Negro since Reconstruction, Rev. Francis Joseph Atlas, the same man who had suffered through the economic boycott. It had taken eighty-four years to regain the right to vote after the last black elected officials were removed from office at gunpoint in 1879, and almost ninety years to elect another black person to office. We had persevered through all kinds of hardships, but we were finally there.

# TWENTY-TWO

# Our Eyes to the Future

*On Friday, May 30, 1980, the Lake Providence community gathered to celebrate John Henry Scott Day as proclaimed by then mayor Rev. L. B. Jackson. Hundreds of people came from far and near to honor and celebrate the life and achievements of a man totally committed to his community. Twenty-three days later, on June 22, 1980, Rev. John H. Scott passed away at the age of seventy-eight. This last chapter is a compilation of the things he wrote and the advice and wisdom he shared with his children at various times during the last nine months of his life. We share his words with you because we believe they have value to anyone who will read them and take heed. As my father would say, "A word to the wise is sufficient."*

Many, many years have passed since that momentous day in the 1960s when a black person was finally elected to public office in East Carroll. The town has changed greatly over the years. Most of the young people, including my own children, moved away to the bigger cities where they could find good-paying jobs and better living conditions than could be found in a poor rural community. Though some victories have been won, there is no time for slowing the fight for equality. In wars, you win the battle, then you take time to establish your position and hold on to what you have. In battles, territories not freely given can and generally will be taken back if you don't remain vigilant.

As I look back and reminisce about those dark years when we groped our way, I am reminded of what the great prophet Jeremiah said, "Walking with God in the dark, still you are not walking alone. Your God can show you the way." So we walked across the years on God's strength until we finally came into the light—not because we could see the light in the distance, not because we had a path laid out to follow, not because someone had given us an instruction book. We were able to walk because we believed in someone greater than mankind. I walked because God had made me know that one person could make a difference in a town, a state, or a country when that person could see possibilities out of impossibilities.

All of us have been on a journey together, but my journey must soon end, as we are fast approaching a fork in the road. I have been struggling with prostate cancer for some time and my doctor has recently advised me that I shall be gone from this place within the next six months. So as we come to the fork, I must take one side and you must take the other. I have asked my children to come back home so that we can talk, so that I can make sure that nothing is left unsaid, so that I can remind them of the lessons I wanted them to always remember and share with their children and their communities.

I used to say all the time that when God created the Negro, he created a beautiful bouquet, with all our different shades of colors. Now that was how I looked at my family—as a beautiful bouquet—all from one family, but all very much individuals in their own right. They had pursued different careers and lived in different cities and different states. The bouquet included a minister and marriage counselor, a master electrician (must have gotten that talent from his mother), a lawyer, a day care center owner, a mental health professional, a college professor, an auditor, and a civil servant. Three had completed their master's degrees, one had a law degree, and one was working on her master's. One daughter would complete her requirements for her doctoral degree in a couple of months. My wife had even gone back to school after most of the children moved away, and she now managed a local day care center. That's a lesson right there. It's never too late to go back and finish school and pursue your dreams. She always loved children and teaching, so now she gets to do both of these every day.

As some of the children made their way in, arriving at different times from Illinois, Texas, New Jersey, North Carolina, and several parts of Louisiana, I sat and pondered what were the most important things I had learned in life. What instructions and directions should I leave behind? Many things flowed through my mind, but I settled on a few that I thought were most important. These are the things I jotted down to share with my children and to pass on to anyone reading my words.

First, God is the foundation. Everything else is built on that foundation. God is the source of strength, wisdom, and vision. Without him, I would have never survived. I would have quit the fight or would have been killed a long time ago, but he gave me the courage and strength to go on. It is a personal relationship with God that makes the difference.

Truth and open communication should come next. In the late 1960s, after the burnings and killings stopped and the buses, restaurants, stores, and schools were integrated, I used to think that after a while blacks and whites would forget about the color of the skin and they were all going to unite and work together. It was only later that I began to see signs that the new peace and harmony between the races wouldn't last. It took some study, but I finally figured out what the problem was. We had tried to build a future without first dealing with the past. So that is why I put communication and truth near the top of the list. A law was passed in the 1960s to make discrimination illegal, but there was little dialogue and few changes to history books, or education of the masses meant to change the hearts of man. And because hearts were not changed, you can see today reflections in our children of the anger, resentment, racial bias, and hatred, and worst of all, the blindness to discrimination that so controlled the parents of the '40s, '50s, and '60s.

So I say to anybody of any race who says "leave the past in the past" that no problem was ever solved by ignoring it. The issues separating the races and leading to discrimination and dislike will be passed down from generation to generation until black people and white people start to talk honestly about the long-term impact of slavery and, even more important, the impact of Jim Crow laws. So I ask everyone to talk and search and seek to acquire knowledge. We seek this knowledge not to feel guilty, not to get angry and lay blame, but to understand how things got the way they are so that we will not be ignorant in decision making and so that we will all *want* to change for the better.

The quest for knowledge may not be simple, as much history is unrecorded or recorded in Afro-American sections of bookstores and libraries where many may never go. Then the information is disturbing to both blacks and whites, especially to southern whites who may be familiar with only one side of their heritage. The natural instinct is to reject truth as an exaggeration. Last, it takes quite a bit of talking about racial issues before one can dig deep enough to reach the truth. Although it might seem like a lot of effort, truth is what the country needs. Truth is the only thing that will break the chains that slavery and Jim Crow still hold around America. Only truth will set our minds free. As a minister, I challenge other ministers of all faiths to take the lead in resolving matters of race in America.

After truth and communication, I thought about the educational system, which is key to everyone's success. Some of my children were involved in teaching, one way or the other, so I had to leave some words about education, my other passion. I am disappointed in the school system and feel that much of the education the Negro has gotten has not been an education—it has been miseducation. Booker T. Washington said that if you educate the Negro, you would unfit him for a slave. But the pattern of education now too often fits the Negro for a slave or for prison.

When I was a boy, an old man told me, "Son, I went to school to learn to be a fool. And I'm going to be a fool all my days." Now in my estimation, when you go to school and it fails to elevate you, it fails to make you want to be a man or a woman, it fails to make you want to respect others, actually it's training you to be what this old man said he was. So that is why I put so much emphasis on education, because knowledge is the one thing that no one can take from you. I believe in and have always taught gaining knowledge for knowledge's sake—not to get a job, but just to be able to understand life itself. We as black leaders and educators in East Carroll Parish promoted the importance of education and taught the children at school, church, and home good study skills, a strong work ethic, and pride in our ability as a race to survive and beat all odds. I believe that is why the black children from the small rural town of Lake Providence competed so well nationally for honors, scholarships, jobs, and senior positions after leaving home.

So I challenge the educators, school board members, and religious and community leaders to make a new commitment to the children. Look and see whether certain groups of children continue to fail or do less under your care. Always be mindful of the amount of power in your hands. What you do as educators and school board members is of extreme importance. You greatly influence the future of this country. Speak to the children and represent them like you understand your power. You have the power to challenge and motivate and to break the chains of poverty, low expectations, and ignorance. You also have the power to destroy a child's future.

Of course I could not leave you without a word about voting. Register to vote as soon as you are old enough and vote in every election. Get to know your elected officials and make sure they know you by name. Hold them accountable for their actions; otherwise, you are just giving your vote away, and politicians will gladly take it and give you nothing in return.

The next important lessons I thought about were all about control—controlling your words, controlling your finances, and controlling your image. Words have great power—written or spoken. Be careful who or what you listen to. Use your own words with care, for in them is the power to break or create yokes, the power to bring a smile or create a tear, the power to create a vision or destroy a dream, the power to give hope or sink a person into despair.

Control your finances. Be careful with what you get. Stay out of debt. Remember, it's not generally what a person needs that puts a person in debt. It's usually what he wants. When we try to live above our income, why then we get into debt, and anybody that's too deeply in debt becomes a slave. Even though he owns his property, he cannot speak up because he is in debt. He's just as bad off as the fellow that doesn't own anything. Don't waste what you have; learn to help others by sharing your time, knowledge, and money too. You're never so poor that you have nothing worthwhile to share. This is what will really help the country.

Control your image as much as you can. Be especially concerned when you start seeing a change in the way people who look like you are portrayed in the media. It doesn't matter whether the image is ignorance, unattractiveness, criminal, or general immorality. If people who look like you are portrayed to the masses in mostly a negative way, it *will* change the way you are treated, and if such a negative image goes unchecked, it will generally lead to discriminatory laws and general persecution. Remember that what you see and hear about yourself, or those who look like you, seeps into your mind and eventually down inside your soul. It is so subtle that the damage is done before you even know it. Then you start to act a certain way and you won't even know why. You become what others see and expect in you rather than what you really are.

Black parents, be careful with how your children see themselves, especially when they are young. Make sure that you teach them who they are. Start teaching them their history early, and if you were never taught, it's a good time for the whole family to learn together. Their history will straighten their backs and make them proud of the strength of their ancestors. History will teach them that their problems are smaller by comparison; therefore, they can conquer their problems too, if they focus on the right things and stop fighting among themselves. Keep in your home black-owned newspapers and magazines that showcase the achievements of blacks. A type of brokenness has remained in the Negro's spirit from Jim Crow days, but it can be purged through exposure to positive images on a regular basis. A positive self-image developed in youth is essential to strength and survival as adults.

After the lessons about control, I thought about the issue of respect. I couldn't leave without reminding you that in life people don't have to like you. It's nice to be liked, but that shouldn't be your primary objective. People should always respect you. Respect is what you should be working to achieve. Always behave in a manner that first says that you respect yourself, both in your conduct and in your dress. If you can't see and appreciate and take care of your own specialness, then how can you recognize some redeeming value in someone else? Respect yourself first, then show respect for others. You must give respect in order to receive respect.

Finally, I must end my journey with some parting words about that all-important subject of forgiveness. We have to let go of any anger and bitterness we may have, no matter how right it feels, no matter whether anyone comes to apologize. Just like a man who neglects his wife and child while totally consumed with hatred for the murderer of his other child, he only creates new problems for himself. Perspective is lost when so much energy goes toward discussing and hating behavior outside one's control, to the detriment of what can be controlled.

Anger and negative feelings should never be directed toward a whole group of people. Every person must be judged on his or her own merit. I hope that because of my story, somebody will see past their anger, and possibly hatred, and see that these are emotions that keep us preoccupied with nonproductive thoughts and keep us separated from the work that will give us our victories.

Anger pulls you down to the other person's level. Never let a hateful or unkind person pull you down to their level. Your behavior should pull them up toward your level—even though sometimes they may be kicking and screaming all the way. Anger and bitterness give other people control over your mind, your thoughts, and your behavior. No one should ever be given that much control. Unforgiveness works on *you* from the inside out. It is inside your heart, but it controls everything you do on the outside. Sometimes unforgiveness can even make you physically sick while the object of your unforgiveness generally is not even being affected. On the other hand, forgiveness works on the *other* person rather than you and it works from the outside in.

It is like I had to explain to one of the men who tried to hurt me. He was in the hospital at the time, and as I made my hospital visitations, I was surprised that he had requested to see me. He said, "You knew I was one of them, didn't you?"

I told him that yes, I knew. "Then why didn't you treat me any differently, why didn't you hate me? You even treated me as nice as you treated everybody else."

He said that it had really worked on his mind. In fact, he had been afraid of me for years. "I didn't know when you would come against me," he said. He thought I should have every right to hate him, but I explained to him that God had made me too precious a vessel for hatred to live inside me. Besides, hating took a lot of time and energy that was better spent planning and changing the things I could change. After the two of us had talked a while, he begged my pardon, as many others had done before him. It's a difficult concept for humans to grasp, because most people can't hold on long enough for results, but it is true that love is stronger than hate.

Now I believe that all has been said and done, so I can now bid you farewell. I close knowing that right now there are leaders in development who will listen to my words and know that they have been given a vision for resolution and healing that can only begin through open, honest discussion about the past. May the truth soon be told in the history books and in the schools, spoken from the pulpits and in the places people work, documented on television and in magazines, until people of all colors, in positions to bring about change, come to know, acknowledge, and properly address the past as it affects the future, with all its generational economic and social implications for all parties involved.

May God bless all who read and listen to my story and may his light shine upon you so that the complicated may be made plain. There is something very important to be done, and you may be one of the chosen for such a time as this. What will you do today that will make a difference for the good?

So I say goodbye to all of you who chose to take a little walk through time with an old man. I leave with you a favorite of mine, an adaptation from an old hymn titled "Only Remembered" by John R. Sweeney and William J. Kirkpatrick:

*Up and away, like the dew of the morning*
*That soars from the earth to its home in the sun,*
*So let me steal away, gently and lovingly,*
*Only remembered by what I have done.*
*My name and my place and my tomb all forgotten*
*The brief race of time well and patiently run,*
*So let me pass away, peacefully, silently,*
*Only remembered by what I have done.*
*I need not be missed if another succeeds me,*
*To reap down those fields which in spring I have sown;*
*He who ploughed and who sowed is not missed by the reaper,*
*He is only remembered by what he has done.*
*Not myself, but the truth that in life I have spoken,*
*Not myself, but the seeds that in life I have sown*
*Shall pass on to the ages—all about me forgotten*
*Save the truth I have spoken, the things I have done.*
*So let my living be, so be my dying;*
*So let my name lie, unblazoned, unknown;*
*Unpraised and unmissed, I shall be remembered;*
*Yes—but remembered by what I have done.*

# Appendix

*John H. Scott's testimony, September 27, 1960, before the United States Commission on Civil Rights hearings on voting rights violations in Louisiana, held in New Orleans, September 27–28, 1960. Excerpt from* Hearings before the United States Commission on Civil Rights. Hearings held in New Orleans, Louisiana, September 27, 1960, September 28, 1960, May 5, 1961, May 6, 1961 *(Washington, D.C.: USGPO, 1961), 15–23.*

Colonel ROSENFELD. If it please the Commission, the oral evidence will be presented according to a topical arrangement. The topic under which a witness testifies represents a particular experience to which that witness was subjected in his effort to register to vote or have his vote counted. Some of the witnesses obviously have had experiences encompassing more than one topic.

The first topic on which evidence will be presented is the requirement exacted by certain registrars to produce registered voters of their precinct for the purpose of attesting to the identity of the applicant, and the first witness to be called under this topic is the Reverend John Henry Scott, of East Carroll Parish. He will also act as a background witness.

Vice Chairman STOREY. Come around, Mr. Scott. Will you please hold up your right hand and be sworn? Will you hold up your right hand?

Reverend SCOTT. Yes. May I make a statement as I made to the Commission?

Vice Chairman STOREY. Or affirmation; I understand.

Reverend SCOTT. Yes, sir.

Vice Chairman STOREY. All right. You have no objection to affirming.

Reverend SCOTT. No objection. I tell the truth. As a Christian, I feel I should tell the truth at all times.

Vice Chairman STOREY. You hold up your right hand. Do you solemnly swear or affirm that the testimony you are about to give will be the truth, the whole truth, and nothing but the truth, so help you God?

Reverend SCOTT. I do.

Vice Chairman STOREY. Have this seat over here, please.

Mr. BERNHARD. If the Commission please, in referring to Reverend Scott's testimony, I would like to point out that Reverend Scott is from East Carroll; that in this particular parish, you will note ———

Vice Chairman STOREY. Point out East Carroll.

Mr. BERNHARD. East Carroll is in the northeastern part of the State. You will observe that the nonwhite age 21 and over—that is, the potential Negro voter—constitutes 4,690. The number of colored who are registered is zero; obviously the percent registered over 21 is zero.

At the same time, whites age 21 and over constitute 2,836. Whites registered are 2,826, and the percentage comes out that 99.7 percent of the white 21 and over are registered in East Carroll Parish.

Vice Chairman STOREY. Thank you, Mr. Bernhard. Now, will you please state your name, your age, and place of residence?

Reverend SCOTT. My name is John Henry Scott. My age is 57.

Vice Chairman STOREY. Where do you live?

Reverend SCOTT. I live in East Carroll Parish.

Vice Chairman STOREY. How long have you lived there?

Reverend SCOTT. I have lived there all my life.

Vice Chairman STOREY. What is your occupation?

Reverend SCOTT. My occupation is minister.

Vice Chairman STOREY. Of what denomination or church?

Reverend SCOTT. Baptist. I am pastoring one of the churches that my great-grandfather organized.

Vice Chairman STOREY. How long have you been pastor of that church?

Reverend SCOTT. I have been pastoring there since 1947.

Vice Chairman STOREY. Will you give, briefly, what your education is?

Reverend SCOTT. I would be afraid to say, as far as public school is concerned. I quit school in the ninth grade, but after I entered the ministry, I have been in school practically every year.

Vice Chairman STOREY. Do you hold any degrees?

Reverend SCOTT. Yes.

Vice Chairman STOREY. What degrees?

Reverend SCOTT. I hold a Th. B. from the United Theological Seminary. Also I have done work at Leland College, and I have attended Southern University 3 years or in the extension work there by the home mission department.

Vice Chairman STOREY. Both of those universities or colleges are in the State of Louisiana, are they not?

Reverend SCOTT. That's right.

Vice Chairman STOREY. Do you own any real property, any real estate?

Reverend SCOTT. No more than heir to property, and my grandfather ———

Vice Chairman STOREY. Do you own any personal property?

Reverend SCOTT. No personal property.

Vice Chairman STOREY. Automobile?

Reverend SCOTT. Just heir. Yes; I own an automobile, and I live on the property of East Carroll Baptist Association on which we pay taxes. I am their president. I represent them.

Vice Chairman STOREY. The church furnishes your home?

Reverend SCOTT. Yes; East Carroll Baptist Association.

Vice CHAIRMAN. Are you a registered voter?

Reverend SCOTT. No.

Vice Chairman STOREY. Have you attempted to register?

Reverend SCOTT. Many times.

Vice Chairman STOREY. All right. Now, tell the first time and where, and the circumstances. What happened? Just tell in your own words.

Reverend SCOTT. Well, the first time that I attempted to register, that is back in 1946. Another young man named Rev. Paul Taylor, we decided we would go and try.

Vice Chairman STOREY. Did you go together?

Reverend SCOTT. We went together. He lives in St. Louis, Mo., now. Well, we didn't know exactly where the registration office was, so finally we went upstairs, and we got to the door, and I said, "Paul, here is the door," and we went to the door, and the registrar of voters say, "Go to the next door." So we went to look for another door, and when we got back, the door was locked. So we didn't make any attempt to go in. We give up that time.

Vice Chairman STOREY. Where was this? What town and what parish?

Reverend SCOTT. That is East Carroll Parish, Lake Providence, La.

Vice Chairman STOREY. All right. Is that all that happened on that occasion?

Reverend SCOTT. That was all that happened on ———

Vice Chairman STOREY. When did you next try to register?

Reverend SCOTT. The next time I tried to register must have been about 2 years later, around 1947; the Reverend Mason and I went together.

Vice Chairman STOREY. Where did you go then; the same place?

Reverend SCOTT. Went to the same place, the same registrar. She was very nice. She gave us the card to fill. When we filled it she looked at it and said, "Well, we wouldn't know where to find you all," or something, so we went out, and a little later on I decided to go back. I don't know whether I am giving them in the order, but I am truthfully stating it. I believe Brother Atlas and I went ———

Vice Chairman STOREY. About how long was that after the second time?

Reverend SCOTT. Well, maybe it would be a year or 6 months before I tried again.

Vice Chairman STOREY. All right. Go ahead in your own way.

Reverend SCOTT. So I decided that probably trying to be a Democrat was making it difficult for me to register.

Vice Chairman STOREY. You mean you belong to the Democratic Party?

Reverend SCOTT. Well, that is the party I wanted to.

Vice Chairman STOREY. All right. Go ahead.

Reverend SCOTT. So I decided to put on my next card "Republican." I didn't want to put "Communist" on there, and so when I put "Republican" on, the registrar of voters looked in the office, and she picked out a card, and she looked at it, and she said, "Well, on this card you said you were a Democrat. On this card you are saying you are a Republican." She said, "What are you?"

I said, "Well, I am not anything until you register me."

So she said, "Well, don't you know you can't change your party that fast?"

So I had to go out.

So, later on, about 1950, somewhere about 1950, I believe, Reverend Mason and several others went in, decided to try again, and she gave us all a card, and we filled them out, and she told Reverend Mason that his was perfect, but he would have to get someone to vouch for him or sign, identify him. All of which he was successful, but that didn't work, either. In fact ———

Vice Chairman STOREY. Could I ask you how many signed recommendations or vouched for him?

Reverend SCOTT. Well, just one.

Vice Chairman STOREY. All right.

Reverend SCOTT. But they didn't accept that one.

Vice Chairman STOREY. That was about 1950?

Reverend SCOTT. Yes.

Vice Chairman STOREY. What did you do at that time?

Reverend SCOTT. I came on out.

Vice Chairman STOREY. Did you attempt to register again?

Reverend SCOTT. Yes. Reverend Henderson and I went together, and she told him his was right, and he was fortunate to get a white person to go up there that had not been brought up to the proceedings. And he was turned away, after he had gone down, and they told him what he should do, I guess, and what he shouldn't do. That is my thinking, what he told Reverend Henderson: "I can't fool with that." So he went away. So we were not able to get anyone to come, and if we got them it was to no avail because they had made their mind up not to register anybody. So recently they put a new man or they put a man in office after our present registrar resigned or went on retirement, and we thought we would try him, I believe last September, and several of us went.

Vice Chairman STOREY. How many went along with you? About how many?

Reverend SCOTT. About five.

Vice Chairman STOREY. All right. What happened then?

Reverend SCOTT. He asked us how long had we been living there. Most of us had been living there all of our life and he said, "Well"—

he handed us a form; he said, "You will have to get two qualified electors from your ward and precinct to identify you."

Vice Chairman STOREY. Did you know the registrar personally?

Reverend SCOTT. I didn't know him ———

Vice Chairman STOREY. And he didn't know you personally.

Reverend SCOTT. Yes.

Vice Chairman STOREY. Go ahead.

Reverend SCOTT. So he didn't register. So the lady that was with me, she said, "I can get two to identify me." I said, "Well, you think you can, but you can't." She said, "But I know I can," she said, "I have some white friends, and we are all Christians." I said. "But Christians and this registration business is different. Nobody's a Christian when it comes down to identifying you."

So she went and tried. She said, "Oh, yes; they say they will go with me Monday," and I thought—and she said, "Well, it is just like you said; they told me that they couldn't bother with it."

So we decided to go back, I believe, in July, possibly July 25.

Vice Chairman STOREY. What year?

Reverend SCOTT. This year. A group of us went.

Vice Chairman STOREY. About how many?

Reverend SCOTT. About 21.

Vice Chairman STOREY. All right. Go ahead. Tell what happened.

Reverend SCOTT. So we went in. The registrar of voters asked us what did we want. We said we wanted to register. He said, "Do you have anybody to identify you?" I says, "We can identify each other." I said, "We identify folk at the bank and at the post office." I say "We have come around and got folks out of jail and signed, went on their bond." I said, "We be here long enough to be known."

He said, "No; you can't do that. You will have to have two qualified electors from your ward and precinct, and you can't take these forms out for them to sign. You have to bring them to this office." So he asked us, he said, "Give me your names." One of the men that was with us, he said, "Oh, sure, we will give you our name," and I said, "There is no use in giving you our name. You give us the card to fill out, and we will sign our names to the card."

I said, "But we didn't come to sign up. We came to try to register."

So we could not register. It seemed to be, in my way of thinking—and I am sorry to have to appear before this Commission; I am sorry to be in New Orleans. I never did think that in America or that a citizen would have to do all of this for an opportunity to vote.

Vice Chairman STOREY. Now, Reverend Scott, the last time you went in July, what was the reason the registrar told you people that you couldn't register? What reason did he give? Because you didn't have these identifying persons?

Reverend SCOTT. That's right.

Vice Chairman STOREY. Now, as I understand, the law as to identity reads this way: "If the registrar has good reason to believe that he"—meaning the applicant—"is not the same person, he may require the applicant to produce two creditable registered voters of his precinct to make oath to that effect."

Now, then, did you each time try to get some registered voter to identify you?

Reverend SCOTT. I did not because, Reverend Mason and Reverend Henderson, the effort that they made, it was turned down, and I had a white friend that was on the police jury at that time, and he told me that it wouldn't be any use because it was strictly made up not to register any Negroes.

Vice Chairman STOREY. Now, tell me how long have you lived in this county? Since what date?

Reverend SCOTT. Oh, I have been there since 1901. That is when I was born.

Vice Chairman STOREY. Did you ever have any trouble being identified at banks or the courthouse or any other place?

Reverend SCOTT. No. My great-grandfather lived there; my grandfather lived there; my grandfather was a minister, and I mean, we are all very well known, everybody. Someone asked me about coming down here ———

Vice Chairman STOREY. Don't tell about coming down here.

Reverend SCOTT. What I was trying to say is that everybody knows everybody. You can't—well, you just can't hide. When you walk down the street, everybody knows everybody.

Vice Chairman STOREY. Well, now, this other question. The records show that there are no Negro registrants in your parish.

Reverend SCOTT. That's right.

Vice Chairman STOREY. Is that true?

Reverend SCOTT. That is true.

Vice Chairman STOREY. According to your own knowledge.

Reverend SCOTT. That is true.

Vice Chairman STOREY. The records show that. Why do you want to vote?

Reverend SCOTT. Well, I have always felt like that was a responsibility that belonged to the citizens, after reading—even Louisiana history and the Constitution of Louisiana and the United States, it says that that belongs to the citizens, and another thing that I noticed, it always gives recognition; I noticed the streets where they vote, they were fixed; I noticed the roads where the people lived on where they vote; it was gravel; I noticed the people that vote, the officers of the law respected them and treated them different from the people that didn't vote, and after reading Negro newspapers, traveling quite a bit, I felt like that it was a responsibility, and after my brothers—I didn't go because I was a minister—went to the Army, and back there in World War I, when the President was talking about making the world safe for democracy, and everybody had the right and privilege to participate, it always had been a burning zeal and desire within my heart, and I have never been able to tell my children the reason why that Negroes should be treated in such a way or be cast about.

Vice Chairman STOREY. Well, now, Reverend Scott, have you been arrested in your lifetime?

Reverend SCOTT. No.

Vice Chairman STOREY. Do you know of any impediment that disqualifies you from voting or registering?

Reverend SCOTT. No.

Vice Chairman STOREY. All right. Are there other questions from other members of the Commission? Father Hesburgh?

Commissioner HESBURGH. Reverend Scott, have you ever had any trouble being identified for taxes?

Reverend SCOTT. I didn't understand.

Commissioner HESBURGH. I say, have you ever had any trouble being identified for tax purposes? Have you ever had any difficulty being identified for paying taxes?

Reverend SCOTT. No, sir; no, sir. I have an old poll tax receipt before they stopped receiving poll tax. I had it.

Vice Chairman STOREY. Have you ever had any suit in connection with voter registration?

Reverend SCOTT. Yes, sir.

Vice Chairman STOREY. When and where?

Reverend SCOTT. In 1951 we filed a suit against the registrar of voters in East Carroll Parish. Our attorney from this city filed the suit for us, Louis Barry, who is out of town. It is quite discouraging.

Vice Chairman STOREY. Just tell us this. What happened to the suit?

Reverend SCOTT. Well, the suit just dragged along until—from one court—not one court to another, but from one attorney in court to another, on technical grounds. I believe it was in 1957, from 1951 until 1957, and at that particular time, Jurist Ben Dawkins put us out of his court, said he had no jurisdiction, it belonged to the three-judge court, and after that our attorney went off to California. So I don't know. He just dropped the suit or whatever.

Vice Chairman STOREY. You didn't get any relief from the suit.

Reverend SCOTT. No, sir.

Vice Chairman STOREY. All right. Any other questions?

Chairman HANNAH. Yes. Reverend Scott, do you have any sons or relatives that have served in the Armed Forces?

Reverend SCOTT. No. I have brothers. My son is still in school.

Chairman HANNAH. Do you have brothers that have been in the Armed Forces of the United States?

Reverend SCOTT. I have a brother in the Armed Forces now; he is in Germany.

Chairman HANNAH. He is a native of East Carroll Parish?

Reverend SCOTT. That's right.

Chairman HANNAH. There are a goodly number of Negroes in East Carroll Parish that are now or have in the past served in the Army and the Navy or the Air Force or Marine Corps?

Reverend SCOTT. That's right. I have two brothers live there that served in World War II.

Chairman HANNAH. Any other questions?

Commissioner JOHNSON. I wonder if I could ask just one question.

Vice Chairman STOREY. Dean Johnson?

Commissioner JOHNSON. Reverend Scott, as a result of your rather persistent effort to get registered over a considerable period of time,

I was wondering, have you ever been threatened or intimidated because of this kind of activity?

Reverend SCOTT. Well, slightly. I don't like to talk about intimidations. I would rather forget them. I always felt if a fellow thought he was doing you some harm or that he was bluffing you or was upsetting you in your mind, that he would go further, so I just let it go. They have told me not to say anything about it. Well, the officer of law at that time, sheriff of East Carroll Parish—I can call his name; he is out of office now—Matt Fowler, and we had a meeting. Our—well, at that time the NAACP was having a membership drive and had invited Mr. Daniel E. Byrd to speak for us, and after he got to town, everything was so excited, and they sent for him to come to the courthouse, and they picked me up, and I picked up several other ministers, and we went to the courthouse, and the sheriff told me come to the office, his office, and don't bring anybody. So I went down, and they seated me around a table like that there, and they wanted to know what kind of meeting we were having. He said he had been called up during the day, and someone said that somebody was coming there to teach us how to vote, and I told him no one had to come there to teach us how to vote, that practically all of us knew how to fill out those forms and figure our age correctly and so on. So the collector of court has passed on now to the Great Beyond. He was across the table from me, he said, "If you don't like our way of doing things, why don't you leave here?"

I said, "Well, I was born here, and if I leave here, I might not like the things that go on where I go, but I think that I could stay here and try to help correct some of the things." So they wouldn't allow us to have the meeting at the schoolhouse, and we went to a church. When I walked out of the sheriff's office, he said, "You be damned sure and tell him don't say anything about voting." So the next day he picked me up, and he asked me to name some of the leaders and those that understand how to fill out those forms. I say, "Is this strictly confidential between you and me and nobody else?" And he said, "No; I am not going to promise you that." I said, "I am not going to tell you the names, either." So then he went on to tell me about going to start a riot and so on, like that; he was sheriff, and he had to furnish protection, and he couldn't put up with anything like that. So times moved on.

I just go on, go on because I feel like I am right, and I know where I am going, I know what I am talking about, and I don't care what happens. Whatever happens, I got to go to heaven, and if I go for my people or for the right to vote I would be perfectly satisfied, so that's the way I feel about it.

Commissioner JOHNSON. No further questions.

Vice Chairman STOREY. No further questions. Thank you, Reverend Scott.

# Index